WEB DESIGN
and
CSS ANIMATION

Web Designing Technicalities | Web Performance | CSS Principles

Web Development Tools HTML5, CSS, PHP | Web Graphics | CSS Techniques

DR. UMAPATHI JANNE

BLUEROSE PUBLISHERS
India | U.K.

For permissions requests or inquiries regarding this publication,
please contact:

BLUEROSE PUBLISHERS
www.BlueRoseONE.com
info@bluerosepublishers.com
+91 8882 898 898
+4407342408967

ISBN: 978-93-5989-958-9

Cover Design: Muskan Sachdeva
Typesetting: Pooja Sharma

First Edition: February 2024

DEDICATION

This book is dedicated to the memory of my father JANNE VENKATARAMANAPPA NAIDU who taught me to be an independent and determined person, to my doting mother JANNE LAKSHMIDEVAMMA without whom I would never be able to achieve my objectives and succeed in life.

From your Son,

Dr. UMAPATHI JANNE

Email: yourspathi@gmail.com

CONTENTS

CHAPTER 1
INTRODUCTION TO WEB DESIGNING

"If You Think Math is Hard Try Web Design"

-Pixxelznet

***Chapter Learnings*:**

After reading this chapter, the reader will get an idea into how the web designing has evolved over the years, about web technologies, the current trends and modern web designing concept, the technical aspects on web development and finally about responsive web designing which is something that is become popular.

1.1 INTRODUCTION:

In the current digital world where people want everything to be available at the comfort of their homes, the dependency on the internet has increased. Websites are quickly becoming the primary medium for finding information, presenting a company, commerce, entertainment, education, and social networking. At a time when visual symbols are becoming increasingly essential, an effective web design is a prime determinant to the success or failure of the content being represented on the website. This book will be focussing on various aspects of web design right from evolution to entire A to Z of web designing.

Since the days of dial-up internet, internet connectivity has come a long way to providing the loading of a website in few seconds. Many incarnations of websites over the last 30 years have been witnessed, from text-only interfaces in the 1980s to blocky layouts in the 1990s to flashy 'web diaries' (aka blogs) in the early 2000s. While it's amusing to reminisce about previous websites and wonder, "What were they thinking?" Looking back at the history of web design has a lot to teach us. Everything old may be made new again by drawing inspiration from vintage websites. Here, a basic outline on how web design has changed in recent years—and how it will continue to develop in the future is seen in brief.

EARLY WEB DESIGNING (1991 – 1994): Tim Berners-Lee, who designed the website at the Swiss research centre CERN, created the very first website on the World Wide Web (European Organization for Nuclear Research). The basic CERN website, which was created to provide information to other researchers, is still available. Berners-Lee is recognised for not only being the first web designer, but also for inventing the Hypertext Mark-up Language (HTML), which he used to develop the CERN website (Beaird, et al. 2020). He went on to form the World Wide Web Consortium, which is still in charge of web standards development today. The HTML <table> function was the only option to organise information by allocating data to columns and rows in the early days of web design. There are no colour blocks, images, or graphics, only text. A far cry from what we now refer to as "web design." The World Wide Web continued to expand, and the world's first search engine was launched only two years later. ALIWEB (Archie Like Indexing for the Web) was a website that categorised connections into computing, entertainment, living, money, magazine, recreation, research, and shopping categories. Colour was also used by ALIWEB as a new method of organisation. The categories were divided by a yellow background, making it easier for users to find what they were looking for. ALIWEB, like the initial website, is still active today. In reality, if you click the "BMW" link in the Auto category, you'll be taken to BMW's current website. The concept of using website design to achieve commercial goals expanded in tandem with the number of websites. Around 1993, landing pages began to appear, enticing readers with bright colours and invitations to "Click Here to Enter" or "Sign Up Now." In 1994, Hotwire (now Wired Magazine) was the first to run a web banner ad, with the subliminal message, "Have you ever clicked your mouse right here?" "You'll do it." Brilliant. In the early 1990s, the popularity of websites skyrocketed. In 1991, there was only one website. In 1994, there were a total of 2,738. To put things in perspective, Jeff Bezos founded Amazon.com in 1994 (Cyr, et al. 2018).

THE EVOLUTION OF WEB DEVELOPMENT (1995 – 2000): It was time to get serious about effective design once the thrill of simply having a website had worn off. From 1995 to 1998, the advancement of web design and development would profoundly alter the history of web design. Enter JavaScript - This is where design and development began to diverge, as JavaScript was the first computer language to allow static websites to be animated with interactive effects. HTML

2.0 was published in 1995, and it included support for graphics, forms, tables, and other features. This offered developers more leeway in terms of page layout. Web users began to expect more from their online experiences as design and development tools became more sophisticated. As a result, at a computer systems conference, Apple coined the phrase "User Experience." Cascading Style Sheets (CSS) were introduced in 1996 and guided the presentation and style of HTML coded design components such as colour, layout, and typography. HTML and CSS were a formidable combination, but CSS tables would eventually supplant HTML tables, with the exception of data that required a real tabular arrangement.

Web animation took centre stage as Macromedia Flash 1.0 swept the internet. However, it was not without flaws. Animations could only be seen if a website had the Flash plugin installed; otherwise, the animation would be blank. For websites developed solely in Flash, this constituted a big difficulty. Furthermore, the hard lifting necessary behind the scenes to bring the animations to life resulted in slower page loading times. Despite its flaws, Flash ushered in a new era of page improvement via movement. It was useful on the web and had a huge impact on the history of web design. However, on December 31, 2020, Adobe stopped support for Flash and Windows deleted Flash from all browsers, putting an end to that role.

Google Beta was developed in 1998 by Stanford PhD students Larry Page and Sergey Brin as part of a research project that looked into indexing page results based on relevant search phrases. Page and Brin had no idea the magnitude of what they had just accomplished, or how Google would influence and revolutionise the internet and site design. As Google grew in popularity, the term "search engine optimization" became popular, and businesses began to look for ways to boost their rankings. Surprisingly, Google was unaware of Flash animation because it required a plugin extension to function. Web capabilities were improving, and ecommerce and online payments enabled firms to transition from analogue to digital payment procedures. PayPal (which was formerly known as Confinity for the first two years) was founded in 2000 and quickly became a market leader in online transactions.

2000 – 2006: Websites were solely made for desktop browser windows till the new millennium. Although "responsive web design," as we now know it, was still a long way off, concepts were brewing. In the year 2000, web designers began generating several versions of websites that could be seen on various browsers and devices.

While this worked in theory, it was inconvenient and time-consuming. Devices and browsers were continuously developing, and having different versions meant that updates for desktop, tablet, and mobile had to be made individually. Three times the effort, three times the time with the passage of time, an increasing number of people began to construct websites for business objectives, information distribution, and a new trend – blogging. Content management systems (CMS) rose in popularity since they permitted dynamic design and smooth content updates. Despite the fact that numerous CMSs existed in the 1990s, the heavy hitter debuted in 2003.

WordPress began as an open source blogging platform, but it has slowly grown and evolved into the world's most popular content management system (CMS). WordPress now runs 35.9% of all websites on the internet. This timeline would be incomplete if it didn't include Myspace (2003) and Facebook (2005). (2004). Myspace was founded by Tom Anderson and Chris DeWolfe with the goal of encouraging self-expression through online profile sites and allowing users to engage with one another online. When Mark Zuckerberg and co. launched Facebook as a student social networking site at Harvard University, it skyrocketed in popularity throughout the world when it went public in 2006. Whether we were ready or not, the dawn of social media, self-expression, and online connection had arrived, and Myspace and Facebook had set the ground for a new level of involvement. This accelerated the growth of web design because there was suddenly a market for developing adverts, website gadgets, and graphics and photos for social networks.

THE MOBILE ERA (2007 – PRESENT): This era has seen major developments right from the first iPhone release to the high end devices that are currently on the market. "We're delivering breakthrough software to a mobile device for the first time," Steve Jobs declared during his famed iPhone presentation, explaining that the Safari browser was "the first completely useable HTML browser on a phone." The iPhone was a one-of-a-kind device that didn't support Flash in more ways than one. While there was no official comment at the time, Steve Jobs wrote a detailed explanation titled "Thoughts on Flash" in April 2010. "...the mobile era is about low-power devices, touch interfaces, and open web standards – all areas where Flash falls short," he writes at the end of the letter. Flash's slow decline and eventual demise was likely affected by Apple's decision.

Responsive and mobile-friendly design has become a necessity as the world has moved toward mobile online experiences. The article "Responsive Web Design," written by web designer Ethan Marcotte in 2010, described how to optimise information dependent on resolution or display size. Not only would having a responsive website increase the Google ranking five years later, but having a non-responsive website would be penalised by Google. Web design has evolved to meet the needs of users over time. Rich design (shadows, depth, colour gradients, textures, flashy animated gifs, etc.) gave way to flat design in the 2010s (clean, minimalistic, bright colours, 2D icons, san-serif typography, etc.). Prior to flat design, rich design's skeuomorphic properties gave it a "real-life" or 3D sense, but the increased design complexity meant longer loading times and more clutter and noise on the website. The move to flat design offered the site a distinct "digital" appearance and provided a more streamlined and efficient user experience. Moving on, the basics of web technology will be discussed in the next section.

1.2 WEB TECHNOLOGY:

Web technology refers to the numerous tools and strategies used in the process of communicating through the internet between various sorts of devices. To access web pages, you'll need a web browser. Web browsers are programmes that use the Internet to display text, data, images, animation, and video.

The World Wide Web has become an invaluable tool for both business and enjoyment in a relatively short period of time. Many individuals now use the Internet instead of the telephone or other traditional methods to find information in their daily lives. Information may be communicated quickly, accurately, and in great detail, thanks to the Internet. Most firms' radio, television, and print advertisements now include web addresses, providing clients with a more tailored and particular manner of information access to aid in learning and decision making. Today's Web, however, is more than just a means for disseminating information. People are increasingly relying on Web-based software programmes to complete their work responsibilities and manage portions of their personal lives. The capacity to link directly with other people and organisations via a widely used and easy-to-use computer network technology has the potential to boost company efficiency and favourably impact our lives by easing many previously complicated activities. It is the role of the Web designer to guarantee that a Website or Web-based application conveys the intended message and is useable by the target audience. As a result, design concepts are just as important as content and functionality in a Website.

Web designers aren't the only ones who should learn about design. People in technical and non-technical professions (as well as those who support them) must be conversant with Web design concepts in order to be competitive. The development of the information infrastructure will be aided by everyone in the modern workplace environment. There are numerous tools and technologies available to make Web page design easier. Designers must be aware enough with the technical aspects of Web design to be able to choose the tools that will provide their organisations a competitive edge, in addition to understanding design and being able to develop useful Websites.

The majority of Website designers take a self-reflective approach to development. They want to use well-known mass advertising analogies to offer themselves to a large audience. The Internet, on the other hand, provides an alternative: the capacity to form one-on-one relationships. Users respond better to information and product options that are suited to their unique demands when they visit a website. Everyone should understand that the Internet is, by its very nature, a medium that allows users to pick which information they want to receive and when they want to view it. As a result, the Internet is a one-to-one medium rather than a broadcast medium. As a result, mass media principles and applications are not always applicable to the Internet. The majority of the media is passive. Its purpose is to pique the viewer's or reader's attention to the point that he or she will finally convert that interest into a desired transaction (such as buying an advertised product). Between the act of reading or viewing and the act of transacting, there is a gap. In other words, the customer does not interact with a television or newspaper directly. As a result, producing information for the mass media necessitates a different approach than producing information for the Internet. The Internet is transactional by definition. User requests and server responses — in other words, transactions and interactivity — underpin the entire Internet experience, from logging on to Web browsing. Furthermore, the Internet is nonlinear by definition. The user makes transactional decisions all the time, from navigating to and arriving at the site, to searching (often within the site's integrated databases), to conducting e-commerce, and eventually deciding to return to the site. Users can, however, transfer to another site — and a different business — at any moment.

1.3 THE INTERNET VERSUS THE WEB:

The Internet is a network of computers that are linked together. The Internet is not owned by any firm; it is a collaborative effort controlled by a set of standards and guidelines. Of course, the point of connecting computers is to share information. Email, File Transfer Protocol (FTP), and many other specialised modes on which the Internet is constructed are just a few of the ways information may be exchanged between computers. Protocols are established techniques for exchanging data or documents across a network.

The Web (formerly known as the World Wide Web, hence the "www" in site URLs) is one of the many ways to transmit information over the Internet. It is unique in that it allows documents to be linked to one another via hypertext links, resulting in a massive "web" of interconnected data. HTTP is the protocol used on the internet (Hyper Text Transfer Protocol). Almost all internet addresses begin with those four characters, so the acronym should be familiar.

In 1989, the Web was born at CERN, a particle physics laboratory in Geneva, Switzerland. Tim Berners-Lee, a computer specialist at the time, presented an information management system that employed a "hypertext" approach to link similar papers via a network. He and his collaborator, Robert Cailliau, developed a prototype and made it available for feedback. Web pages were text-only for the first several years. It's hard to believe that there were just roughly 50 web servers in the world in 1992. The introduction of the first graphical browser (NCSA Mosaic) in 1992 gave the Web a major boost in popularity, breaking it out of the sphere of scientific study and into the realm of mass media. The World Wide Web Consortium is in charge of overseeing the continued development of web technologies (W3C) (http://www.w3.org/History.html).

1.3.1 SERVING UP INFORMATION – SERVERS:

Let's go over the machines that make up the Internet in further detail. These computers are called servers because they "serve up" documents when requested. The server, more precisely, is the software (rather than the computer itself) that allows the computer to communicate with other computers; yet, the term "server" is sometimes used to refer to the computer. Server software's job is to wait for an information request, then retrieve and return that information as rapidly as feasible.

The computers themselves are nothing exceptional...Consider anything from a powerful Unix machine to a basic home computer. All of this is made possible by server software. A computer must run special web server software that allows it to process Hypertext Transfer Protocol transactions in order to be part of the Web. "HTTP servers" is another name for web servers. Although there are numerous server software solutions available, the two most prevalent are Apache (open source software) and Microsoft Internet Information Services (IIS). Apache is a free Unix-based web server that comes pre-installed on Macs running Mac OS X. There is also a Windows version. Microsoft IIS is a server solution offered by Microsoft.

Every computer and equipment connected to the Internet (modem, router, smartphone, automobiles, etc.) is given a unique numeric IP address (IP stands for Internet Protocol). The IP address of the machine that hosts oreilly.com, for example, is 208.201.239.100. Because all those numbers can be confusing, the Domain Name System (DNS) was created to allow us to refer to that server by its domain name, "oreilly.com." The domain name is more accessible to humans than the numeric IP address, which is helpful for computer applications. A different DNS server is responsible for mapping the text domain names to their numeric IP addresses. One can set up their own web server such that many domain names are mapped to a single IP address, allowing multiple sites to share a single server.

1.3.2 WEB BROWSERS:

We've established that the server is in charge of serving, but what about the other side of the equation? The client is the piece of software that does the requesting. Clients for accessing documents on the Web include desktop browsers, mobile browsers, and various assistive technologies (such as screen readers). The pages are returned by the server to the browser (also known as the user agent in technical circles).

The HTTP protocol, as explained before, is used to handle requests and responses. Despite the fact that we've been discussing "documents," HTTP may also be used to send photos, movies, audio files, data, scripts, and any other web resource that makes up a website or application. A browser is commonly thought of as a window on a computer monitor that displays a web page. These are known as graphical browsers or desktop browsers, and they were once the sole way to see the internet. Internet Explorer for Windows, Chrome, Firefox, and Safari are the most popular desktop browsers as of this writing, with Opera coming in last. These days, however, a growing number of people use browser clients integrated into their mobile phones or tablets to access the Internet on the go. It's also crucial to consider different web experiences. Users with vision impairments may be listening to a screen reader reading a web page (or simply making their text extremely large). Users with limited mobility can browse links and type using assistive equipment. All users, regardless of their browsing expertise, must be able to access and use the sites we create. Pages may look and operate differently from browser to browser, even on desktop browsers that initially introduced us to the vast world of the Internet. This is due to varied levels of web technology support and the ability of users to customise their surfing habits.

When you think of a website, you probably imagine that it can be accessed by anyone who is surfing the Internet. Many businesses, on the other hand, use the incredible information-gathering and sharing capabilities of websites to share information only within their own company. Intranets are web-based networks with a specific purpose. They're designed and function like regular websites, but they're protected from the outside world by special security mechanisms called firewalls. Intranets can be used for a variety of purposes, including sharing human resource information and providing access to inventory databases. An extranet is similar to an intranet, but it permits access to a limited number of people from outside the corporation. A manufacturing firm, for example, might give its clients passwords that allow them to check the progress of their orders in the firm's orders database. Naturally, passwords define which parts of the company's data are accessible.

1.3.3 WEB PAGE ADDRESSES:

Every page and resource on the Internet has its own unique address, known as a URL (Uniform Resource Locator). It's practically difficult to go a day without seeing a URL (pronounced "U-R-L," not "erl") on the side of a bus, on a business card, or on a television commercial. Web addresses have become ingrained in modern slang.

Some URLs are succinct and to-the-point. Others may appear to be a jumble of characters separated by dots (periods) and slashes, yet each component serves a distinct purpose. Let's take a look at one of them.

1.3.4 THE PARTS OF A URL:

As demonstrated in Figure below, a complete URL is made up of three components: the protocol, the site name, and the absolute path to the document or resource.

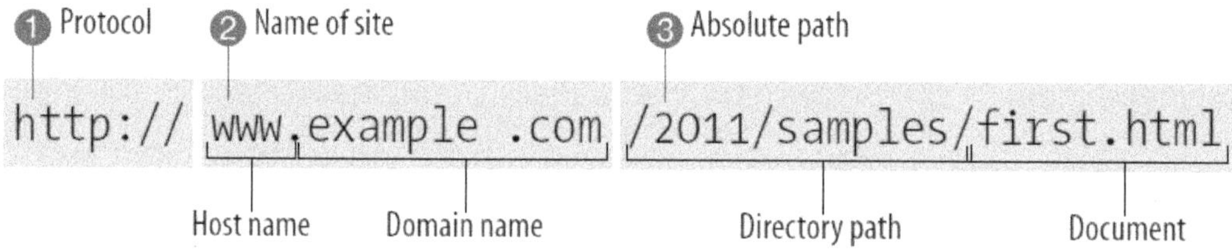

Figure 1.1: The parts of a URL.

- http://

The URL's initial function is to provide the protocol that will be utilised for that specific transaction. The letters HTTP tell the server to use Hypertext Transfer Protocol, or "web mode," as the case may be.

- www.example.com

The domain name is used to identify the website in the following part of the URL. The domain name in this case is example.com. The "www." component at the start denotes the specific host name for that domain. The use of the host name "www" has become customary, but it is not a rule. In fact, the host's name may be removed on occasion. At a domain, there might be multiple websites (sometimes called subdomains). There might also be domains like development.example.com, clients.example.com, and so on.

- /2012/samples/first.html

This is the absolute path to the requested HTML page, first.html, through the server's folders. The directory names are separated by slashes, commencing with the host's root directory (as indicated by the prefix /). Because the Internet was founded on computers running the Unix operating system, we still follow many Unix rules and customs today, hence the use of / to separate directory names.

To summarise, the URL in Figure 1.1 states it wants to connect to a web server on the Internet named www.example.com using the HTTP protocol and request the document first.html (which is located in the samples directory, which is in the 2012 directory).

Obviously, not every URL you encounter is this long. Many addresses, like these, do not include a filename and instead lead to a directory:

http://www.oreilly.com

http://jendesign.com/resume/

When a server receives a request for a directory name rather than a specific file, it looks for a default document, usually named index.html, in that directory. So, if you type the aforementioned URLs into your browser, you'll see something like this:

http://www.oreilly.com/index.html

http://www.oreilly.com/index.html

The default file (also known as the index file) may have a different name depending on how the server is set up. It's called index.html in these samples, although some servers call it default.htm. If your site generates pages using server-side programming, the index file will be titled index.php or index.asp. Just double-check with your server administrator or your hosting service's tech support department to make sure you've named your default file correctly.

Another thing to note is that the original URL in the first example did not include a trailing slash to indicate that it was a directory. The server just adds a slash if it discovers a directory with that name when the slash is absent. The index file is also beneficial in terms of security. If the default file cannot be found, some servers (depending on their settings) display the contents of the directory. The documents in the housepics directory are exposed as a result of a missing default file, as seen in Figure 1.2. One technique to keep individuals from looking through your files is to make sure each directory has an index file. Other protections may be added by your server administrator to prevent your directories from being displayed in the browser.

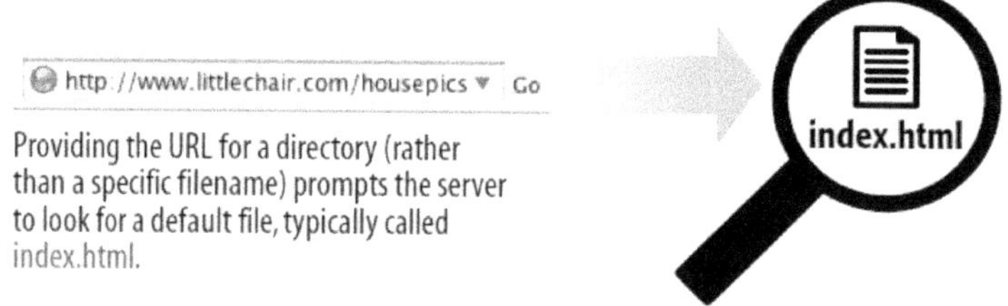

Some servers are configured to return a listing of the contents of that directory if the default file is not found.

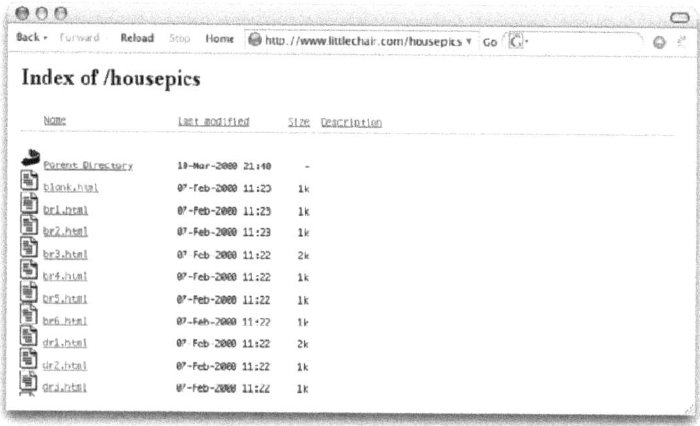

Figure 1.2 Some servers display the contents of the directory if an index file is not found.

1.4 CURRENT TRENDS:

The most recent Web content trends have been toward more up-to-date information and collaborative ease. Web services are an example of such technology that is now transforming Web development. Web services technology is a collection of XML-based technologies that allow computers running various operating systems and software to share information and functionality via the Internet using a common language. Microsoft's .NET and Sun's Sun One are two development platforms that presently offer Web services.

A Web developer benefits from Web services because he or she can use third-party services on his or her own site or Web application without having to understand the nuances of each service's functionality. Only the information required to connect to the service is required of the developer. A search engine, for example, may make its Web services available to subscribers, allowing them to access its search technology. The search engine service does not provide users with any information about its search technology or capabilities, simply the information needed to use it.

Web logs, or blogs, are another example of contemporary Web content trends. A blog is a personal Web journal that is ordered chronologically. Many free or low-cost Web-based tools make it possible for anyone with no technical knowledge to create blogs. As a result, everyone from teenagers to CEOs may — and can — self-publish their opinions on the Internet through blogs. One of the most appealing characteristics of emerging technologies and trends like XML, Web services, and blogs is that they have been unanimously accepted and enthusiastically adopted by the World Wide Web community. As a result, communication and collaboration on the Internet is advancing at a breakneck pace.

1.4.1 TOOLS AND TECHNOLOGY:

There has been substantial controversy over the usage of specialist tools to assist in the Web development process for years. The majority of Web designers consider today's graphical user interface (GUI) Web page-editing tools to be beneficial, if not essential, for Web development. Web developers must still grasp the underlying technologies (including Hypertext Mark-up Language [HTML]) while employing tools to automate development processes, but they should also leverage the tools available to assist them in executing their jobs more effectively.

Challenges for the Web Developers:

- Adapted to new frameworks in order to remain competitive in the industry.
- Website scaling and optimization
- Performance check of the websites.

Latest Technologies for Web Development:

First and foremost, let's go over some of the web development technologies. These are the following:

- Artificial Intelligence:

Artificial Intelligence (AI) will allow programmers to design programmes that act and think like humans — without the need for human labour. Grid is a web design application that makes beautiful websites, and Molly is the AI programme that is used.

- Internet of Things:

The Internet of Things (IoT) is increasingly being used on our household appliances, not just our smartphones. So we use timers to turn on lights, turn on our heaters and refrigerators remotely, and even schedule the settings on our kettle to make a hot cup of coffee as we walk through the door. For a comparable system at home, Facebook's Mark Zuckerberg uses an iOS voice app and a messenger bot.

- Conversational UI with Bots:

The rise in popularity of messaging services has influenced web design and development. The year 2018 has been dubbed "the year of conversational commerce." Conversational interfaces have begun to appear on webpages. Websites that are built with a conversational-first strategy are getting a lot of traction. Chabot's are used on a variety of websites. Chabot's are useful for delivering customer service, offering individualised responses to questions, and increasing online sales.

Web Development Tools:

The web development tools that help the developer to ease the workflow of development are:

- JavaScript Libraries:

For the developer community, JavaScript is one of the most widely used programming languages. The library includes a collection of pre-built libraries that make web development more accessible. Backbone JS, React, jQuery, jQueryUI, and jQuery Mobile are examples of popular JavaScript libraries.

- Front-end Frameworks:

Folders and files make up the front-end frameworks. Some examples to mention include JavaScript, CSS, and HTML. Bootstrap is a nice example of a framework that developers may use to create responsive, mobile applications.

- Databases:

For data storage and retrieval, web developers should be familiar with databases such as MongoDB, PostgreSQL, MariaDB, and MySQL.

- Programming Languages:

Web development tools are built on the backbone of languages. PHP, Python, Ruby, Scala, CSS2, and, above all, JavaScript are some of the most popular.

- Task Runners:

These tools are used for workflow automation. Functions are created to speed up the web development process. All packages in use are checked and maintained by package managers. This will enable the required version to be updated. Grunt is described as a JavaScript-based Task Runner that ensures automation.

- Icons:

All web developers need this tool. As a customizable and scalable vector icon, Font Awesome is worth highlighting. Finally, web developers are responsible for creating user-friendly web apps that are seamless. The goal is to incorporate innovative features that will make clients' lives easier and more enjoyable.

1.5 WEB DESIGNING BASICS:

The process of thinking, designing, and constructing a collection of electronic files that decide the layout, colours, text styles, structure, graphics, photos, and use of interactive features that deliver pages to one's site visitors is known as web design. In the creation and management of websites, web design involves a wide range of talents and disciplines. Web graphic design, interface design, authorship, including standardised code and proprietary software, user experience design, and search engine optimization are all components of web design. It also covers a variety of topics such as webpage layout, content creation, and graphic design. Despite the fact that the phrases web design and web development are sometimes used interchangeably, web design is a subset of web development.

1.5.1 DEFINITION OF WEB DESIGNING:

Web design is a Web development process that focuses on aesthetic considerations such as layout, user interface, and other visual imagery to make a website more aesthetically appealing and easier to use. Various programmes and tools, such as Dreamweaver, Photoshop, and others, are used in web design to obtain the desired aesthetic. Web designers must consider their audience, the website's function, and the design's visual appeal while creating a winning design. The majority of webpages are coded in the Hypertext Mark-up Language (HTML). A website must follow the rules of this language in order to be shown correctly on the client browser. Every page's HTML tags indicate the website's content. The overall visual design of each page is then defined using Cascading Style Sheets (CSS). The end outcome is the result of combining these factors. Because hand coding can be tiring for some designers, they choose to use software such as Adobe Dreamweaver.

1.5.2 ROLE OF MULTIMEDIA:

There are many parallels between web and print design. The Web, like printed media, was created with the intention of disseminating text that could be read by a large number of people. As multimedia became more widely available on the Web, many individuals began to draw parallels between the Web and television. The introduction of push technology, which sends content to the user automatically, was intended to make the Web more of a passive medium. The comparison between the Internet and television, however, is still inaccurate.

One of the most popular Web design misunderstandings is that a good site must dazzle the user with a multimedia experience, and that the content of the site is secondary. As a Web designer, you want your site's visitors to have a positive experience, but wowing them isn't always your goal. In Web design, the fundamental purpose is to provide users with what they want, not what you think they want. This goal can be met by a delicate balancing act of well-thought-out design, high-quality content, and effective use of available media. You should employ multimedia if it makes sense and improves the usability of a website. You should not utilise multimedia if it does not improve the user experience or if it damages the user experience by causing an unreasonably long download.

1.5.3 USER EXPERIENCE, INTERACTION, AND USER INTERFACE DESIGN:

When we think of design, we frequently consider how something appears. The first order of business on the Internet is to design the site's functionality. Before choosing colours and fonts, think about the site's aims, how it will be used, and how visitors will navigate it. Interaction Design (IxD), User Interface (UI) design, and User Experience (UX) design are the disciplines that these responsibilities fall under. There is a lot of overlap between these tasks, and it's not uncommon for one individual or team to be in charge of all three.

The Interaction Designer's purpose is to make the site as simple, efficient, and enjoyable to use as feasible. User Interface design is closely related to interaction design, but it focuses on the page's functional organisation as well as the specific tools (buttons, links, menus, and so on) that users use to access material or complete activities. The User Experience Designer is a more contemporary job term in the web design world. The UX designer takes a more holistic approach, ensuring that the entire site experience is positive. Founded on observations and interviews, UX design is based on a deep understanding of users and their needs. User experience design, according to Donald Norman (the term's creator), encompasses "all aspects of the user's contact with the product: how it is seen, learned, and utilised." This encompasses the visual design, user interface, content quality and messaging, and even overall site performance for a website or application. To be successful, the experience must be in line with the organization's brand and commercial objectives.

1.6 WEBSITE DEVELOPMENT – THE PRINCIPLE & THE PLAN

1.6.1 WEB SITE DEVELOPMENT – THE PRINCIPLE

A wide range of individuals with knowledge in several areas is required for good website design. When a key decision must be made, their combined efforts must be put in. In this section, we'll go through the eight fundamental characteristics of good website design that must be considered while creating a website. These design concepts will undoubtedly aid web designers in creating stunning designs and improving a website's usability. The following are eight good design concepts that will make your website more appealing, user-friendly, effective, and engaging:

- **Simple is the best**

A website that is too developed may not work. Having too many items on a page can cause users to become distracted from your website's core goal. Simplicity is always a good thing when it comes to web page design. Your website's clean and fresh design not only looks good, but it also makes it easier for users to move from one page to the next. It can be aggravating to load a website with design features that aren't useful. Keep your design as simple as possible so that visitors can get a sense of how easy it is to use and navigate.

- **Consistency**

The consistency of a website's design is quite important. Pay close attention to how the design components on each page match. It's obvious that your fonts, sizes, headings, subheadings, and button styles must be consistent across the board. Everything should be planned ahead of time. Finalize the fonts and colours for your messages, buttons, and other elements, and stick with them throughout the development process. CSS (Cascading Style Sheets) would be useful for storing all of the information about design elements and styles.

- **Typography & Readability**

Regardless of how excellent your design is, text still reigns supreme on the web, as it offers visitors with the information they seek. Along with the clever use of keywords and meta-data, you should make your typography visually appealing and readable for visitors. Consider employing easier-to-read fonts. For body text, current Sans serif fonts such as Ariel, Helvetica, and others can be utilised. Make appropriate typeface combinations for all design elements, such as headlines, body texts, and buttons.

- **Mobile compatibility**

With the increasing use of smartphones, tablets, and phablets, web design must be adaptable to many screen sizes. If your website design doesn't accommodate all screen sizes, you're likely to fall behind your competitors. There are several web design studios or service points where you may get your desktop design converted into a responsive and adaptive design for all screen widths.

- **Colour palette and imagery**

A good colour mix attracts users, however a bad colour combination can distract them. This entails selecting a colour palette for your website that can generate a pleasant ambiance and so make a positive impression on visitors. To give your website design a balanced look, choose complementary colour palettes to improve the user experience. Remember to use white space to avoid visual clutter and disorder on your page. Also, stay away from utilising too many colours. For a pleasing and clear design, 3 or 4 tonnes for the entire website are sufficient. The same is true with photos. Don't utilise a lot of colourful graphics.

- **Easy Loading**

Nobody loves a website that takes an excessive amount of time to load. So take care of that by reducing HTTP requests by minimising picture sizes and combining code into a central CSS or JavaScript file. Compress HTML, JavaScript, and CSS as well for faster loading.

- **Easy Navigation**

Visitors spend more time on websites with straightforward navigation, according to research. Consider building a logical page structure, employing bread scrums, and making clickable buttons for effective navigation. The "three-click-rule" should be followed so that visitors can receive the information they need in three clicks.

- **Communication**

The main goal of visitors is to obtain information, and if your website is able to effectively connect with them, they will most likely spend more time on it. Organizing information by making appropriate use of headings and sub-headlines, reducing the waffle, and using bullet points instead than long windy phrases are all tricks that may serve to develop easy contact with visitors.

1.6.2 WEB SITE DEVELOPMENT – THE PLAN

Before beginning any project, it's critical to communicate and ensure that everyone has a clear understanding of the goals. The best way to avoid scope creep, which can influence budgets and deadlines down the road, is to have a defined strategy and detect any red flags.

- **Determine Goals:**

What exactly is one attempting to achieve? What is the website's primary goal? When creating a website, it's critical to grasp the ultimate purpose. One wants to ensure that their "dream home" is functional and designed with the proper aims and target audience in mind. Whether the goal is to grow membership, convert more visitors into leads, or provide important information to investors, these goals must be established from the start so that everyone knows what the developer is striving for.

- **Define the Target Audience:**

What are the demographics of the audience you want to reach? Understanding the target market is essential for developing website plans that will appeal to them. Conduct market research, develop buyer personas, and assess the competition. Examining websites that the target market might frequent is also a good idea. Make a list of what you enjoy and don't like. It is much easier to develop a website that resonates with the target audience if you keep them in mind.

- **Search Engine Optimisation (SEO):**

Always keep SEO in mind because it has a direct impact on your online performance and success. When constructing a website, there is no better moment to focus on SEO because it can save a lot of effort in the long run. It's easier to incorporate into the site design and architecture if they know what keywords they want to try to rank for. It's also critical to have a mobile-friendly or responsive website these days, as Google favours them over those that aren't.

- **Plan for Content:**

The right content that communicates to the target audience is essential for a successful website. Not only must material be present, but it must also be instructional and entertaining to the audience, as well as search engine optimised. A developer can create a beautifully structured and designed website, but if the content to back it up isn't there and people aren't seeing it, it's a waste of time.

- **Develop Use Cases, Sitemap and Wireframes:**

Use cases aid in the definition of project requirements. They are a technique of detailing the stages a user will take to accomplish their objective or task, as well as determining how various users will act on the site. It will be easier to move forward if it can better describe and understand diverse use cases. Creating a sitemap might help you organise the content you want on your website. It lays the groundwork for the pages the developer intends to include. The goal while creating a site map should be to keep it as simple and intuitive as feasible.

It's critical, though, that all of the features and functionality are described. A wireframe is a visual representation of your website's skeletal framework. It allows the client to examine the site's layout, overall navigation, and functionality before construction begins. Wireframes also give the designer a clearer concept of where different components should go and how the website should function, as well as where different features should show.

1.7 WEB DEVELOPMENT – THE TECHNICAL ASPECT:

Web material must be stored on a dedicated computer with an Internet connection in order to be available on the Internet. A "web server" (Figure 1.3) is the name given to this machine. Any number of individual Websites can be "hosted" by the web server. The web server allows individuals to access and read the information connected with a website, but it prevents unauthorised users from altering the content.

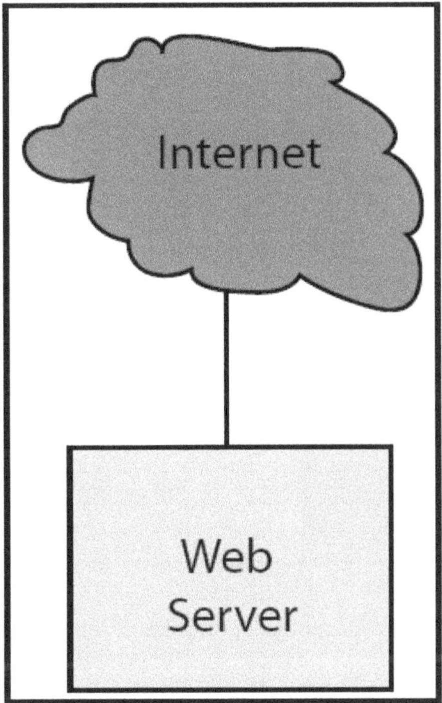

Figure 1.3 Web Server

User has two choices for getting your material to the server if one is producing web content and the server is located remotely (Figure 1.4). One can either transmit it to someone at the remote place on a storage medium (CD, etc.) and have them publish, or one can send it over the Internet also. The most frequent way is to use the Internet to upload web data to the server. A special computer programme known as an FTP (File Transfer Protocol) client is utilised to make this possible. Some websites will necessitate the use of SFTP (a secure version of FTP). FTP and SFTP technologies allow you to connect to a remote web server via the Internet and transfer data to it. Before you may upload data to the server, you must first reach an agreement with the entity that owns it. A user name and password will be provided that may be used to access the remote server and upload your data.

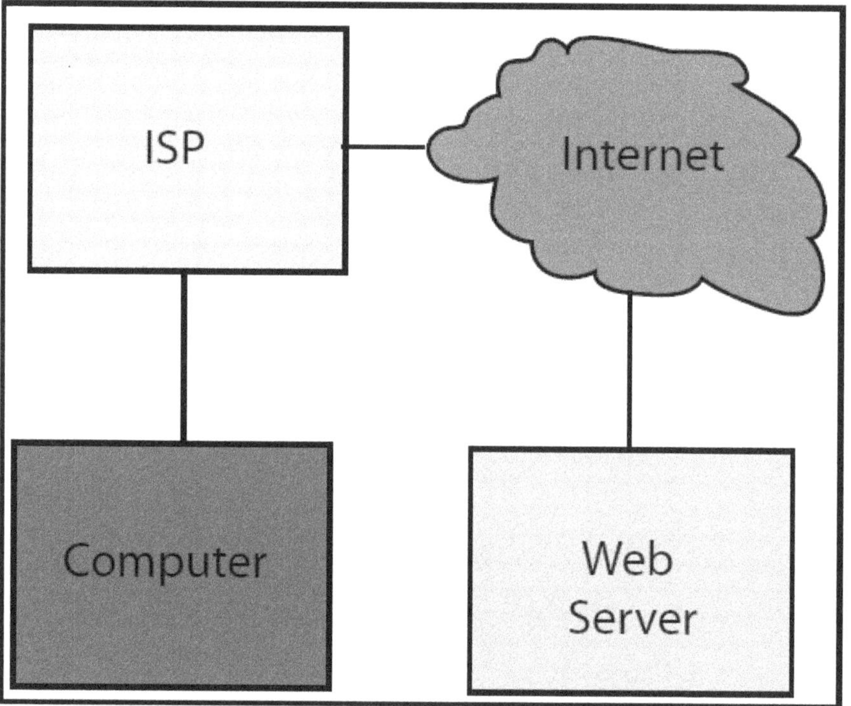

Figure 1.4 Communication between computer and server

Until 2007, one could reasonably assume that our visitors were using our sites while seated at a desk, staring at a huge display, and connected to the Internet via a fast connection. We all pretty well agreed on 960 pixels as a good web page width. Our main issue back then was dealing with the dozen or so desktop browsers on the market, as well as leaping through a few extra hoops to support odd old versions of Internet Explorer. We thought we had it bad before!

Although web pages and web content could be accessed on mobile phones prior to 2007, the introduction of the iPhone and Android smartphones, as well as a more widely available 3G network, signalled a significant shift in how, when, and where we surf the web (especially in the United States, which lagged behind Asia and the EU in mobile technology). Since then, we've witnessed the emergence of various-sized tablets, as well as web browsers on televisions and other devices. And it's only going to get more diverse.

Designing for all of these devices involves more than just dealing with different screen sizes. Using a site on a broadband connection vs a 3G or EDGE network is a completely different experience. There are also different circumstances to think about. Users could be seated at a desk, surfing for fun at home, or looking for information fast on the go. Designers must avoid making network speed and context assumptions depending on screen size. It's not ordinary to use a smartphone to access the web while sitting on the couch at home with a strong Wi-Fi signal. New iPads with high-resolution displays may be using a sluggish 3G connection to get to the Internet. To put it another way, it's difficult!

So, what are our options for dealing with this diversity? Following the World Wide Web Consortium's HTML, CSS, and JavaScript standards is a smart place to start (W3C). Web standards are your major tool for ensuring that your site is as consistent as feasible across all standards-compliant browsers (about 99 percent of current browsers). It also aids in the future compatibility of your content as web technologies and browser capabilities advance. Standards compliance may appear to be a no-brainer now, but it used to be that everyone, including browser developers, messed around with HTML and scripting. Incompatible browser implementations and the need to design sites twice to ensure they function for everyone were the price we paid.

With so many browsers, there are so many different levels of compatibility for web standards. In fact, no browser has fully integrated all of the standards, and new technologies are constantly gaining traction. Users can also customise their browser choices, so they may have a browser that supports JavaScript but have elected to disable it. The point is that we're dealing with a wide range of browser capabilities, ranging from basic HTML support to everything.

One approach for coping with uncertain browser capabilities is progressive enhancement. When using progressive enhancement, you start with a foundational experience that makes content and functionality accessible to even the most basic browsers and assistive devices. Then, for the browsers that can handle them, you layer on more advanced functionality. You could finish with some "nice to have" elements like animation or rounded corners on boxes, which improve the user experience for experienced browser users but aren't crucial to the brand or message. Progressive enhancement is a design and production technique that considers all aspects of a page, including HTML, CSS, and JavaScript.

1.7.1 AUTHORING STRATEGY:

When an HTML document is created in a logical order and its elements are marked up in a meaningful way, it may be seen in a variety of browsers, including the oldest browsers, future browsers, mobile and assistive devices. Although it may not appear identical, the crucial issue is that your material is accessible. It also guarantees that search engines such as Google correctly catalogue the information. The cornerstone for accessibility is a clean HTML text with its elements clearly and thoroughly documented.

1.7.2 STYLING STRATEGY:

Simply by exploiting the way browsers digest style sheet rules, you may create multiple layers of experiences. Without delving into too much technical detail, you can write a style rule that turns an element's background red, but also include a style that gives it a cool gradient (a transition from one hue to another) for browsers that support gradients. Alternatively, you can utilise a cutting-edge CSS selector to limit specific styles to only the latest browsers. Knowing that browsers discard properties and rules they don't understand offers you the freedom to experiment without putting older browsers out of business. Simply remember to style the baseline experience first, then add improvements once the bare needs have been met.

1.7.3 SCRIPTING STRATEGY:

JavaScript is a programming language for creating interactive and dynamic web pages (content that updates on the fly or in response to user input). Without it, the

Internet would be a lot of static brochure ware. There are differences in how browsers handle JavaScript (particularly on non-desktop devices), just as there are with other web technologies, and some users choose to disable it entirely. The first criterion of progressive enhancement is to ensure that core functionality is preserved even when JavaScript is disabled, such as linking across pages or completing vital activities like data input via forms. As a result, you can ensure the baseline experience while also improving it when JavaScript is accessible.

1.8 WEB DESIGNING IN THE MODERN WORLD:

This section will discuss the modern technologies needed to create an effective web app, with a focus on user pleasure as well as the ease with which developers may create their web designs, both frontend and backend.

1.8.1 CASCADING STYLE SHEETS (CSS):

CSS is a W3C standard for specifying the presentation of HTML and XML documents. The way the document is displayed or delivered to the user, whether on a computer screen, a cell phone screen, printed on paper, or read aloud by a screen reader, is referred to as presentation. HTML may handle the business of defining document structure and meaning, as intended, with style sheets taking care of the presentation. CSS is a distinct programming language with its own set of rules. This section introduces you to CSS vocabulary and basic principles, which will help you prepare for the following chapters.

BENEFITS OF CSS:

The advantages of employing style sheets are summarised below.

- **Precise type and layout controls:** CSS can be used to produce print-like precision. There's even a set of characteristics tailored to the printed page.
- **Less work:** By altering a single style sheet, you can modify the design of an entire website.
- **More accessible sites:** When CSS handles all aspects of appearance, you may meaningfully mark up your information, making it more accessible to non-visual or mobile devices.

- **Reliable browser support:** Every browser in current use supports CSS Level 2 and many cool parts of CSS Level 3.

When you think about it, there aren't many drawbacks to using style sheets. There are still residual issues due to browser inconsistencies, but if you know where to look for them, you can avoid or work around them.

THE POWER OF CSS:

We're not talking about small changes like changing the colour of the headlines or adding text indents. CSS is a robust and effective design tool when used to its full capacity. The variety and richness of the designs at CSS Zen Garden first opened our eyes to the possibilities of using CSS for design (www.csszengarden.com). David Shea's CSS Zen Garden site showcased exactly what could be done with CSS alone in the misty days of yore, when developers were still unwilling to give up their table-based layouts for CSS. David made an HTML document public and requested designers to contribute their own style sheets to give it a visual appearance. A few instances are shown in the diagram below. The HTML source document is used in all of these designs.

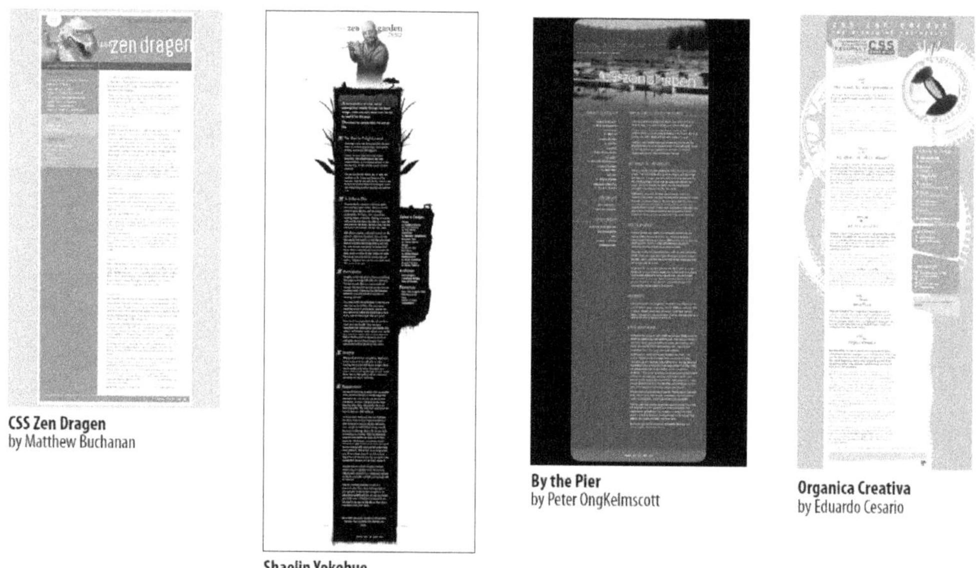

Figure 1.5 These pages from the CSS Zen Garden use the same XHTML source document, but the design is changed using exclusively CSS

Furthermore, there isn't a single image element (all of the images are used as backdrops). But take a look at how different—and sophisticated—each page is. All of this is accomplished through the use of style sheets. It demonstrated the value of keeping CSS and HTML separate, as well as presentation and structure. The CSS Zen Garden is no longer updated and is now regarded as a historical record of a watershed moment in the adoption of online standards.

1.9 RESPONSIVE WEB DESIGNING:

Websites were constructed with a set width, such as 960 pixels, until 2011-2012. The expectation was that all users would have a similar experience. Tablets, netbooks, and cell phones are now available. People are using their mobile devices to access the Internet more than they used to. As a result, it's critical for the end user to have a positive experience on the small screen. The term "responsive web design" was coined by Ethan Marcotte (2014), in which, a responsive web design, refers to the use of HTML5 and CSS3 in its design, that allows a website to adjust to numerous devices and displays, and is the solution to the ever-expanding browser and device environment.

Responsive design has now become the standard for all websites, solving a problem that was once thought to be a web designer's nightmare. With the rise of mobile technology, the days of creating websites solely for desktop displays are numbered; now we must also consider smartphones and tablets. Businesses don't want to lose those valued visitors, so we're also tasked with creating web experiences for them. Prior to flexible design, web designers had to create various versions of the same site for different screen sizes to accommodate the growing number of mobile devices. This was obviously not an ideal approach. The goal of responsive design is to build a single site that can modify its content to appear fantastic on all devices. An example of a responsive website can be found in Figure below. The site adapts to different screen sizes, but the content remains accessible and the style remains consistent and attractive across all three.

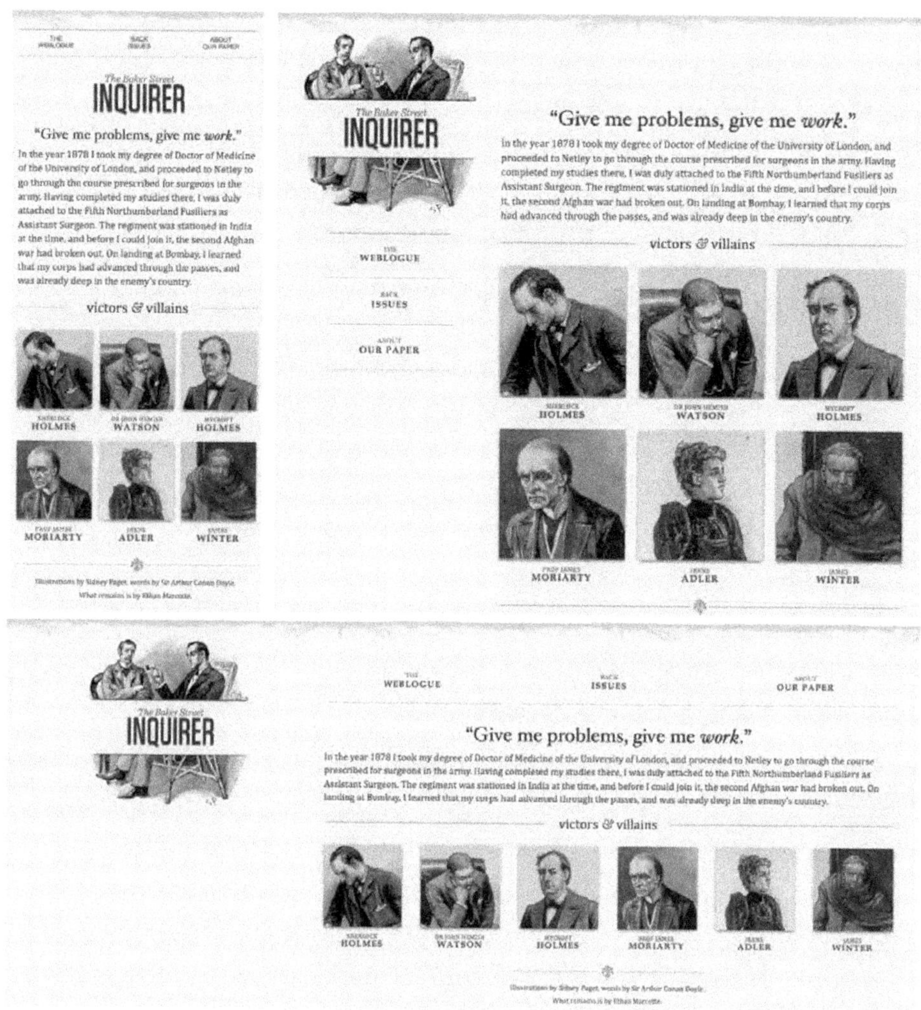

Figure 1.6 A layout that adapts to mobile, desktop, and Jumbo Tron

HOW IT WORKS?

CSS is used in responsive design to regulate how content appears depending on the screen size of the device displaying it. Media queries are one technique to accomplish this. The webpage is supposed to figure out what a device's screen resolution is. Breakpoints are defined in the CSS and are used to describe the size and structure of elements based on the device's screen width. These breakpoints are pixel width ranges for the various screen sizes you'd like to target. For mobile devices, for example, you can specify breakpoints ranging from 0 to 568 pixels. This is how the CSS for this particular breakpoint would look:

```
@media only screen and (min-device-width: 320px)
➥and (max-device-width: 568px)
```

Then, for the next breakpoint, choose a range that fits most tablet devices, followed by a desktop. Breakpoints and media queries have the advantage of allowing you to specify as many breakpoints as you wish.

1.9.1 WEB TYPOGRAPHY:

In layman terms, web typography is the process of using various typefaces on the Internet. Web typography, on the other hand, is a lovely art of designing and arranging various sorts of online fonts, letters, phrases, and paragraphs to produce outstanding web design based on priorities. A decent online typography primarily aids a designer in establishing an effective visual hierarchy as well as providing strong visual punctuation and graphic accents.

Web typography makes it simple for online readers to connect text and graphics. It is common knowledge that TEXT plays an important function in web design. Surprisingly, more and more internet users prefer text to colour, photos, graphics, or sound when visiting a well-designed website. Site fonts, in reality, allow all web designers to effectively employ multiple fonts that are not installed on the end user's computer system. Web typography is an essential component of web design. In the last few years, there has been a lot of progress in web typography.

There are a few key areas where a person can simply improve his online typography by concentrating on them. Font, size, scale, and hierarchy are among the many suggestions, as are vertical rhythm of line spacing, measurement, well-planned grid and alignment, white space, colour, and contrast. Aside from that, proper application of techniques such as CSS image replacement, Scalable Inman Flash replacement, cufón, Facelift Image Replacement, and so on. Last but not least, the CSS3@font-face rule is the most advanced feature. A decent web typography plays an important role in web design and aids a professional web developer in creating a flawless web portal. However, there are some key principles about web typography that a web designer should keep in mind, which are outlined below:

- ✓ Strong horizontal movement
- ✓ Simple but strong typography
- ✓ Good management of white space

- ✓ Upsizing of typography
- ✓ Fun fonts add spontaneity

To fully appreciate the power of type, we must first comprehend it. This isn't an easy process, to be sure. Over decades of research and expertise, the minute intricacies of letterforms and the spaces around them have been meticulously determined. Every letter of every typeface had to be carved into wood or cast from lead, inked, and then pressed into paper in the early days of print. It was a professional trade that demanded meticulous attention to detail. Despite the fact that modern printing methods have long surpassed the physical craft, many colleges and universities still offer letterpress classes so that future graphic designers can appreciate the benefits of working with type on a computer while also seeing the potential for typographic exploration.

Everyone enjoys the variety of voices provided by different fonts, as well as the expressiveness of typographic collages like the one shown below. After all, typography is made up of two root words: typos, which means impression or mark, and grapheia, which means writing; typography literally translates to "creating impressions with writing." Working with type also requires puzzle-like problem-solving. Font and colour selections are merely the tip of the iceberg when it comes to type. In fact, rather than the type itself, the majority of the decisions we must make in our work with type concern the space around the letterforms and text blocks. Choosing a suitable typeface is, nevertheless, a key step.

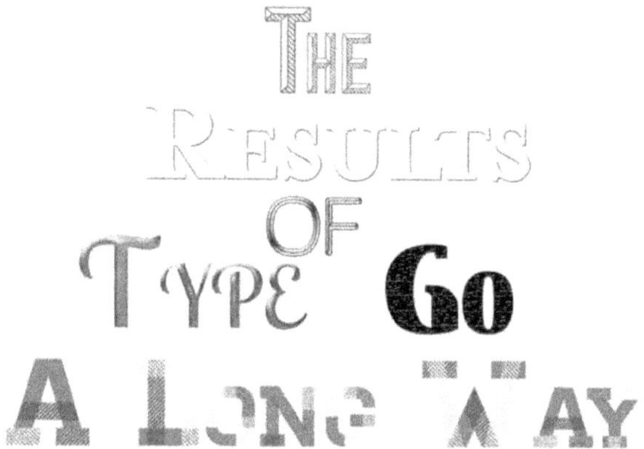

Figure 1.7 A Collage of Typography

1.10 CONCLUSION:

Web design is the process of thinking, planning, and constructing an electronic file collection that determines the layout, colours, text styles, structure, graphics, photos, and use of interactive features that deliver pages to one's site visitors. In the creation and management of websites, web design involves a wide range of talents and disciplines. It also covers a variety of topics such as webpage layout, content creation, and graphic design. All of the basic topics covered in this chapter are discussed in more detail in the upcoming chapters.

CHAPTER 2

WEB DESIGNING– THE TECHNICALITIES

"A designer knows he has achieved perfection not when there is nothing left to add, but when there is nothing left to take away."

-Antoine de Saint-Exupéry

Chapter Learnings:

After reading this chapter, the reader will have a better understanding of the web designing technicalities which includes routing to multiple web servers, web server accelerators, efficient dynamic data serving, load balancing and high availability of Websites, the effects of active queue management on web performance and finally Website usability and design approaches.

2.1 INTRODUCTION:

Websites that receive a great number of requests must prioritise performance and availability over other things. Performance and availability may be improved using numerous strategies that include redundancy hardware, load balancing, web server acceleration, and efficient management of dynamic data, all of which are discussed in this chapter. A case study is also presented that describes how several of these strategies were implemented at the official Website for the 1998 Olympics in Nagano, Japan, which was one of the most popular sites in existence at the time of its deployment. As a result, the site was officially recognised by the Guinness Book of World Records on July 14, 1998, for having set two world records.

- Based on an officially audited total of 634.7 million inquiries throughout the 16 days of the Olympic Games, the Olympic Games were named the "Most Popular Internet Event Ever Recorded."
- According to an officially audited statistic of 110,414 hits received in a single minute around the time of the women's freestyle figure skating competition, "Most Hits on an Internet Site in One Minute" was established.

Due to the high visibility of the site, the massive number of queries, and the amount of data, performance and high availability were essential design considerations. The architecture of the site was developed as a result of experience in developing and implementing the Olympic Summer Games Website in 1996. In this chapter, some broad approaches that can be used to increase the performance and availability of Websites are discussed followed by explaining how several of these were implemented at the official Website in Nagano.

2.2 ROUTING TO MULTIPLE WEB SERVERS:

Multiple servers running on various machines are required by Websites in order to cope with high traffic volumes. The servers can exchange information by using a shared file system, such as the Andrew File System (AFS) or the Distributed File System (DFS), or by using a shared database; alternatively, data can be duplicated over multiple servers using a distributed database.

2.2.1 RR-DNS:

The Round-Robin Domain Name Server (RR-DNS) methodology, which was employed by NCSA for their server, is one method of distributing queries to many servers that has been proven to be effective (Dias et al. 2000). A single domain name can be associated with several IP addresses, each of which could represent a separate Web server, thanks to the RR-DNS technology. Client requests that include a domain name are routed to the appropriate servers in a round-robin method (Mockapetris, 1987). RR-DNS, on the other hand, has a number of drawbacks.

Server – Side Caching: A load imbalance can occur as a result of name server caches storing name-to-IP address mappings. Numerous name servers typically save the resolved name to IP address mapping between clients and the RR-DNS in order to speed up the resolution process. Forcing a mapping to alternative server IP addresses is possible through the use of RR-DNS, which allows you to provide a time-to-live (TTL) for a resolved name. Requests sent after the specified TTL will not be resolved in the local name server. As an alternative, they are routed to the authoritative RR-DNS, where they are remapped to the IP address of a different HTTP server.

Multiple name requests made during the TTL period will all be mapped to the same HTTP server, which is a security feature. Given that a little TTL might result in a considerable increase in network traffic for name resolution, name servers will frequently disregard a very small TTL specified by the RRDNS and impose their own minimum TTL in its place. As a result, even with short time-to-live (TTL) values, there is no way to prevent intermediate name servers from caching the resolved name to IP address mapping. One or more name servers may be shared by a large number of clients, such as those served by the same Internet service provider. As a result, many clients may be directed to a single unique Web server (Kwan, 1995).

Client – Side Caching: Load imbalances can also be caused by the caching of resolved name-to-IP address mappings on the client side. The amount of load placed on HTTP servers cannot be regulated; rather, it will fluctuate depending on how clients visit the servers. Furthermore, because each Web page often includes requesting numerous items, including text and images, clients submit requests in bursts; each burst is directed to a single server node, which raises the skew. These effects can result in large imbalances, which may require the cluster to operate at lower mean loads in order to handle peak loads, if the effects are severe enough.

One further issue with RR-DNS is that the round-robin mechanism is frequently oversimplified in terms of providing effective load balancing. We must take into account things such as the demand placed on individual servers. For example, requests for dynamic data created from numerous database accesses at a single server node can cause a certain Web server to become overloaded.

Node Failures: The caching of resolved names to IP addresses by both clients and name servers makes it difficult to maintain high availability in the event of a Web server node failure, and this is the final point to mention. It is possible that clients and name servers will continue to make requests to failed Web servers since they are not aware of the issues. It may also be necessary to bring down a specific Web server node in a cluster when doing online maintenance tasks. This is made more difficult by the fact that individual node IP addresses are provided to the client and name servers. While we can configure backup servers and perform IP address takeovers in the event of a suspected Web server node failure or for maintenance, it is difficult to keep track of all of these actions at the same time. Furthermore, if a primary node fails, an active backup node may be burdened with twice the amount of work. This gives the common processes involved in webserver routing. The next section, gives the different aspects of TCP Routing.

2.2.2 TCP ROUTING:

The figure below depicts a load-balancing system that uses TCP routing (rather than normal IP routing) to distribute traffic. In this case, a node in the cluster acts as a TCP router, delivering client requests to the Web server nodes in the cluster in a round robin (or other) fashion. The identity and IP address of the router are made publicly available, however the addresses of the other nodes in the cluster are kept secret from customers. The RR-DNS service maps a single name to numerous TCP router nodes in the event that there is more than one TCP router node. The client sends requests to the TCP router node, which in turn routes all packets belonging to a specific TCP connection to one of the server nodes in a ring configuration. It is possible for the TCP router to choose which node to route to using a variety of different load-based methods, or it can utilise a basic round-robin system, which is often less successful than load-based techniques. The server nodes do not communicate with the TCP router and instead respond directly to the client. Note that, because the response packets are larger than the request packets, only a little amount of overhead is added by the TCP router.

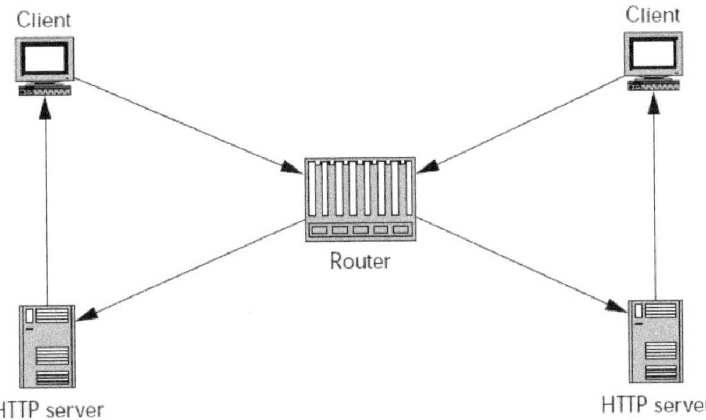

Figure 2.1. The TCP router routes requests to various Web servers. Server responses go directly to clients, bypassing the router

The TCP router system provides better load balancing than DNS-based solutions, and it avoids the problem of client or name server caching that can occur with other solutions. The routers are capable of employing complex load-balancing algorithms that take specific server loads into consideration. The failure of one or more Web server nodes can be detected by a TCP router, which can then route user requests to only the remaining Web server nodes. The system administrator has the ability to modify the TCP router settings in order to delete or add Web server nodes, which makes Web server cluster administration easier. It is possible to handle failure of a TCP router node by setting a backup TCP router, and the backup router can also serve as a Web server when the system is in normal operation. If the backup TCP router detects that the primary TCP router has failed, it will route client requests to the remaining Web server nodes, sometimes removing itself from the process.

TCP routers are widely accessible on the commercial market. Consider IBM's Network Dispatcher (ND), which runs on standard hardware and is compatible with a variety of operating systems (OS), including Unix, Sun Solaris, Windows NT, and a proprietary embedded operating system (EOS). By streamlining the TCP communications stack and eliminating the scheduler and interrupt processing overheads that are present in a general-purpose operating system, an embedded operating system can significantly increase router performance. When running under an embedded operating system on a uniprocessor platform, the ND is capable of routing up to 10,000 HTTP requests per second, which is far more than the request rate experienced by most Websites.

If a single TCP router does not have enough capacity to route requests without becoming a bottleneck, the TCP-router and DNS systems can be coupled in a variety of ways to increase capacity. An IP address can be assigned to a number of router nodes using the RR-DNS mechanism, for example. This hybrid scheme can withstand the load imbalance caused by RR-DNS because the appropriate router will route any burst of requests mapped by the RR-DNS to different server nodes, allowing the hybrid scheme to withstand the load imbalance caused by RR-DNS. A lengthy time-to-live (TTL) can ensure that the node executing the RR-DNS does not become a bottleneck, and numerous router nodes can be used in conjunction to achieve good scalability.

2.3 WEB SERVER ACCELERATORS:

One significant distinction between Accelerator and other caching solutions is that our API allows application developers to explicitly add, delete, and update cached data, which helps to maximise hit rates while still maintaining existing caches. Because apps have the ability to explicitly invalidate any page once it becomes obsolete, it is always recommended to allow caching of both dynamic and static Web pages. Web page caching, particularly dynamic Web page caching, is critical for boosting performance for websites with a lot of dynamic content. We are not aware of any additional accelerators that allow for the caching of dynamically generated pages at this time.

As shown in the diagram below, the accelerator serves as a front end for the collection of Web server nodes. The accelerator and a TCP router are both located on the same node (although it could also run on a separate node). If the client requests a page that is already in the cache, the accelerator returns that page to them. If this is not the case, the TCP router selects a Web server node and forwards the request to that server instead. Persistent TCP connections between the cache and the Web server nodes can be maintained, resulting in a significant reduction in the overhead associated with satisfying cache misses from the server nodes. It is possible to reduce the number of Web servers required for a site by utilising the accelerator to handle a substantial portion of requests from the cache.

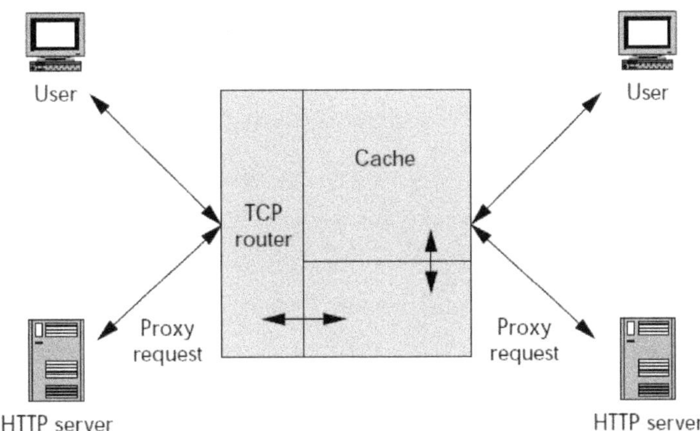

Figure 2.2: Web server acceleration. The cache significantly reduces the server load

Due to the fact that the accelerator must review each request to determine whether or not it can be serviced from cache, it must disconnect from the client. To resolve caching issues, the accelerator requests and returns data from a server, which is then cached by the server and then returned to the client. Due to the fact that the accelerator must act as a proxy for the client in the event of a miss, caching imposes some overhead when compared to the TCP router shown in Figure 1. This overhead is considerably minimised, however, by maintaining permanent TCP connections between the cache and the server. In fact, the overhead on the server is smaller than it would be if the server dealt with client requests directly, as shown in the diagram.

You can use the cache in one of two modes: transparent or dynamic. When using transparent mode, data is automatically cached if a cache miss occurs. Also included are cache policy options, which allow the webmaster to control which URLs are automatically cached. In the case of static image files, different settings define whether they should be cached along with static no image files and dynamic pages, as well as the default lifetimes for each type of file. HTTP headers supplied in a server response can then be used to modify the default behaviour of a certain URL, as defined by the cache policy parameters.

In dynamic mode, the contents of the cache are expressly controlled by applications that are running on either the accelerator or a remote node, rather than by the cache itself. API functions enable programmes to cache, invalidate, query, and determine lifetimes for URL content using the URL's contents as parameters. Although dynamic mode makes the job of the application programmer more difficult, it is frequently essential for best performance. It is particularly useful for prefetching popular things into caches and for invalidating objects whose lives were unknown at the time they were cached while using dynamic mode.

For performance reasons, caching items on disc would significantly delay the accelerator; therefore, all cached data is saved in memory. As a result, cache sizes are restricted by the amount of RAM available. It is necessary for an accelerator to seek information from a back-end server before delivering it to the client in the event of a cache miss. Requesting information from a server necessitates the execution of a significantly greater number of instructions than retrieving the object from cache. As a result, by maintaining permanent connections between the accelerator and the back-end servers, cache miss performance can be increased significantly.

2.4 EFFICIENT DYNAMIC DATA SERVING:

When computing resources were limited, web pages were frequently provided as static text files. This form of static content is incredibly efficient, but if it isn't maintained, it can quickly become outdated. Developers devised server-side platforms and architectures that could generate user-specific content on the fly as low-cost computing and higher Internet bandwidth became more common. Dynamic content is a term for this type of content.

Dynamic content is the primary source of power for some of the world's most popular websites. Dynamic content is used by search engines, social media networks, wikis, and even some blogs to deliver pages to users. These websites would have to pre-generate practically all of their original content if they didn't have dynamic content. If all of Wikipedia's pages were saved as static files, it would require the management of about 40 million unique HTML files.

The majority of dynamic content is generated by programmes and scripts that operate on the website's server. When a user makes a request, these apps work with the web server to process the request, generate content based on it, and present it to the user as if it were static content. Dynamic pages, on the other hand, are frequently supplied at speeds that are orders of magnitude slower. The generation of a single dynamic page by a software can take more than a second on the CPU, which is not uncommon at all. When it comes to Websites with a high proportion of dynamic pages, the CPU cost involved with generating them is frequently the bottleneck in terms of performance. Dynamic pages are vital for websites that give data that is constantly updating. An application that generates pages dynamically can return the most up-to-date version of the data; but, if the data is kept in files and served via a file system, it may not be possible to keep it up to date. This is especially true when there are several files that need to be updated on a regular basis.

2.4.1 CACHE MANAGEMENT USING DATA UPDATE PROPAGATION (DUP):

Caching pages the first time they are created is one of the most essential approaches for boosting performance when dealing with dynamic information. Subsequent requests for an existing dynamic page can retrieve it from the cache rather than having to invoke a programme to generate the same page over and over and over again. The determination of which pages to cache and when they become obsolete is a significant challenge with this strategy. It is once again necessary to do explicit cache management by invoking API operations in order to optimise speed and ensure consistency.

Data Update Propagation (DUP) is a technique that may be used to precisely detect which cached pages have been rendered obsolete by newly available information. DUP determines how changes to underlying data influence cached Web pages and how they are affected by changes to cached Web pages. If, for example, a collection of cached pages is generated from tables belonging to a database, the cache must be kept in sync with the database so that pages do not include out-of-date information about the database. Aside from that, cached pages should be as precisely correlated with parts of the database as feasible; otherwise, objects whose values remain unchanged may be wrongly invalidated or modified following a database change. The frequency of such needless cache updates might increase miss rates and negatively impact performance.

DUP is responsible for maintaining correspondences between objects—defined as items that may be cached—and underlying data, which changes on a regular basis and has an impact on object values. It is a trigger monitor that keeps track of the data dependence information between objects and underlying data, as well as determining when the underlying data has been modified. The system queries the stored dependence information when it becomes aware of a change to determine which cached objects are affected and if they need to be invalidated or updated. It is possible to describe dependencies using a directed graph known as an object dependence graph (ODG), in which each vertex typically represents an item or some other underlying data. An edge connecting a vertex v to another vertex u indicates that a modification to v has an impact on u as well as v. The trigger monitor used its knowledge of the application to construct the ODG depicted in the illustration below. For example, if node *go2* changed, the trigger monitor would be notified about it. The system makes use of graph traversal algorithms to determine which objects are affected by the change to *go2*, which in this example includes *go5, go6*, and *go7*, and which items are not affected. In this case, the system can either invalidate or update any cached items that it considers to be no longer relevant.

Weights can be assigned to edges to aid in determining how outdated underlying data updates have rendered an item in a given scene or scene type. The data reliance from *go1* to *go5* is more significant than the data dependence from *go2* to *go5* in the figure below because the weight of the former edge is five times more than the weight of the latter. As a result, a modification to go1 would normally have a greater impact on *go5* than a change to *go2.*

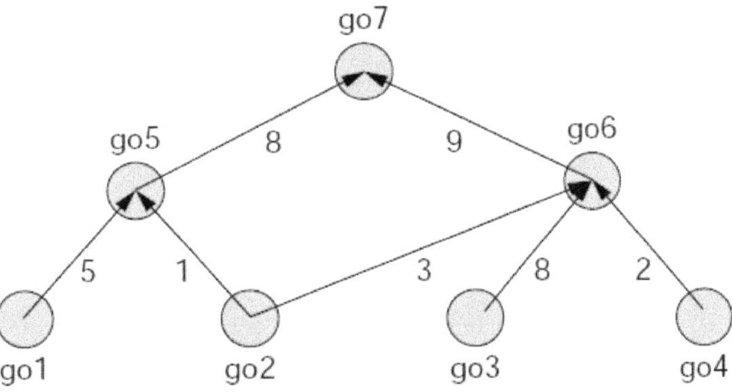

Figure 2.3. Object dependence graph (ODG). Weights are correlated with the importance of data dependencies

2.4.2 INTERFACES FOR CREATING DYNAMIC DATA:

The interface used for launching server programmes that generate dynamic pages has a substantial impact on the overall performance of the site. The Common Gateway Interface (CGI) operates by spawning a new process for each request, resulting in a significant increase in processing time and overhead. CGI, which was once the most extensively used interface, is being phased out in favour of more efficient techniques. Fast CGI processes do not require overhead process creation, although there is some communication overhead between the Web server and the Fast CGI process as a result of this. As a result, the number of simultaneous connections a server can handle is limited by the number of physical processes that a system is capable of supporting.

Server extensions are invoked through interfaces provided by Web servers such as Apache, the IBM Go server, and those from Netscape and Microsoft rather than by forking off new processes each time a server programme is invoked or by connecting with respawned processes. Server tasks are executed in distinct threads within the Web server and may be either dynamically loaded or statically bound into the server, depending on the configuration. An example of this method is IBM's Go Web server API (GWAPI), Netscape's server application programming interface (NSAPI), and Microsoft's Internet Server API (ISAPI). Another example is Apache's low-level "modules," which are a subset of the web server API. Another benefit of efficient thread administration is that many more connections can be handled than there are serving threads, resulting in reduced total resource use while simultaneously boosting capacity. Due to concerns such as portability, thread safety, and memory management that can arise in practise when using the interfaces provided by the GWAPI/NSAPI/ISAPI/Apache modules in particular, the development process can be made more difficult.

Java Server Pages (JSP), Active Server Pages (ASP), Java Servlets, and Apache's mod Perl are examples of more recent approaches that hide the underlying interfaces in order to make the job of the Web author easier. Java, Visual Basic, and Perl are examples of programming languages that are used to create these interfaces. These services also disguise many of the challenges associated with thread safety, and they have built-in garbage collection, which relieves the programmer of the burden of dealing with memory management issues. The ease of programme creation, maintenance, and portability, combined with higher application reliability, can more than make up for the modest performance difference compared to extensions written directly to the native interfaces.

2.5 LOCAL LOAD BALANCING AND HIGH AVAILABILITY:

The employment of load balancers (LB) was critical in the implementation of the complicated network management techniques that were employed. While we picked IBM NDs, we could have also used alternative load balancers, such as those from Radware or Resonate, if we had wanted to save money. They received requests for traffic from the Internet, routed them to a complex, and then forwarded them to accessible Web servers for processing to be completed. The LB (Load Balancing) servers were responsible for running the gated routing daemon, which was designed to broadcast IP addresses to the routers. Depending on whether an LB was the primary or secondary server for an IP address, we assigned various costs to each LB in turn. These routes were subsequently redistributed throughout the network by the routers. Using the information about the routes published by each of the complexes, routers might determine where to direct incoming requests to the LB at the lowest possible cost. A classic example would be the local branch (LB) that served as the primary source for the address allocated to incoming requests at the nearest complex.

If the primary LB for a certain address was unavailable for some reason, the request would only be routed to the secondary LB for that location. Traffic would be diverted to the primary LB in a different complex if the secondary LB fails as well as the primary LB. This approach provided load balancing server operators with complete control over load balancing among complexes. The routers, in addition, did not require any modifications in order to support the concept because they learnt routes from the LB servers using a dynamic routing protocol. It was necessary to connect each of the LB servers to a pool of frontend Web servers that were scattered throughout the SP2 frames at each of the sites. On the basis of load information provided by so-called advisers running on each Web server node, traffic was dispersed across the Web servers in real time. Whenever one of the Web nodes went down, the advisers removed it from the distribution list immediately.

This strategy contributed to high availability by avoiding the creation of a single point of failure in a site. In the event of a Web server failure, the LB would automatically route requests to other servers in its pool, and in the event of an SP2 frame failure, the LB will automatically direct requests to the other frames at the site as well. The router would route requests to the backup LB server if one of the primary servers failed, and if the entire complex went down, traffic was automatically routed to a backup location. The result was what we term elegant degradation, in which the numerous failure sites within a complex are promptly identified and traffic is smoothly reallocated to system elements that are still operational.

2.6 THE EFFECTS OF ACTIVE QUEUE MANAGEMENT ON WEB PERFORMANCE:

The random early detection (RED) method has prompted a shift in the focus of congestion control research to the domain of active queue management as a result of its development (AQM) (Athuraliya, 2002). All AQM designs have one thing in common: they all want to keep the average queue size in routers as minimal as possible. The benefits of this include providing queue room to absorb bursts of packet arrivals, minimising lock-out and bias effects caused by a small number of flows dominating queue space, and giving lower delays for interactive applications such as web browsing and email.

Each and every AQM architecture works by detecting impending queue build up and notifying sources before the queue in a router overflows, as described above. The many designs for AQM that have been proposed differ in the processes that are used to detect congestion as well as the types of control mechanisms that are utilised to reach a stable operating point for the queue size. One further aspect that has a substantial impact on performance is the manner in which the congestion signal is given to the sender. Nowadays, in an environment where TCP is the primary transport protocol (which responds to segment loss as an indicator of congestion), the signal is typically supplied implicitly by rejecting packets at the router when the AQM algorithm detects a growing backlog of traffic. Specific congestion notification (ECN), as recommended by the Internet Engineering Task Force (IETF), would be implemented by assigning bits in the IP and TCP headers for this purpose. With ECN, a router can signal congestion to an end system by "marking" a packet and sending it to the end system (setting a bit in the header).

2.6.1 WEB-LIKE TRAFFIC GENERATION:

It is based on a recent large-scale examination of online traffic that the traffic that drives is based on the resulting model is a high-level description of the critical features that describe the way the HTTP/1.0 and HTTP/1.1 protocols are used at the application level. It is based on empirical data and is intended for use in the generation of synthetic Web workloads on a computer system. Among its key characteristics is that it accurately represents the use of persistent HTTP connections, which are common in many modern browsers and servers. A further distinction is made between Web objects that are "top-level" (usually an HTML file) and those that are embedded objects, according to the analysis that has been presented (e.g., an image file). At the time this data was collected, approximately 15% of all TCP connections carrying HTTP protocols were effectively persistent (that is, they were used to request two or more objects at the same time), but more than 50% of all objects (and 40% of all bytes) were transferred over these persistent connections. The model presented here is expressed as empirical distributions characterising the ingredients required to construct synthetic HTTP workloads, which are described in more detail below. Table 1 summarises the model elements that have the most significant impact on the produced traffic. Virtualization is used to simulate the majority of the behaviour of Web browsing in the client-side request-generating application (also known as the "browser"). Its primary parameter is the number of simulated surfing users that it can accommodate (typically several hundred to a few thousand). The programme creates a basic state machine for each user that will be mimicked, which represents the user's current state as either "thinking" or requesting a web page. Whenever a web page is requested, a request is sent to the server-side portion of the software (which is running on a remote machine) in order to obtain the primary page. Then, for each embedded reference, requests are made to a certain number of servers (the number of servers and the number of embedded references are chosen at random from the relevant distributions). It also defines how persistent and non-persistent connections should be used; 15% of all new connections are randomly picked to be persistent, and the remainder are non-persistent. In order to determine how many requests will be served by each persistent connection, a second random selection from the distribution of requests per persistent connection is performed. In addition, one of the program's parameters controls the number of parallel TCP connections that can be established on behalf of each browser user in order to make embedded requests within a page. This setting is used to simulate the parallel connections that are available in Netscape and Internet Explorer.

Element	**Description**
Request size	HTTP request length in bytes
Response size	HTTP reply length in bytes (top-level & embedded)
Page size	Number of embedded (file) references per page
Think time	Time between retrieval of two successive pages
Persistent connection use	Number of requests per persistent connection
Servers per page	Number of unique servers used for all objects in a page
Consecutive page retrievals	retrievals Number of consecutive top-level pages requested from a given server

Table 2.1: Elements of the HTTP traffic model.

A message of random size (sampled from the request size distribution) is delivered over the network to a server programme instance for each request. The number of bytes the server should return as a response is specified in this message (a random sample from the distribution of response sizes depending on whether it is a top-level or embedded request). The server returns this number of bytes to the browser via the network. After the specified number of requests have been performed, the browser is responsible for terminating the connection (1 request for non-persistent connections and a random variable greater than 1 for persistent connections). The server's "service time" is set to 0 for the tests detailed below, so the response starts as soon as the request message is received and parsed. This closely resembles the behaviour of a Web server or proxy with a large main-memory cache and a hit-ratio of around the browser application records the response time for each request/answer pair. The time between the socket connect () operation (for a no persistent connection), the initial request (on a persistent connection), or the socket write () operation (for successive requests on a persistent connection) and the time the last byte of the response is returned is known as response time. This reaction time refers to the time it takes for each element of a page to load, not the overall time it takes to load all of the page's elements.

When all of the request/response pairs for a page have been finished, the emulated browsing user enters the thinking state and does not make any further requests for a random period of time drawn from the think-time distribution. The distribution of consecutive page requests is sampled to determine the number of page requests the user performs in succession to a given server machine. When that number of page requests has been completed, the following top-level request is handled by a server chosen at random and uniformly among the active servers. Throughout each experiment, the number of mimicked users remains constant.

2.7 WEBSITE USABILITY AND DESIGN:

A growing body of literature in both the human computer interface (HCI) and web-specific usability studies has focused on how well websites are designed and usable. Usability has traditionally been approached from an engineering perspective, with the goal of identifying a set of rules and standard practises that will ensure that usability is a result of system design.

For a long time prior to the widespread usage of the internet, the usability of information systems was defined by a set of design principles that articulated five important characteristics, including:

- Consistency of the interface
- Response time
- Mapping and metaphors
- Interaction styles
- Multimedia and audio-visual

Consistency suggests the necessity for navigational tools such as buttons and bars to be placed in a consistent manner. When measuring response time, it is important to consider how quickly the system responded to a user activity. Mapping and metaphors are important in usability since they emphasise navigation from one location to another within the system as well as the use of specific metaphors such as shopping carts to aid in the user activity within the system. The focus of interaction styles is to focus on system messages that are generated in response to user engagement. The degree to which multimedia capabilities are included into the system design is the fifth usability factor to take into consideration.

Navigating around a website is a crucial design element since it allows visitors to gain more of the information they are seeking while also making the material more easily accessible. As a result, one of the most difficult challenges in developing a useful Website is developing effective links and navigation methods. The visual design, the layout, and the actual information all play a role in making the page easier to use and navigate. Text linkages are essential; navigation and content are inextricably linked; therefore, the navigational structure, searching, readability, and graphics are all important considerations.

As online sites have developed, there has been some uniformity, with de facto standards beginning to emerge as a result of this. Changes in technology have also had an impact on the character of design, but because these changes are typically not disruptive, fundamental design principles have tended to remain.

2.7.1 USABILITY AND WEB INTERFACE DESIGN:

A user interface design process begins with an analysis of who will be using the product and how it will be utilised to assist in the completion of specific tasks. While designing a web page, activities such as profiling user classes, which are often undertaken during the design of user interfaces, can also be performed (Calongne, 2001). While web pages may appear to be straightforward to create, a more in-depth assessment of their target audience, category, and content allows for a better understanding of their usability goals. Important tasks involved in Website design include identifying target audiences and dividing them into user classes, selecting what style of Website will be created, and determining the content of the site as well as any limits or boundaries that will be imposed on it. Every web page designer should take into consideration the user profiles of these different user classes, as well as the categories they choose and the nature of the material. The specifics of how to carry out these responsibilities are less clear.

- **Audience:** Who will be the target audience for the website now under construction? The designer will benefit from addressing certain critical questions regarding the nature of this audience in order to make smart desktop publishing and layout decisions, such as the use of colour, background pictures, fonts and styles, and multimedia components. Through the activation of objects and hypertext options, it also aids in determining the level of control that the user will require.

It is unlikely that a site established for the Young Republicans will be well received by kids who identify as Goths and who prefer a lifestyle that includes a certain degree of pathos, passion, and the sense that the world is a very dark place. Although the sample audiences may be comparable in terms of age, gender, and demographics, and they may have many things in common, their preferences and what appeals to them may be wildly dissimilar. Only the colour palettes will differ; for example, the Goths will prefer a black background with startling images and font techniques, whereas the Young Republicans' site will most likely include metaphors that foster the notion of patriotism and will use red, white, and blue fonts and images to emphasise their patriotic feelings. How does one categorise users into user classes based on their characteristics? Mayhew [Mayhew 1999] covers user profiles, which are used to identify the psychological traits of a representative user population as well as their knowledge, general experience, and task experience. User classes are created to gather together individuals who are similar in their behaviour. Users' motivation, reading level, colour sensitivity, culture, primary language, software knowledge, and previous experiences are all significant factors to consider since they influence the solution set for the design process.

- **Category:** What is the significance of the category or type of Website? The category defines the fundamental objectives that must be completed in order for the website to be effective. For example, a Website designed to sell products will have goals that are vastly different from a Website designed to promote one's ego or to inform the public about a health threat, among other things. The solutions, approaches, and design processes employed by the two groups will be vastly different. Common categories for Websites include:

- Sites that Sell Products or Services
- Information Sites
- Entertaisnment Sites
- Ego-Based Sites

The major usability aim is determined from the choice of a category for the application. If the site is intended to sell things, the performance requirements for the site will place a greater emphasis on fast load times than on high-quality multimedia components that cause the overall load time to slow down. It will have an impact on judgments about colour and desktop publishing layout, how product isnformation is structured, and the use of successful metaphors, among other things.

- **Content:** Once a category has been established, the designer must gather as much information as possible about the site's content before finishing the design of the site. However, content is not limited to the theme of the site, which is its very reason for being. User-friendly content covers the solutions and techniques that are implemented to make it simple for users to complete critical tasks such as information retrieval and navigation, making a purchase, and receiving feedback. There are a number of important design questions that must be addressed, including the following:

- What are the mental models common to the target audience?

- What analogies can be employed to make the Website easy to use?
- What information needs to be included?
- How should this information be organized across the collection of web pages?
- Which desktop publishing styles will best communicate the message?
- Which multimedia components will effectively communicate this information?
- How will the user navigate the site?

Metaphors instruct the user on how to complete critical actions on the website while reducing the need for specific instructions to be provided. They can help to reduce the amount of complexity and the need for extensive instructions, but they must be chosen based on the identification of mental models that the target audience is likely to recognise and understand. When the icon of a pair of scissors is displayed in a user interface, this icon represents the task of cutting some text or a graphic from a document. As part of our mental image of how the work is performed, we see the scissors being applied to the paper, and we understand that something on the paper must be selected before the activity can be completed. Not all users will have the same mental models, and some users will have mental models that are incorrect or poorly understood. Making strong mental models needs a great deal of consideration and knowledge of how one activity in the real world might link to another activity on a web page, among other things.

The shopping cart metaphor and the checkout metaphor are two examples of typical metaphors that are used to teach individuals how to successfully purchase things, to continue with the product sales example. Users have expectations of how the site will behave in order to assist them in the accomplishment of a sales task based on the basic descriptions provided. If the site has been designed in a way that is compatible with the mental model of a shopping cart and checkout, they will be aware that they have not paid for a purchase until they have visited and finished the checkout job. Finding good mental models, comprehending their corresponding metaphors, and mapping them to the user's cognitive model is not an easy task. The way in which users see and respond to a mental model is closely related to the notion of a cognitive and conceptual model. Each of these words builds on the user's experience of considering a task, identifying a correlation in the real world, mapping that activity in the Website, and determining how they have grasped the task when their contact with the metaphor is complete.

2.7.2 USABILITY GOALS:

It is difficult to know how to create a website if there are no objectives. It is hard to test and assess whether anything is useful with a high degree of confidence unless there are quantifiable usability goals. Every Website designer should strive to achieve the skill to build a site that is both visually appealing and functionally effective, and to replicate this process across multiple sites. As a result, usability objectives must first be determined, and then they must be quantified. In order to quantify them, a numerical value must be assigned to each objective. High task performance, for example, might be one of the usability objectives of a Website. In a topic area other than web design, this aim can relate to the number of transactions that are completed each day. As applied to Websites, the speed at which a web page loads and displays the requested information under specific hardware conditions, with sufficient bandwidth, and taking into account traffic congestion may be defined by the Website designer as follows: One possible value for this quantifiable target is ten seconds. Users who represent the target audience would be measured in terms of the time it takes for the web page to load during a usability study. Assigning a number to define a performance metric provides the designer with a baseline for measurement, comparison, and analysis, as well as the ability to determine what to do next in the design process.

The following are some examples of usability goals: easy to learn (measured by the time it takes to perform common tasks); subjective satisfaction (measured by a survey instrument); low usability error rate (noting when the user falters in the performance of a task, goes to the wrong location, makes a typographical error, fails to successfully complete the task); high task performance; and retain ability (measuring the interface usage over time, assessing whether the user retains knowledge).

2.8 CONCLUSION:

Web speed is crucial because it has the potential to cause problems for both the user and the developer if not handled properly. The majority of people who use the internet favour speedier web page loading times. The failure to achieve faster web page load times will have a significant financial impact on the developer. There are numerous techniques that can be employed in order to improve web performance, the most significant of which are those that are linked to HTTP, HTML, CSS, JavaScript, cache, and images. HTTP, HTML, CSS, JavaScript, caching, and images are among the most important. Each and every one of these plays a significant function, and the inability to recognise them will have an impact on the overall performance of the website. Apart from that, there is a more straightforward method of analysing online performance, which is through the use of web performance analysers and other tools. Yottaa Site Optimizer, YSlow, Google Page Speed online, and web page test are the four web performance analysis tools available. This type of tool provides the user with more detailed reports on specific websites or pages, and by utilising it, the user may learn more about the general performance of a webpage rather than having to go through the tiresome process of modifying codes or resizing an image. When using a web performance analyser tool, one of the most significant benefits is that some of the tools also provide excellent ideas that are thought to be beneficial in improving online performance.

CHAPTER 3

WEB PERFORMANCE & ITS INTERCONNECTIONS WITH WEB DESIGNING

"A successful website does three things:
It attracts the right kinds of visitors.
Guides them to the main services or product you offer.
Collect Contact details for future ongoing relation."

— Mohamed Saad

Chapter Learnings:

After reading this chapter, the reader will have a better understanding of the web performance and its interconnection with web designing. This chapter includes Importance of web performance optimization, web performance measurement criteria's, its testing and finally explain the concept based on a case study.

3.1 IMPORTANCE OF WEB PERFORMANCE OPTIMIZATION(WPO) IN WEB DESIGNING:

Web Performance Optimization (WPO), often known as website optimization, is the branch of expertise that focuses on boosting the speed with which web pages are downloaded and shown on a user's internet browser. The performance principles outlined by Souders (2008) must be followed in order to increase the speed of a web page. These web pages must load quickly because all websites with faster download speeds have been proven to boost visitor loyalty and happiness. This is especially true for users with sluggish Internet connections and mobile devices, who rely heavily on these websites. Web performance also results in less data being transmitted via the internet, which helps to reduce website power usage and environmental impact, among other things.

The first decade of the internet's existence saw web performance progress focusing mostly on optimising website code and pushing the limits of available hardware technology. Early techniques, such as the use of simple servlets or Computer-

Generated Imagery (CGI), increased server memory and improved the ability to detect and retransmit packets in the event of a loss. These ideas, while they currently form a large part of the optimised foundation of internet applications, are distinct from contemporary optimization theory in that there was far less of an effort made to increase the browser display performance during their development. Souders coined the name "World Peace Organization" (WPO) (2008). WPO as an emerging industry is expected to have a significant impact on the web, with sounders predicting a number of outcomes such as websites that are fast by default; consolidation; Web performance standards; environmental impacts associated with optimization; and speed as a competitive differentiator. One of the most important points made by Souders is that the front-end structure is responsible for at least 80% of the time it takes to download and browse a website. This lag time can be reduced by being aware of standard browser behaviour as well as the workings of the Hypertext Transfer Protocol (HTTP).

There were numerous performance challenges, with three of the most prominent being the sheer size of web pages, the way in which the sites are constructed, and the way in which it is consumed by different browser types. A second issue is that users' page-load expectations outstrip the capabilities of most websites to deliver on their promises.

The performance of a website has a significant impact on both the user and the developer. Customers care about the speed of a website. A survey of 1500 consumers determined more than 75% of online consumers chose to visit a competitor's website rather than wait for delays. After having a negative experience on a website, around 88 percent of online shoppers are less likely to return to the site. Following a single negative experience, half of those polled indicated a less positive overall impression of the organisation. Poor availability and page load time have a direct and negative impact on the customer's satisfaction. Because of their lack of loyalty, visitors are willing to switch to another website if their present web page takes an excessive amount of time to load. This is unquestionably unworthy of the developer and has the potential to result in a significant loss of revenue.

3.1.1 WAYS OF INCREASING WEB PERFORMANCE:

There are a few things you can do to help improve the performance of your website. One method is to reduce the number of HTTP queries. In other words, this will reduce the number of times the browser must make a round trip to the server to retrieve the information. All files on the website must be downloaded to the browser before it can be seen. The page's performance is greatly improved as a result of reducing the number of requests it receives. It is more advantageous to put all of the CSS in a single style sheet for the site rather than separating it into distinct sections. The same may be said about JavaScript and other resources, among other things.

Some people style the code they write in order to make it easier to read and understand. This is done in order to make it more intelligible. Despite the fact that the code is easier to read, it contains a large number of superfluous characters. When a large-scale site with hundreds upon thousands of lines of code is involved, however, it will have an impact on the overall web performance. Characters like as empty space, comments, and new line characters are examples of unneeded characters. It is possible to remove it without harming the performance of the code. The benefit of removing the code is that the file size of the code can be lowered, which reduces the amount of data that needs to be downloaded to the browser by the user. Additionally, data can be utilised to reduce the number of HTTP requests made by the images in addition to the Uniform Resource Locator (URL) and the images themselves.

Images are one of the most critical things that most browsers need to download before they can function properly. As a result, the site is extremely slow. An alternative method of avoiding this is to generate visuals using CSS rather than pictures. However, while this is fantastic for items such as buttons, in some circumstances CSS may not be able to accurately recreate the design, such as in the case of a photograph or a detailed decorative element. In this instance, photos must be correctly formatted and compressed in order to be effective. This is done in order for the data to be retrieved and turned into visually appealing images for the web.

HTML CSS Sprites is a process of combining many backdrop pictures into a single composite image, which is then displayed using the CSS background position property. This strategy is used in order to reduce the amount of time it takes for a page to load, hence reducing the number of requests made to the server and saving bandwidth. CSS sprites were utilised by Yahoo! to minimise the amount of HTTP requests for the little ivories that appear on the Yahoo! site. It can assist in minimising the amount of data used on the web by decreasing the number of HTTP requests and enhancing the speed of web performance. CSS Sprites are tough to generate, but there are online tools, such as Sprite Pad, that may assist you in creating the sprites by dragging and dropping the images and having them available, as one Portable Network Graphic (PNG) Sprite CSS code, immediately. Figure 3.1 shows examples of CSS sprites in two known websites, Facebook and Yahoo!

Figure 3.1 CSS Sprites used in Facebook and Yahoo! websites

There are several photos on the planned website that would not be convenient or practical to use as a CSS sprite. As a result, it is critical to understand how to compress the photographs. By properly structuring and compressing photos, it is possible to save a significant amount of data. Because of the usage of tools such as Photoshop or Fireworks, the resulting image contains additional data, including colour data that may or may not be used in the image. It is possible to reduce the amount of data that must be downloaded by compressing photographs without sacrificing their appearance or visual quality.

Both web browsers and web servers have the capability of caching information. Previously requested items such as photos, web pages, CSS/JS files, and other data such as cookies are stored in these caches on the browser or on the server side. By storing these responses, the amount of bandwidth used is reduced, and the overall speed of the website is improved.

In addition to attempting to enhance online speed on your own, it is possible to analyse web performance through the use of special applications. These four pieces of software can be used to assess the overall performance of a website: Yottaa Site Optimizer, YSlow, Google Page Speed, and Web Page Test are some of the tools available.

In addition to offering an easy-to-use site optimizer, the company Yottaa also offers a service that increases the performance, scalability, and security of any website. It speeds up the site, resulting in faster page loads and a better user experience, as well as preventing the site from going down under heavy demand or attacks. It expands the web infrastructure to become a worldwide cloud network with more than 20 data centres around the world (Huang, 2005).

Web pages are analysed and suggestions for speed improvements are made using YSlow, a tool developed by Yahoo outstanding performance team. This is based on a set of guidelines for high performance websitesWebsite and may be used to analyse and offer performance improvements. It works by utilising the Firebug plugin on the Firefox web browser. Marcel Duran, on the other hand, has built plugins for YSlow Chrome, Opera, and Safari over the course of the previous year. In addition to grading web pages according to one of three predetermined rule sets and providing advice for enhancing the page's performance, YSlow summarises the page's components and displays statistical information about the page.

Google page speed online is a Google webpage performance tool that aims to assist in optimising the performance of a website's page load time. It assists in the identification of performance best practises that can be used to the site as well as optimization tools to assist in the automation of the process. A simple, user-friendly interface that is simple to understand is provided (Killelea, 2002).

Web page test is a free tool that includes a variety of basic and complex analysis tools that allow the user to have a level of control over how the website is actually tested and evaluated. The advanced features include the ability to customise the test to account for the various real consumer connection speeds, the ability to change the browser depending on the target location within the website, the ability to ignore Secure Socket Layer (SSL), which is a protocol used over the internet for the security of transactions made between clients and servers, and the ability to stop the test from running after a specific item, component, or document has been loaded.

3.2 WEBSITE PERFORMANCE MEASUREMENT: PROCESS AND PRODUCT METRICS:

Website metrics can be gathered either manually or automatically through the use of tools on a website. A large number of technologies are being developed to collect measurements and attributes in an automated manner. Some attributes and metrics, on the other hand, necessitate the participation of surveyed users or testers in order to provide their "personal" opinions on those features, owing to their subjective nature. In this section, we will go through some of the features and measurements that have been described.

3.2.1 PRODUCT ATTRIBUTES:

- Websites usability: Usability is one of the most often used software characteristics, and it has been extensively researched in the literature. The usability of a website and its information or services is measured in terms of how easy it is for people to use the website and its information or services. Several internal characteristics that can be evaluated as part of the usability evaluation process are as follows: (which is an external attribute). This may involve the following:

- Success rate (i.e. whether users can perform the intended tasks or not).
- The time each task on the website requires to be accomplished. In some cases, a similar metric called "ease of use" is evaluated by users. It can also be measured subjectively through users' response or satisfaction.
- The time it takes for users to know, get used, and complete tasks with the website features and services (i.e. training time).
- The error average or rate for typical or average users. This can be also measured based on a ratio between successful to failure tasks executed by the users.
- User satisfaction.
- Number of features or commands used from the website by users (also called usefulness).

- The number of available help files, documents and any other features that can help users perform tasks easier and faster.

In addition to usability, there are several other characteristics that are components of or connected to usability, such as efficiency, efficacy, user pleasure, learnability, and memorability. Efficiencies include all previous internal attributes that have been linked to the ability of users to complete tasks quickly, such as the time it takes to complete a task, the amount of time it takes to learn a task, the amount of time it takes to make mistakes, the percent or number of mistakes made, the frequency with which help or documentation is used, and the number of repetitions or failed commands. The following are examples of effectiveness-related attributes: the percentage of tasks accomplished, the ratio of successes to failures, the workload, and the number of features or commands employed. The following user satisfaction-related attributes are measured: a rating scale for the usefulness of the product or service, a rating scale for satisfaction with functions and features, the number of times the user expresses frustration or anger, a rating scale for user control of the task versus technological control of the task, and the perception that the technology supports tasks as required by the user The learnability of a website reveals how easy it is for users to complete fundamental tasks the first time they encounter the features of the website. The memorability of a website indicates how well it aids a user in recalling its elements (i.e. from previous visits). On the other hand, memorability can refer to the ability of a website to remember and accelerate the ability of a user to execute tasks on the website in question.

- Performance metrics: In most cases, the term "performance" is used to describe characteristics such as correctness and speed. In this section, we will discuss attributes that are relevant to the speed with which transactions are processed. In other words, some of those measures may be related to usability in some way. In some circumstances, the number of persons who visit a website is included in the performance indicators for that website. Other classifications include it in the category of traffic measurements. According to the dictionary definition of performance, "the capability of a website to provide its services accurately and swiftly," then such a characteristic may not be directly tied to traffic metrics like visits. Some websites have become well-known because of the services they provide to their visitors. Of course, if such services are delivered incorrectly or in a sluggish manner, this will have an impact on traffic statistics. The only performance metrics that will be considered are those that relate to the speed with which pages and images are downloaded, as well as the reaction time that is required when a user initiates a transaction and waits for the website to respond. Depending on the performance attribute, it may be time dependent, meaning that it may differ depending on the time of day or on specific days of the year. They can also be influenced by the quantity of people who are now requesting services from a certain website in question. Interactivity and responsiveness are two related measures that measure how quickly and how long it takes for a user to interact with a website's services through ping pong dialogues. Interactivity and responsiveness are both measured in milliseconds.

- Traffic and usage metrics: These measures are quite popular, and they have been the focus of numerous articles, tools, and reviews. The popularity of a website, or the number of people who visit that website, is one of the most important success metrics for that website. There are a variety of characteristics that can be grouped together under the headings of website traffic, popularity, or usage metrics. These include web usage, web and page visits, website and web page rankings, visitors (unique, repeat, and first-time visitors), most viewed pages, most requested pages, single access pages, user average time or stay on website or pages, page refreshes, page views per visitor, and top Directories, to name a few examples. In addition to the previously mentioned qualities, there are a number of sub attributes that are related to traffic metrics. For example, stickiness is a traffic statistic that can be used to determine whether or not a website is appealing to users by analysing the ratio of unique visitors to page views on a website. The higher the ratio of unique visitors to page views, the stickier a website is considered to be. Another indicator to consider is the relevant track, which indicates how long visitors spend on a certain website. The longer people are on the webpage, the more track relevant it becomes.

There are various metrics that can be classified as either customer or financial metrics, or as traffic metrics, depending on how they incorporate aspects from both categories. Cost per visitor, cost per lead, cost per customer, bounce rate, revenue per visit, page attrition, path weight, and proxy scoring are just a few examples of the attributes or metrics that can be measured.

- Business or Financial metrics: As mentioned earlier, there are many metrics that are common with traffic metrics. Other metrics include:

- Operational efficiency: Measuring and quantifying Web content management (WCM) benefits.
- Revenue optimization. Connecting WCM with revenue.
- Time to market

- Customer Metrics: There is no direct relationship between those measures and the website and its relevant qualities. Those are associated with services that may be offered on those websites. Typical metrics include: reach, product profitability, brand equity, acquisition of services (such as the cost of acquiring a new service), market share, conversion and retention based on customer communication and interaction with the website, its pages and services, abandonment, attrition, and churn (see below). outline the process of user migration

- Process Quality Metrics: Those are associated with the actions and operations that take place on the websites in question. In website activities, this may include properties linked to memory, such as the maximum amount of memory that can be used. The length of time necessary to complete specific tasks on the website may also be included in this figure. Process quality measurements can include metrics for defects and defect tracking, which can be grouped together as defect and defect tracking metrics (e.g. defect arrival and defect fix rates, and trends).

- Structural Metrics: All of those metrics can be acquired through the website's various components. These numerical values for website structural elements such as the number of links (internal links), web pages, forms, frames, text boxes, and other elements are described in the Website structural attributes section of this document. Some metrics that can be classified as web structural metrics, and these are listed below. Among them are metrics such as centrality (or compactness) and consistency (or consistency), which are all connected to determining how much a Website's components are consistent with one another and with web standard design.

- Web Content Metrics: Web pages and their components are evaluated for their format and conformance with Web design standards, as well as for their content. Web content metrics are used to track the evolution of a website, such as the amount and rate at which web components are added to the website on a weekly, monthly, or other basis. The report also includes details about the website's physical files, database, and the kind of software applications that were utilised to create the website.

- Complexity metrics: These are metrics that are connected to either maintainability or effort) measurements. A large number of previously mentioned features, such as those found in structural metrics, are also found in complexity metrics when it comes to Website complexity. This means that the majority of those features are recycled from other measures and used for a variety of distinct metrics types. The following are some examples of complexity and maintenance-related metrics: testability, error proneness, dependability, fault tolerance, and so on. The complexity metric takes into account those components that may incur maintenance overhead or that may cause a web page to load slowly. Another feature to consider is the measure of calculating the number of dynamic pages in comparison to the number of static pages. This metric may have an impact on the performance and maintainability of websites.

- Quality and Marketing metrics: Many measures and traits are associated with quality, including but not limited to: In this context, we will consider only those issues that are particularly linked to page errors, unsuccessful logins, errors, crashes, and so on. Some of such indicators are combined with metrics derived from popularity or traffic statistics, for example. Many sources, on the other hand, cited measures that were solely for marketing purposes. This includes the following:

- Brand impact (i.e., increased product or brand awareness, intent or favourability)
- Number of impressions
- Position of organic and paid listing
- Click through and number of clicks by users.

- Number of pages indexed
- Number of overall inbound links
- Authoritative citations/links
- Referring traffic sources
- Cost per lead
- Customer acquisition cost
- Customer life cycle
- Referring search engines
- Top keyword referrals
- Top keywords by revenue
- And many more items found in good analytics packages
- Churn rate.
- Website grade (i.e. through grader tools, e.g. websitegrader.com).
- Ratio of new to returning visitors
- Amount of increased website traffic
- Duration of website visits (i.e. new, returning, etc)
- Amount of increased traffic to physical store
- Amount of increased volume to call centre
- Number of leads generated for products sold online
- Number of leads generated for products sold offline
- Number of immediate sales generated for products sold online

- Web Security Metrics: Recently, it has been gaining more and more attention. The calculation of website security metrics is based on the number of weaknesses (also known as vulnerabilities) that exist on that website. SQL injection, session hijacking, Cross Site Scripting (XSS), Cross Site Request

Forgery (CSRF), Remote File Include (RFI), Denial and Distributed Denial of Service (DOS, DDOS), IP, content, packet and form spoofing, phishing, code injection, broken access controls, information leakage, insufficient authentication and authorization, and other types of attacks are examples of how these weaknesses can be exploited and abused. Several metrics are proposed in light of the threats that have already been mentioned. This includes the following:

- Exposure or discoverability. E.g. Number of weaknesses, or number of days a website is exposed per month or year.
- Exploitability or threats.
- Impact severity.
- Annual expected loss or exposure rate

3.2.2 PROCESS ATTRIBUTES:

To understand quality factors in website project development, we must first identify the primary actions that take place during the website design project's development. For the most part, web page design has goals that are similar to those of software design. The goal is to create a website that is simple to learn and use, appealing to browse and use, allows its users to efficiently complete their activities, and is simple to maintain. According to some website designers, the website design process is divided into phases based on the primary features of a website design, which include:

- Accessibility design
- Colour design.
- Image design
- Navigation design.
- Database or storage design.
- Text design.
- Sound design.
- Look and feed design.

- Content design
- Behaviour design.

For each of the elements described above, there are a number of quality factors that can be examined in order to determine the overall quality of the element. When comparing the metrics defined here and those established in the product metrics, one significant distinction is that those defined in the product metrics were defined at a higher degree of abstraction than those defined here. For example, performance and security are two characteristics that are interwoven and cumulative. It serves no use to have some sections of a website that are secure while the others are not. In order for a hacker to bring down a website, he or she needs only one weak point. The same may be said for other factors such as performance, dependability, and so on. As an alternative, portions of the process metrics stated earlier can be measured individually or on a page by page basis, rather than for the entire website, allowing for more precise measurement.

It is also possible to divide the webpage design process according to the development team: user experience team, visual and animation design team, database design team, system design, design production and documentation teams are all examples of sub-teams. Websites, by their very nature, are evolving in nature. The process of constructing a website (especially active websites) can therefore continue even after the website has been launched or is being used. Therefore, design quality attributes are critical in enabling users to quickly update, modify, and maintain all pages of a website, among other things.

3.3 WEB PERFORMANCE TESTING:

Before going into testing, first the basis of Web performance is discussed, the objective metrics of load time and runtime, as well as the perceived user experience, make up web performance. Web performance refers to how quickly a site loads, becomes interactive, and responsive, as well as how smoothly the material scrolls throughout user interactions. Is it possible to click on buttons? Is it easy to load and display pop-ups, and do they animate smoothly while doing so? Web performance encompasses both quantitative metrics such as time to load, frames per second, and time to become interactive, as well as subjective experiences such as how long it took the content to load.

The longer a website waits to respond, the more users will abandon it. Making the experience as available and engaging and feasible, as soon as possible, while asynchronously loading in the longer tail elements of the experience, is critical to minimising loading and reaction times and adding additional features to disguise latency.

It is possible to measure and enhance web speed with the use of tools, APIs, and best practises. With Web Performance Testing, the goal is to analyse the performance of a web application as well as all of its back-end systems (such as the database and application server) under varying load conditions. Performance testing ensures that a system's performance is consistent under a set load, while also finding areas where reaction time is excessive.

The load generated and emulated by the end users is done through the use of automated methods. These kind of tests are quite beneficial for verifying, in a test plant, new updates of the application or stressing it with a higher level of stress (useful, for example, before the launch of a new advertising campaign). In order to imitate the activity of a specific number of users of different sorts and, if long response times are detected, to identify all of the system bottlenecks, false traffic is manufactured. Following the completion of the initial tuning activity, all of the tests should be rerun. All testing tasks can be carried out on-site or remotely, depending on the situation. The application is the primary focus of the first type of activity (the entire network between the server web and the browser is not taken into consideration), and it is possible to extract a great deal of relevant and comprehensive information from it (especially if, during the test, all the resources of the systems involved are under monitoring). Because all of the factors involved (user browser, ISP, network, and application) are taken into consideration, it is possible to acquire an end-to-end assessment of performance with a remote test; however, it is not possible to obtain a great deal of detail on each aspect.

There are several different types of tests that can be performed depending on the type of load and the timing:

- Smoke Test – A brief test, just to check if the application is really ready to be tested (e.g. if it takes 5 minutes to download the home page it isn't worth going on to test other pages)

- Load Test – For these kinds of tests, the application is subject to a variable increasing load (until the peak load is reached). It's useful to understand how the application (software + hardware) will react in the field.
- Stress Test - For these kinds of tests, the application is subject to a load bigger than the one actually expected. It's useful to evaluate the consequences of an unexpected huge load (e.g. after an advertisement campaign)
- Spike Testing – For these kinds of tests, the application is subject to burst loads. It's useful to evaluate applications used by lot of users at the same time (high concurrent user rate)
- Stability Testing – For these kinds of tests, the application is subject to an average load for a long period of time, It's useful to find out problems like memory leaks.

Automatic tools are used to execute performance testing when you need to simulate real user activities. They work as follows:

- Identify transactions and pages to test;
- Record user activity (tool feature). A script will be generated;
- Identify the data and parameters of the application (workload characterization);
- Modify the script according to the data just identified, in order to reflect the activity of several users (e.g. in an e-commerce site, every user buys different things);
- Playback the script increasing the numbers of simulated users (virtual users);
- Extract response time of main user transactions or pages.

When creating workloads, it is critical to ensure that they are both very accurate and as realistic as feasible. This necessitates an accurate understanding of the genuine user profile. The most up-to-date Web Log Analysis methodologies and technologies can assist in resolving this issue.

Figure 3.2 Performance Testing Tools

3.4 IMPROVING WEB PERFORMANCE BY CLIENT CHARACTERIZATION DRIVEN SERVER ADAPTATION:

Over the last few years, web performance has been a major focus of academic and industry study. Longer user sessions on a Website, as well as more frequent visits, are both influenced by the perceived latency of the site by its visitors. Consequently, a Website that wishes to retain users has a strong incentive to lower the time to glass" (the time elapsed between the user clicking on a link in the browser and delivery and display of the resource on the user's screen). There is a strong incentive to offer material to users as rapidly as possible for Websites that have a vital requirement to keep people once they have reached the rest page. Because of the inconsistencies of network latency, the presence of intermediaries, and the user's network connectivity, the server has a strong incentive to transmit the most appropriate (either dynamically created or statically selected) content to the user as soon and efficiently as possible.

Here we will learn about the quality of the connection between a client and a web server, which will assist the server in making an informed decision about the material to deliver. Everyone is attempting to gather information about the client's connectivity based on information that is already available at the server. The active collection of information on the more dynamic components of the end-to-end latency, such as the bandwidth of the client or network delays, is an alternative to the passive collection of information. A significant quantity of active information collection in many locations would be required for this to be possible, though.

It is possible for a Website to contain many variations of the same resource. A more appropriate variation of a resource may be supplied in the response if the Web server on the site was aware of the client's poor (or abundant) connectivity, according to the site's policies. A different method of delivering the same content could be used by the server instead. In some cases, a faster or higher-quality response may result in greater user satisfaction, which may help the Website retain more customers. It is not necessary for the Website to know the exact degree of connectivity of the client; it is sufficient to be able to classify the client into one of a few categories, such as poor, normal, or wealthy. Additionally, the number of various variations of the response that can be given back is not likely to be more than a few in number. By mapping the different versions of the resource to the different categories of customers in advance, the relevant response may be provided to the appropriate category of clients as soon as the client category is determined (Barford, 1999).

For example, the server can select between delivering only the base document, sending only the base document plus a few embedded resources, or sending the entire container document to the client. Aside from merely returning a different answer, the server can use the information obtained from identifying the client to drive a range of policies on the server's end. It is possible that a server will elect to keep an HTTP persistent connection open longer with clients who have poor connectivity in order to limit the number of times they must establish a new TCP connection with the server. Alternatively, the server can piggyback cached information to lessen the requirements for future validation requests in the future. In order to meet this issue, we must first be able to reliably classify customers into a few useful categories and then identify a set of methods in which the classification can be used to make meaningful improvements. Because the content or access pattern of a given Website may or may not lend itself to benefiting from such a classification, we must determine the fraction of retrievals that are able to benefit from such a classification. Another important indicator to track is the number of clients that are eligible to get assistance. Once a client's characteristics have been determined, we must associate them with the relevant action that the server should do. Clients who are well-connected may not require any modification to the operations conducted by a server. In addition, we can look at how clients are grouped for the purposes of classification and application of server operations.

3.4.1 CLIENT CHARACTERIZATION:

The final stage in being able to customise information or the method in which it is delivered for a customer is to identify the characteristics of the client. Customers can recognise their own traits as one method of approaching the problem. Clients are already able to accomplish this to a certain extent by selecting the categories of content that they are willing to allow. As an alternative, clients could indicate their network connectivity preferences, such as dial-up or cable modem versus T-1 or other options, similar to how they do so presently when they first start using a multimedia player. By using the CC/PP (Composite Capabilities/Preferences Pro les) protocol, the clients can communicate their connectivity information to the server. The CC/PP specification allows user agents and proxies to indicate their capabilities, and it also allows for HTTP content negotiation between servers. Although these technologies are available, the problem with them is that many clients may not use them for typical Web browsing even if they are available. The experience of a client may also differ depending on the time of day or the number of network hops between the client and the server, among other factors. It is advantageous for a Web server to be able to characterise a client in the absence of explicit classification information from the client. There are a variety of different bits of information that a server could use to make such a classification decision. We take into account three different sorts of classification based on network connectivity, reaction time, and various other factors.

- **Network Connectivity:**

It is necessary to characterise the nature of network communication between a client and a server in order to provide the first type of information. It would be ideal if the server could obtain information about the round-trip time (RTT), the bandwidth available, and the degree of congestion present on the path to the client. As a practical matter, the Web server can only draw conclusions based on the network traffic that it receives from the client. For example, the server can estimate the RTT by measuring the time elapsed between accepting a TCP connection from a client and receiving the first byte of an HTTP request from the same client in the following session. This period necessitates only a single round trip of an IP packet. This solution is straightforward and does not require the installation of a new network track, albeit it would necessitate the instrumentation of common Web servers in order to measure this value.

In contrast to RTT estimates for the client by the server, estimation of bandwidth characteristics for the network connection is more difficult to do with each TCP connection made by the client to the server. In most cases, tools for estimating bandwidth between two nodes function by delivering packets of varying sizes between the nodes and measuring the resulting round trip times between them. Bing, path char, and measuring end-to-end bulk transfer capacity are all examples of such technologies. Both the web server and the client will incur additional overhead as a result of this strategy.

The Web server can also utilise an HTTP redirect response (302 Found) to estimate the RTT at the HTTP level. This would normally lead the client to retrieve the redirected content as a result of the initial answer (302 Found). The difference between the two request timings can then be used to estimate the RTT between two consecutive HTTP requests, as shown in Figure 1. Due to the fact that this solution involves the creation of an additional HTTP transaction, the response time for the client is significantly increased.

A second approach at the HTTP level takes advantage of the fact that browsers often immediately request the set of embedded objects for a page after loading the container object for a Web page, as opposed to the previous approach. When measuring the time between the retrieval of the base item and the retrieval of the first requested embedded object, it is not necessitated to make extra requests or redirection simply for the purpose of measuring, as is the case with most other methods.

- **Response Time:**

Aiming to characterise the RTT or bandwidth of the network connection between client and server, each of the previous measurements is described in detail below. When classifying a client, an alternative method is to concentrate on the reaction time perceived by the client rather than being directly concerned with the type of the network connection itself. This outcome-oriented definition is less concerned with finding the specific causes of poor performance and more concerned with defining the contexts in which bad performance occurs.

One method of measuring the response time of a Web page is to make use of the fact that most browsers immediately download embedded objects on a page, as was the case previously. With this observation in mind, the recorded time between serving the base object and providing the last embedded object on the Web page approximates the overall response time of the Web page to the client. This measurement can be carried out without the need to generate any additional Web-based traffic.

When a page is instrumented using JavaScript, which runs within the client's browser and measures the entire download time and reports it back to the Web server, it is possible to gain a more accurate assessment of the total delay experienced by the client (in comparison to the server). Due to the requirement that JavaScript be supported by browsers, this strategy is not without its drawbacks, including the need for intentional instrumentation of pages and the introduction of additional HTTP traffic. The Web server can also count the number of connection aborts and resets from the client, which may indicate the presence of clients that are not well-connected or who are impatient with the process.

- **Additional Factors for Characterization:**

There are a variety of different factors that could be considered when categorising a client. Information contained in the client request header, such as the allowed content types, the HTTP protocol version, and the client software itself, might all be used to classify the capabilities of the client and determine its classification. A client's classification could be stored in cookies generated by a server and included by the client in subsequent requests to that service after the client has been classified. The caching of a client's information by the browser or by a proxy server can also have an impact on its classification. A plausible inference can be drawn from the fact that a client requests only a handful of the embedded objects on a Web page that is known to have dozens of embedded objects, indicating that the client or an intervening proxy has cached many of the objects. Clients who have or are behind an effective cache may be regarded richer if a large number of the objects they require are already in the client's cache. However, a proxy in the path between a client and the Web server may cause additional delays for requests from that client to the Web server, making that client appear worse. The third point to examine is determining which clients should be classified. The most obvious candidates for categorization are those for whom response speed is important users who use browsers as their primary means of communication. Clients who are automated, such as spiders, should be screened out and should not be considered for classification, on the other hand. Most recently, researchers looked at the detection of spiders on a Web server.

3.4.2 POTENTIAL SERVER ACTIONS:

The server could potentially execute a variety of actions after determining a client's characteristics. Here are some examples. In general, there are two types of actions: those that alter the content, which can be used to either wealthy or impoverished clients; and those that affect the delivery of the content, which are primarily applicable to the latter. For the purpose of determining which action to take, the server can use client-specific features as well as the characteristics of a client group, such as the characteristics created by network-aware clusters.

When presented with a variety of content variations, a server could choose a larger and perhaps enhanced variant to provide to richer clients and a smaller and presumably less enhanced variant to serve to poorer clients. By incorporating fewer, if any, embedded objects or by including "thinner" variants of embedded images, the server could give a more condensed version.

When a server receives a request, the first action it takes is to determine whether or not the request will be handled on the machine from which the request was received. When a Website is busy, it is common to have a big collection of machines behind switches or redirectors, where the material is stored or generated. This strategy is used by popular search engines and other heavily trafficked news websites. If the content stored or generated in those machines is partitioned on this basis, the front end server can use the client's connectivity information to influence selection of the back-end machine.

Following the selection of the appropriate mirror, the manner in which the Request-URI is mapped to a specific resource can be further customised in accordance with the connectivity of the client. Additionally, sites that make use of Content Distribution Networks (CDNs) may have some materials provided to them via mirror sites that are scattered throughout the Internet. When it comes to choosing a particular mirror site, the CDN is frequently left in charge; however, the origin server can give information about the client's connectivity that can be used by the CDN in making the selection.

Clients and proxies that are well-connected are more likely to prefect or revalidate content in order to reduce user-perceived delay. Servers can customise the heuristic assignment of expiration meta-information to resources in order to guarantee that clients with bad network connections do not have to do unnecessary validation on resources that change infrequently. Origin servers could use headers to provide indications of proxies between poorly connected clients and the origin server, allowing proxies to increase the freshness interval for resources on their behalf. It is possible for the origin server to assist in guiding caching rules at intermediate nodes by providing information to caches along the path

Once a server has returned a response, it continues to be able to use the information provided by the connection information. In HTTP/1.1, connections between a client and a server can last longer than the duration of a single request-response transaction. In terms of determining when a persistent connection should be terminated, the HTTP protocol does not provide any guidance. A server can decide when to stop a persistent connection depending on a variety of variables, including fairness, the possibility of future connections from the same client, the length of time the connection has been open, and other considerations, among others. If a server is aware that a client is experiencing poor connectivity, they may choose to keep the connection open for a longer period of time than is customary in order to avoid the overhead of having to tear down and re-establish a new connection for the client. A client with a large number of connections might be able to afford the overhead of creating a new connection. Additionally, the server can assign a higher priority to clients who are not properly connected, allowing their requests to be processed more quickly and reducing overall latency.

3.5 CASE STUDY - 1998 OLYMPIC GAMES SITE:

The architecture of the 1998 Winter Games Website was developed as a result of our previous experience with the 1996 Olympic Summer Games Website. The server logs that were collected in 1996 offered valuable information that was used to impact the architecture of the site that was launched in 1998. Users have spent an excessive amount of time looking for fundamental information, such as medal standings, the most recent results, and current news headlines, according to the site's creators, who determined that this was the case. A minimum of three queries to the Web server were required by clients in order to navigate to a result page. There was a lot of overlap in the browsing behaviours for the news, photographs, and sports areas of the site. Furthermore, when a client arrived at a leaf page, there were no direct links to relevant information in other areas of the document. The intermediate navigation pages were among the most often visited due to the hierarchical nature of the site. Hit minimization was a primary goal for the 1998 site, as the designers anticipated that using the 1996 Website's design in conjunction with the additional information given by the 1998 site would result in more than 200 million hits per day, according to the designers. In order to make it easier for clients to acquire vital information while reviewing fewer Web pages, designers revamped the layouts of the pages. We previously published a full description of the Olympic Games Website for the 1998 Summer Olympics in Athens.

There were two major changes: the creation of a new home page for each day and the establishment of a top navigation level that allowed clients to visit the home page from any previous day. They estimate that enhanced page design resulted in a reduction of at least thrice in visits to the site. More than a quarter of users found the information they were looking for with a single hit, according to web server log analysis, and they did it by browsing no further than the current day's home page.

The Website made use of four IBM Scalable Power Parallel (SP2) servers located at various locations across the world, with a total of 143 processors, 78 Gbytes of memory, and more than 2.4 Tbytes of disc space. In order to ensure high performance and availability, we built this level of hardware because not only was this an extremely popular site, but the data it provided was continuously changing. Within seconds of any new content being entered into the system, updated Web pages reflecting the changes were made available to everyone around the world. The latest results, stories, images, and other information from the games may thus be found on the Website and relied on by customers. Even during peak periods, the system was able to serve pages fast, and the site was accessible at all times.

It was possible to achieve high availability for this site by using mirrored information and redundant hardware to serve pages from four separate geographic locations at the same time. The failure of a server resulted in requests being automatically directed to other servers, while the failure of a whole complex resulted in requests being routed to the other three. The network was designed with redundant paths to eliminate the possibility of single points of failure. For high data volumes to be accommodated in the event of a network failure, it was built to handle at least two to three times the anticipated bandwidth.

Dynamic pages were created using the FastCGI interface, and dynamic pages were cached by the Website using the DUP algorithm, which was implemented in PHP. Because of the importance of DUP, we were able to achieve cache hit rates of more than 97 percent. The 1996 Website, on the other hand, made use of an earlier version of the technology and cached dynamic pages without the use of dynamic URL caching (DUP). As a result, it was impossible to determine which pages had changed as a result of the addition of new material. While ensuring that all stale pages were eliminated, many current pages were invalidated, leading to high miss rates when the system was updated with fresh data.

The cache hit rates for the 1996 WebsiteWebsite were in the neighbourhood of 80%. Prefetching was another important factor in getting hit rates that were close to 100 percent. New versions of hot pages were automatically added to the cache as old versions became obsolete, so that old versions were not invalidated. As a result, there were no cache misses on these pages. Responding times were not significantly affected during peak update times since the modifications to the underlying data were performed on separate processors from those providing the pages. Processors acting as Web servers at the 1996 Website, on the other hand, were also responsible for updating the underlying information. Response times are increased as a result of this architecture, which is combined with high cache miss rates during peak update periods.

3.6 CONCLUSION:

Anyone can create a Website that loads and works quite effectively, and that may even be visually appealing to the untrained eye if done correctly. Nevertheless, the assessment of the target audience, the identification of the common tasks that they will perform, and the empirical evaluation of the Website's usability are all necessary for determining whether or not the usability objectives have been met in the design and development of a useful and measurably usable Website The sequence in which activities are carried out is less critical than if the growing

Website has been thoroughly evaluated at each stage of the process and is progressing toward these quantitative usability objectives as a result of the testing. An accomplished professional web designer strives to forecast the design of a useable Website that fulfils clearly specified needs and to be able to repeat this activity on future projects in order to maintain a high level of competence. In order to ensure the usability and productivity of future Websites, it is advised that design approaches that have been shown to be effective in user interface design for other topic domains be applied during the Website design process.

CHAPTER 4

WEB DEVELOPMENT TOOLS

"Website without visitors is like a ship lost in the horizon."

—Dr. Christopher Dayagda

Chapter Learnings:

A greater grasp of web development tools is gained by reading this chapter, which includes the procedures involved in web development, as well as technologies such as HTML5, CSS, and APIs, which are utilised in the building of websites.

4.1 INTRODUCTION:

Applications for the Internet in domains like electronic commerce, digital libraries, and distance learning are characterised by an unprecedented combination of features that distinguishes them from previous information technology applications [Myers et al. 1996]. Individuals with low or no abilities in the use of computer programmes will have more access to information, which will need the development of novel man-machine interfaces capable of catching the customer's attention while also facilitating access to information. It is necessary to integrate the management of structured and unstructured content, which may be stored in a variety of systems (databases, file systems, multimedia storage devices) and distributed across a number of locations in order to ensure global availability of heterogeneous information sources.

Due to its powerful communication paradigm based on multimodality and browsing, as well as its open architectural standards, the World Wide Web has been selected as the ideal platform for developing Internet applications in recent years. These standards facilitate the integration of various types of content and systems. In a nutshell, modern Web applications can be regarded as a mix between a hypermedia [Nielsen 1995] and an information system. Information is accessed in an exploratory manner rather than through "canned" interfaces, as is the case with hypermedia, i.e., applications commonly found on CD-ROMs, kiosks, information points, and other similar devices. The manner in which information is navigated and presented is also extremely important. Data and application distribution require integrated architectural solutions that are based on technologies such as database management systems and client-server computing, which are similar to information systems in terms of size and volatility.

As a result of its hybrid character, the creation of a Web application must address a variety of applicative needs, including but not limited to:

- the necessity of dealing with both structured data (for example, database records) and nonstructured data (for example, multimedia content);
- Through navigational interfaces, the support of exploratory access is made possible.
- an exceptionally high level of graphic quality;
- the personalization and, in some cases, dynamic adaption of content structure, navigation primitives, and presentation styles;
- For example, suggestion and filtering are two examples of proactive activity that can be supported.

These requirements build up, and they typically contend with the technical and managerial challenges that plague every software and data-intensive application, which are evidently applicable to large Web apps as well:

- security, scalability, and availability;
- interoperability with legacy systems and data;
- ease of evolution and maintenance.

As with other emerging technologies such as databases and object-oriented programming languages, methodologies and software tools can greatly aid in mastering the complexity of innovative applications by fostering a correct understanding and application of a new development paradigm, increasing productivity, and lowering the risk associated with application development and migration.

The concept of the World Wide Web is inextricably linked to the Hyper Text Mark-up Language (HTML), which is the language used to describe web pages on the

World Wide Web. HTML makes use of mark-up tags to describe the structural semantics of a web page by identifying the parts that make up the page, such as sections, paragraphs, headings, tables, lists, interactive forms, and so on and so forth. Elements and their accompanying attributes can be nested within one another, resulting in a standard tree structure of elements and attributes. HTML also allows for the incorporation of external resources into web documents, such as images, videos, and other objects, which become part of the web page as a result of their inclusion.

One of the best practises in modern web development is to define the structure and aesthetic of the website separately from one another. Websites are defined in HTML by the fundamental structure of the pages and the material they include, while the final presentation and style of the pages are established by CSS (Cascading Style Sheets). It is possible to have greater flexibility and control over the final design of a web page when these elements are separated, and it also decreases the complexity of an HTML record by eliminating redundancy in style definitions. The separation of content and style allows for multiple web pages to share the same style while also allowing a single page to utilise many different styles at the same time due to the separation of content and style.

A scripting language called JavaScript is frequently used in conjunction with HTML, in addition to the CSS style sheet. JavaScript is a scripting language that is processed by a web browser and that allows web pages to be interactive and dynamic. The method of user-triggered events allows the JavaScript code to communicate with the DOM (Document Object Model) through the many API (Application Programming Interface) libraries available.

Most online pages in the 1990s were static and meant primarily for reading and browsing, but web pages and applications that are more dynamic are introduced in the first decade of the twenty-first century. Instead of simply browsing the Web, users can also contribute to it by creating and uploading their own content, which is referred to as "browsing." The so-called Web 2.0 has evolved and brought about significant advances in a variety of fields, including web development. It is necessary to evolve web languages in order to codify some of the already known best practises in web development in order to accommodate the changing way people engage with the Web.

Several key changes in the procedures involved in web development tasks, as well as new web standards and protocols, will be discussed in detail in this chapter. We concentrate our attention mostly on the latest version of HTML, introducing its new elements and extensions in the process. As well as a list of the most important JavaScript APIs, this chapter contains information on how to create an entirely new way of developing websites by providing a browser-based database, geolocation information, full duplex communication between a browser and a server, and other exciting new features. This chapter also discusses several new CSS syntax choices that have been added. Many new design options are introduced by the latter, which also simplifies and standardises other capabilities that were previously available but were not supported by all browsers at the time of its introduction.

4.2 STEPS INVOLVED IN WEB DEVELOPMENT:

The creation of a Web application is a multidimensional process that includes not only technological considerations but also organisational, managerial, and even social and creative considerations.

4.2.1 PROCESS:

Although there is no consensus on a generic model of a Web application's lifecycle, a scheme of typical actions involved in building a Web application can be derived by interpolating existing information system lifecycle models and ideas for structured hypermedia architecture. The lifecycle model used as a reference in this section is depicted in Figure 4.1.

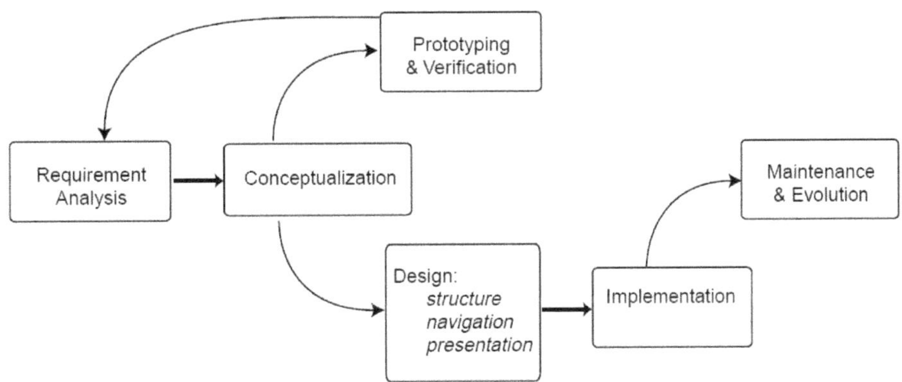

Figure 4.1 The lifecycle of a Web application (Atzeni, et al. 1998)

- REQUIREMENT ANALYSIS: In order to create the purpose of the application, it is necessary to identify prospective users and define the nature of the information database. Additionally, web applications designed for universal access require special attention in the identification of human-computer interaction requirements, in order to determine the interaction mode that is most appropriate for each expected category of users, as well as for each type of output device that users are expected to use to connect to the application. This is in addition to the customary requirement collection and feasibility assessment tasks (ranging from hand-held personal communicators to high definition screens).
- CONCEPTUALIZATION: There are a number of abstract models that reflect the major components of the envisioned solution that are used to depict the application. It is important to note that in the context of the Web, conceptualization differs from the similar activity in information system design since the emphasis is on capturing objects and connections as they will appear to users, rather than how they will be represented within the software system. However, despite the fact that the notation (for example, the Entity Relationship Model [Chen 1976]) may be identical, the schemas arising from the conception of a Web application and a database application are typically distinct.
- PROTOTYPING AND VALIDATION: Users are provided with simplified versions of the applications in order to get early feedback. Since the Web, as well as other hypermedia, has an inherent complexity that necessitates an evaluation of the combined effectiveness of structure, navigation, and display in real time, the relevance of prototyping is particularly highlighted in these contexts. An application prototype is typically developed prior to design and on a simplified architecture, such as a set of manually implemented pages containing samples of the application content, which simulate the expected appearance and functionality of the finished application.
- DESIGN: A higher-level representation of conceptual schemas is translated into a lower-level representation that is more in line with the requirements of implementation while remaining independent of the actual content of the information base. Applications are typically mapped to the schema of a storage repository, the navigational view to a set of access primitives over the content

repository, and the presentational view to a set of content-independent visual requirements. However, there are certain exceptions (styles). The latter activity, known as visual design, is extremely important in the development of Web-based applications and is rapidly becoming a distinct subject in its own right.

- IMPLEMENTATION: New material created by domain experts and/or existing data housed in legacy systems are added to the repository; the actual interfaces, or pages in Web language, are built by embedding repository content and navigational directives into the appropriate presentation style. A decision on the network language in which the application will be delivered (e.g., HTML, Java, ActiveX, or a combination thereof), as well as the decision on the time of "binding" between content and application pages, which can be either offline or online, are all required for the mapping of design to implementation to be successful.
- EVOLUTION AND MAINTAINANCE: Following delivery, changes in requirements or bug patches may necessitate a rewrite of the structure, navigation, display, or content to accommodate the changes. When possible, changes are implemented at the highest level possible in the development chain, and they are communicated downward to the implementation level.

In the example provided, the process model caters to a variety of actual processes, the applicability of which is dependent on the specific development context, which includes the availability of tool support, financial and time constraints, the complexity of the application, and the frequency of changes. According to general practise, when dealing with applications of limited scale and with requirements that are relatively stable, requirement analysis is followed immediately by implementation, potentially after a number of iterations through prototyping. As the complexity and volatility of the application rise, the importance of conceptualization and design increases proportionally.

4.2.2 MODELS, LANGUAGES, AND NOTATION:

The design of a Web application is characterised by three primary characteristics:

- The structure of the information handled by the application explains the organisation of the information managed by the programme in terms of the bits of content that make up its information base and the semantic relationships that exist between them.

- Information access and movement throughout the application's content are addressed by the navigational features of the application.
- The presentation of application content and navigation commands to the user has an impact on how they are displayed to the user.

There are several languages with varying degrees of formality and abstraction that can be used to aid in the representation of application features throughout the development lifecycle, including High-level primitives specify the structural, navigational, and presentational views of applications at the conceptual level, hence abstracting the application from any underlying architectural concerns. It is not necessary to commit to any specific technique for storing, retrieving, and preserving actual instances of such object kinds when using structural modelling primitives to define the sorts of objects that make up the information base as well as their semantic relationships. A few examples of notation that can be used to convey structural characteristics include some of the most well-known conceptual data models, such as the entity-relationship model and numerous object models.

The access paths to objects in the information base, as well as the accessible inter- and intra-object navigation facilities, are governed by navigation modelling primitives, which are not tied to any specific technique for implementing access and navigation, as was the case in the previous section. It is possible to apply the vast range of notation and techniques proposed for the more general problem of human-computer interaction specification to navigation modelling: data models that have been extended with built-in navigation semantics or that have been explicitly annotated with behavioural specifications, first order logic, Petri nets, finite state machines, and formal grammars are among the viable options.

Presentation modelling is concerned with expressing the visual features of application interfaces in a way that is independent of the particular language and device used in the delivery of the programme. It is possible to employ a wide variety of strategies, each with a changing degree of formality and rigour. Techniques can range from simple storyboard definition to the use of software tools and formal procedures. When it comes to the Web, the independent specification of presentation, separate from structure and navigation, is especially important because the final rendering of the interface depends on the browser and display device, and it may be necessary to map the same abstract presentation scheme to different designs and implementations.

Structured or semi-structured data models are used at the design level to describe the features of an application in a fashion that is accessible to manipulation, query, and validation. To take advantage of the capabilities of database management systems, design representations are typically preserved as relational or object-oriented schemas, or as semi structured objects, which may deal with information that has partial or missing schemas, depending on the design representation.

Implementation-level languages, such as network languages, are used to represent programmes at the lowest level of abstraction. Network languages, in particular, are directly interpretable by users' browsers. When the application is at this stage, the content, navigation, and display are all directly embedded in the physical marked-up texts or programmes that make up the application's physical structure.

4.2.3 REUSE:

The ability to create a unique application from existing artefacts is a key part of the reuse process, just as it is in any other software development process. At all stages of the development process, reuse is possible. For example, conceptual schemas and design schemas can be reused across applications, as can content and actual physical application pages.

As with hypermedia, the most common type of reuse on the Web is content reuse, which may be helped by the presence of a structured repository, which allows the development of several applications on top of the same information base. Component-based libraries of self-contained pieces (for example, JavaBeans or ActiveX components) can be plugged into application pages to provide specified functionalities (e.g., an electronic payment facility). As an alternative, generation-based reuse focuses on reusing transformation techniques from design frameworks or partially instantiated implementations to full implementations (for example, through the generation of application pages by starting with page skeletons and adding database content).

4.2.4 ARCHITECTURE:

The spatial arrangement of application data and the spatial-temporal distribution of computation are reflected in architecture, which is the subject of design and execution. The different architecture types are discussed in this section. The two-tier architecture, represented in Figure 4.2, is the simplest spatial setup for a Web application and closely follows the classic client-server paradigm. This differs from client-server solutions, in which the two-tier solution clients (i.e., browsers) are thin, lightweight applications that are simply responsible for rendering the presentation. The server is where the application logic and data are stored.

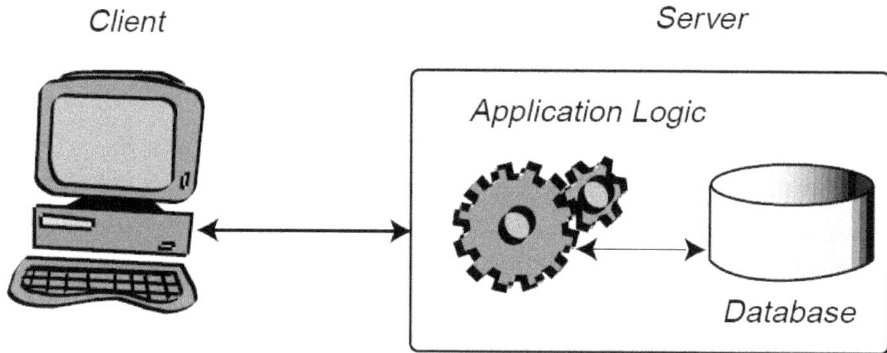

Figure 4.2 Two-Tier Architecture

Three-tier architecture (Figure 4.3) is a more complex arrangement that isolates application logic from data, resulting in an additional separation of duties on the back-end side. Three-tier advanced architectures that merge the traditional HTTP protocol with client-server application distribution protocols for improved performance, scalability, reliability, and security are made possible by the presence of one or more separate application tiers in the architecture.

Figure 4.3 Three – Tier Architecture

The time of binding between the content of the information base and the application pages delivered to the client, which can be static when pages are computed at application definition time and are immutable during application usage, or dynamic when pages are created just in time from fresh content, is an orthogonal architectural issue. There are other nuances to dynamicity: it can involve only content (navigation and presentation are static), or it can apply scale to both presentation and navigation.

4.2.5 USABILITY:

Usability is the most crucial feature of a Web application from the customer's standpoint. Despite a detailed examination of the nascent topic of Web usability engineering, a set of generic criteria for evaluating Web usability can be identified:

- ✓ The overall coherence of the presentation and navigation metaphors, as well as the individual quality of the graphic resources, are indicated by the degree of visual quality.
- ✓ The ability to adjust the application interface to individual users or user groups is measured by the degree of customization. Applications may have a fixed interface on one end of the spectrum, while content, display, and navigation may be individually customised on the other.
- ✓ The degree of additivity is related to the interface's runtime flexibility; on one, the application may remain immutable; on the other hand, it may track the user's activities and adjust accordingly.
- ✓ The ability of an application to interact with the user on its own initiative is measured by its degree of proactivity. Applications can be passive, in the sense

that they only provide information in response to user queries, or proactive, in the sense that they can provide information to users when relevant events occur.

4.3 WEB DEVELOPMENT TOOLS:

HTML5, Cascading Style Sheets, and APIs are the most common programming tools nowadays. The tools are briefly described in the following section.

4.3.1 HTML5:

Since its inception in the early 1990s, HTML has been in constant evolution. The majority of its features and functionalities are based on specifications, but some are also the consequence of good development practises and HTML implementations in popular browsers.

HTML4 – the current HTML version - has been in use for almost a decade. One of the major drawbacks of HTML4 is that it "does not supply enough information to design implementations that interoperate with one other and, more crucially, with a critical mass of deployed content," according to the W3C (World Wide Web Consortium). XHTML1, which defines an XML serialisation for HTML4, and DOM Level 2 HTML, which defines JavaScript APIs for both HTML and XHTML, are the same..."

The development of HTML5 began within the WHATGW (Web Hypertext Application Technology Working Group) initiative and the W3C organisation in order to improve the flexibility and interoperability of HTML implementations while also making web pages more interactive and offering a better user experience. The development is based on a review of existing HTML4 implementations, best practises, and studies of web material that has previously been distributed.

HTML5 will support both HTML and XML (eXtensible Mark-up Language) syntax and will be backward compatible with HTML4 and XHTML1. It will also bring new user interfaces to accommodate current trends like rich internet apps (RIA). These interfaces rely heavily on complicated JavaScript code and proprietary plug-ins like Adobe Flash, Microsoft Silverlight, and Sun JavaFX at the moment. The fundamental notion proposed by web developers is to build key functionality for such interfaces into browsers themselves, eliminating the need for proprietary plug-ins. HTML5 is scheduled to reach candidate status for recommendation in 2012 and become a recommendation in 2022. Despite the fact that HTML5 will not be finished in the next few years, web browsers are increasingly supporting its features.

- CHANGES IN THE LANGUAGE: The semantic structure of most web pages today is denoted by common structures such as headers, footers, and sidebars. Web developers utilise div and span elements, assigning them a unique id and/or grouping them into classes, because current HTML versions do not provide special mark-up for this purpose. HTML5 introduces a collection of new elements that enable for semantic document structure marking. They act as a more precise substitute for the div and span components. Figure 4.4 depicts the present and new approaches to web page structure.

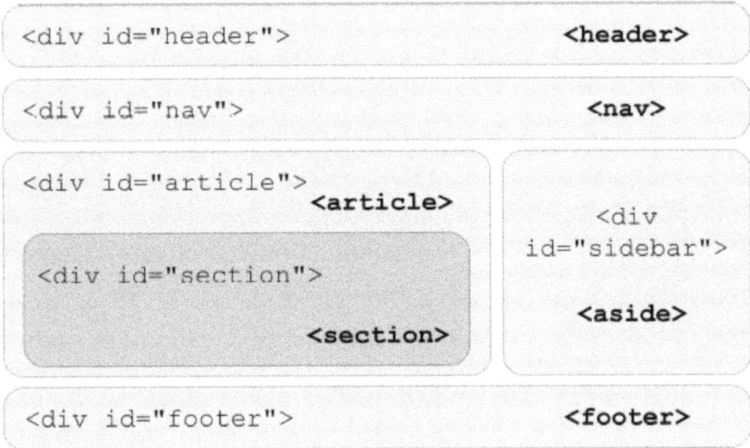

Figure 4.4. Current (using div elements) and the new approach (using new elements which are presented in bold text) to structuring a web page.

HTML5 provides a number of new elements, the most interesting of which are:

- ✓ video, audio, and canvas are elements that support multimedia and graphic content.
- ✓ embed is used for content that is embedded and processed by plug-ins;
- ✓ quantity display elements (progress, metre, time, and so on);
- ✓ Ruby is employed to specify annotations in East Asian typographies.

The absence of presentational characteristics (e.g. align, height, border, size) and elements in HTML5 promotes strict separation of content and design of a web page (e.g. font, centre, strike, u). CSS is the sole way to style and design a page. Due to its poor impact on a web page's usability, HTML5 does not support frames.

A new attribute called ping has been added to the elements an and area. It specifies the URLs (Uniform Resource Locators) to which a browser can send an alert when a user clicks on a hyperlink. User tracking is now largely done via server-side redirects, which results in a significant wait for a specific page. The user agent can utilise the ping attribute to tell the user which addresses will be notified. Users can turn off notifications if they are concerned about their privacy, but they have no control over redirects. New global properties, relations in the elements link and a, events, and many more features are included in HTML5.

- WEB FORMS: Web forms allow a web client and a web server to communicate. The data supplied by the user in the forms is transferred to a server, which responds to the values received (e.g. returns the results of the search). However, the number of widgets available for usage in forms is limited. Validation of more complicated data on the client side is one of the best web development practises. The latter is accomplished through the use of JavaScript or another client-side scripting language. Several custom form widgets have been developed that can be used through third-party JavaScript libraries to provide additional form widgets and prevent data validation on both sides.

  The requirements of developers prompted the development of a new generation of Web forms, known as Web Forms 2.0, which eventually found their way into the HTML5 specifications (see below). Widgets are added to the input element as new values of the attribute type of the input element (tel., search., url., email. date time., date, month, week, time., date time local, number, range, colour.) Along with the addition of new widgets, HTML5 also includes improvements to current widgets, as well as automatic validation of the data entered into the widget.

  Two further novelties should be addressed in this context when it comes to forms. For starters, form elements no longer have to be descendants of the form element; instead, they can be their own elements. Instead, they can be inserted anywhere in the HTML content and connected to a suitable form using the new form property that they have introduced. Using the HTTP (Hypertext Transfer Protocol) protocol techniques for transferring data to the server is the second innovative aspect of this implementation. In addition to the GET and POST methods, HTML5 also supports the PUT and DELETE methods.

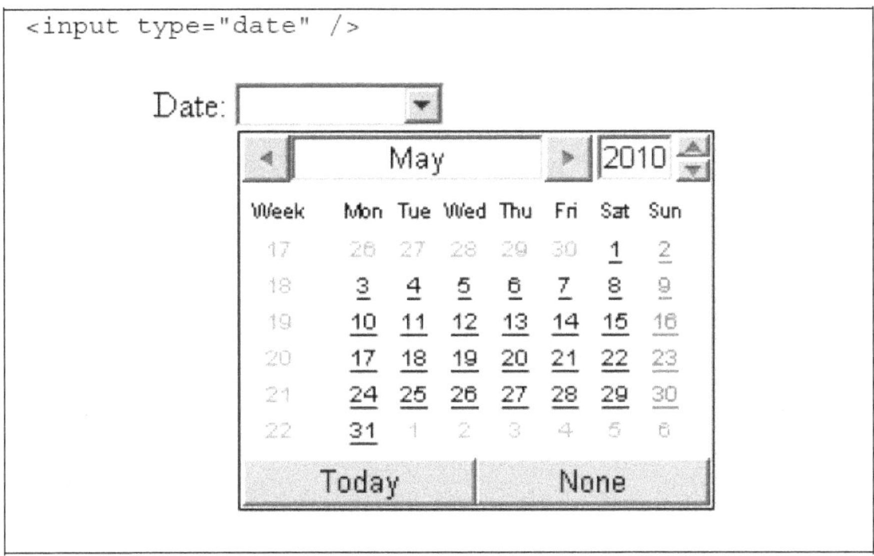

Figure 4.5 New date form widget.

- SEMANTICS: While the HTML tags are intended to describe how the information is displayed, they are not intended to describe what the information signifies. The incorporation of semantics into web resources is a significant trend on the internet nowadays. In addition to specifying the document structure in HTML5, semantic mark-up is also used for capturing microdata and enabling assistive technologies for impaired users, among other things.
- MICRODATA: By using microdata, information in HTML documents that is primarily intended for end users (such as contact information and location information) can be made machine-readable and thus be used for automatic processing (e.g., indexing and searching, storing, cross-referencing, and analysing) by using machine-readable information. The concept of microdata is made up of groups of properties that are referred to as items. It is provided in the context of the existing elements so that the objects and their features are more easily understood. Any element can contain the item scope attribute, which can be used to construct an item. Each item has a unique type (item type), a unique global identifier (item id), and a collection of name-value

combinations that are unique to that item. The itemprop attribute can be used in any of the item's descendants to express a property, and the value of this attribute reflects the value of the property expressed by the itemprop attribute (Figure 4.6).

```
<div itemscope itemtype="http://example.org/band">
   <p>My name is
      <span itemprop='name'>Janko</span>.
   </p>
   <p>My band is called
      <span itemprop='band'>Four Parts</span>.
   </p>
   <p>I am
      <span itemprop='nationality'>Slovenian
      </span>.
   </p>
</div>
```

Figure 4.6: Example of using microdata.

- ACCESSIBILITY: For users with disabilities, a considerable chunk of the Web's information is currently inaccessible, particularly for those who rely on assistive technologies such as screen readers and Braille keyboards. Such tools confront significant challenges in reading and interpreting text that is presented in advanced, regularly updated user interfaces generated by the mix of technologies such as AJAX (Asynchronous JavaScript and XML), HTML, and JavaScript, among other things. Assistive technologies are unable to correctly understand the responsibilities, states, and properties of such widgets, and thus are unable to keep up with the dynamically changing content on the web pages that they are presented with.

  To address this issue, the Web Accessibility Initiative (WAI) launched the ARIA (Accessible Rich Internet Applications) project, which is now in its third year. The ARIA requirements offer a semantic model, which allows for the semantic description of widgets and their behaviour, document structure, and the sections that will be modified in a semantically meaningful manner. This would allow assistive technology to gather enough information to make complex web apps usable by persons with impairments as a result of their efforts.

```
<li role="menuitemcheckbox"
    aria-checked="true">Sort by Last Modified</li>
```

Figure 4.7: Example of using ARIA attributes.

The list item element (li) is assigned a role (with the role attribute) of an element that acts as a checkbox item. Its initial property 'checked' is set to true (using aria-* set of attributes). Using JavaScript, the attribute could be changed according to user actions. Establish the functions that the elements play on the page, as well as their states and qualities, in accordance with the semantic model of the page. When the page updates, states and properties determine the element's current semantic state and property, and as a result can vary from time to time, whereas a role does not change when the page updates.

- AUDIO AND VIDEO: Prior to HTML5, the ability to play audio and video material in a browser was only possible through the use of third-party plug-ins, with Adobe Flash being the most widely used. As well as defining an interface to manipulate audio and video content without the need for third-party plug-ins, HTML5 introduces new elements for embedding audio and video content in a web page.

Overall, the answer consisted in the selection of a standard format that was supported by all browsers. The most important need for such a format was that it not be proprietary in any way. Aside from that, it should have good compression and picture quality, as well as low processing requirements and requirements. In addition, a hardware solution for decoding should be available. Opting for Ogg Vorbis for audio and Ogg Theora for video records over the more popular MP3 and H.264, the World Wide Web Consortium chose them primarily because they are both license-free, which is not the case for the competing MP3 and H.264 formats.

The HTML5 specifications do not specify a default format, nor do they identify any other formats that should be supported by browsers, despite the fact that everything said above is true. The ultimate agreement between the World Wide Web Consortium and browser vendors has never been achieved. As a result, suppliers make individual decisions about the formats that are integrated into their browsers.

As a result of a lack of hardware acceleration and some uncertainty around patents, Apple does not support the Ogg Theora format in its Safari browser. The Mozilla Foundation and Opera, on the other hand, are opposed to the usage of H.264 due to the high cost of licencing it requires. Both Theora and H.264 are supported by Google's Chrome browser. It is maintained mostly because it is utilised by Google's YouTube, which is the world's most popular video portal, and hence cannot be included in the open source project Chromium, which is a fork of the Chromium operating system.

- GRAPHICS: In contemporary web development, graphic rendering on Websites has only been possible through the use of plug-ins, such as Flash or Silverlight, which are available for free. As a result of HTML5, the capability required for graphical rendering is provided in browsers through the use of the Canvas and SVG (Scalable Vector Graphics) technologies, respectively. In HTML, the graphical components are fully integrated, and they are also a part of the document object model (DOM). CSS may be used to determine their appearance, and JavaScript can be used to alter their behaviour.

Canvas allows scripting to be used to dynamically render graphics, such as graphs, bitmap images, animations, and games, on the go. In JavaScript code, the canvas element, along with its width and height attributes, defines a display region that can be accessed through the Canvas API drawing functions.

Canvas cannot distinguish between the components in the graphic and does not contain the relationships that exist between these things (such as DOM). Pixels are the fundamental building blocks of a canvas graphic. As a result, the displayed visual is final and cannot be resized down or up. Individual graphic items can't be accessed, altered, or interacted with since they are protected. It is necessary to completely redraw the graphic in order to make any adjustments.

The Canvas API's most basic feature is the ability to render in 2D. 3D rendering will be available through the use of the WebGL web standard. Despite the fact that WebGL is still in its early stages of development, it is currently supported in most mainstream browsers on an experimental basis. SVG-based browser-native rendering is supported by HTML5 as well (Scalable Vector Graphics). SVG (Scalable Vector Graphics) is an XML-based language for defining two-dimensional vector graphics.

Because of its vector nature, SVG, in contrast to Canvas, allows for high-resolution rendering at any level of magnification without sacrificing performance. With the help of browser plugins, SVG is now mostly used for presenting static content (maps, blueprints, and so on) on the web. A unique XML object model called SVG is used to store and manipulate the individual graphic objects, which may then be accessed and altered using JavaScript. SVG also allows for interactivity through the use of event-handlers that may be applied to any SVG visual object.

4.3.2 PRESENTATION AND CASCADE STYLE SHEETS (CSS):

On the one hand, mark-up languages are used largely to define the basic structure of online documents and pages, while on the other hand, CSS – a style sheet language that defines presentation semantics – is used to define the final presentation and rendering. In nearly 14 years, the technique of designing web pages with CSS has been around, with CSS 2.1 serving as a de facto industry standard for the last 12 years. Currently, it is supported by the vast majority of online browsers, and it has advanced significantly over the last decade. It is also being proposed that new CSS be used in conjunction with the new mark-up languages. CSS3 is a new possible standard that is now in the form of working draught or candidate recommendation, according to the International Standards Organization. The enormous specification of the CSS3 standard has been broken into various modules, each of which is being developed at a different pace and with a varied degree of dynamism. The use of several modules allows browser vendors to incorporate new features in stages. There are already a number of CSS3 modules that are supported by the vast majority of recent browsers. With the addition of new features and functionalities, the new standard is totally backwards compatible with the old one.

The new Selectors module introduces a variety of new methods for attaching elements to the corresponding style. The most exciting addition is the ability to select mark-up elements based on their placement in the DOM. The :last-child, :nth-child(n) and :nth-lastchild(n) commands enable the targeting of elements based on their positions in a parent's list of child elements. For example, the command: n^{th}-child(3n+2) would Mach a group of three elements after the second element. Other commands also enable the matching of elements which are checked, without children or elements that do not match the specified declaration. The mark-up elements can also be selected based on the existence of specific attribute and also just a part of an attribute. For example, the img [alt*=" good"] would select all images that have an alt attribute containing the word "good".

Background and Borders is a module that allows you to utilise numerous backgrounds that may be scaled and positioned relative or absolute. It allows for the reuse of photos in a variety of scenarios as well as more precise filling of certain sections. Gradients, rounded corners, shadows, and even border pictures are all possible with this module. The border-image property allows you to utilise an image file as an object's border. Figure 4.8 depicts one example. The gradient attribute allows you to programmatically change the colour of the borders or backgrounds.

Figure 4.8. Use of one image as a border of the other image

The Colour module defines several possibilities for adjusting all of the document's colours. The new *rgba* command allows you to specify an element's colour as well as its opacity. The alpha value should be between 0.0 and 1.0, and the red, blue, and green colours must be defined with an integer value or percentages. The alpha value of 0.8, for example, denotes a 20 percent transparent element.

Since then, all web designers have required to be familiar with a collection of fonts known as Web-safe fonts. The font file can now be included as an external file and accessed using the font-family property in the new Fonts module. The new @fontface rule allows fonts to be called from an internet directory, such as

@fontface font-family:'myFont'; src: url (../myFonts.ttf') format('truetype'); for example, If the browser does not support the command, it defaults to the font-family property's next specified font. Font licencing and copyright are the two most significant concerns with the new font types. The fonts contained in the page can be simply downloaded from any page.

Transitions and Animations are two exciting new modules that allow you to modify and manipulate page elements in 2D or 3D space. The developer can use transitions to specify a single CSS property to animate from one state to another in a smooth transition. A click on an image, for example, can cause the image's size to alter. On the other hand, animations allow for the iteration of many CSS properties at the same time for a number of times. Keyframes can be used to divide the animation into stages. The browser approximates individual phases of components between key frames automatically.

4.3.3 APIs:

HTML5 adds a number of APIs that standardise functionalities that are already available in today's browsers.

- OFFLINE FEATURE: The Internet has progressed from a collection of simply hyperlinked pages to a collection of web apps. These apps are becoming increasingly comparable to desktop applications, necessitating the use of similar tools. To use local storage, the first step is to see if the user agent is connected to the internet. The Offline Web Applications specification from the W3C recommends dispatching two events ("online" and "offline") to the Window object, as well as an IDL (Interface Definition Language) attribute named "online" on the Navigator object. This allows an application to choose whether or not to interact with remote resources on its own or to be alerted by the browser when its status changes.

In the past, the only option to keep data locally was to use cookies. Cookies have been frequently used to save small bits of data on the client, despite being a hack to the stateless nature of HTTP. Cookies have two drawbacks: limited storage (about 4kB) and the fact that they are delivered to the server with each request.

With the Web Storage proposal, HTML5 introduces the concept of simple storage. Storage is accessed via an IDL attribute and is limited to simple key/value storage.

The document considers two forms of storage: local and session storage. Data in session storage expires shortly after the browser window closes, whereas local storage was designed to preserve data indefinitely even after a user stops the browser. Session storage also overcomes the problem of several programme instances running at the same time because each window has its own session storage. This form of storage is not without its detractors. Because data can contain sensitive information, user agents must handle it with caution, denying access to apps running on different domains and erasing data as soon as the application requests it.

Most major browsers support web storage, with varied degrees of conformance to standards. When it comes to more complex types of storage, there is a lot less room for compromise. SQLite is a SQL-compliant database that was popularised by Google as part of Google Gears, a browser extension that enabled support for various features that were not available to user agents at the time. This sort of transactional storage was also suggested to the W3C for standardisation, however the draught was halted since it was overly biased against SQLite and there were no other implementations. SQLite is supported by Google Chrome and Opera, although Mozilla and Microsoft publicly oppose it.

Indexed Database API (renamed from Web Simple DB in late 2009) is another W3C draught for enhanced storage. This draught may look similar to the Web Database draught in terms of API, but it is a key/value store implementation. This specification extends much beyond Web Storage, defining database, object stores (also known as tables in DBMS jargon), indexes, relationships, cursors, and transactions. At the time of writing, no user agent supported the Indexed Database API, despite the fact that the Google team began working on it in March 2010 and Mozilla plans to release it in Firefox 4.0.

- GEOLOCATION: In recent years, HTML has become an increasingly popular technology on mobile devices, and it has emerged as a solution to cross-platform issues on mobile devices. When it comes to mobile operating systems, the HTML technology ecosystem is the only genuine counterbalance to native applications in a market that is becoming increasingly fragmented (iOS, Android, Maemo/MeeGo, Symbian, etc.).

Global positioning systems (GPS) are one of the "killer technologies" in the mobile industry. It has spawned an ecosystem of applications, and it has also enhanced the capabilities of currently available applications. While geolocation has been accessible on many mobile platforms for quite some time, it is only now that it is being standardised by the World Wide Web Consortium (W3C). A wide range of technologies, including the GPS (Global Positioning System), Wi-Fi, RFID (Radio Frequency Identification), and mobile radio technologies, are used to determine the location of a device when software is used to determine the location of the device.

```
//output last cached location
navigator.geolocation.getCurrentPosition(
    function(pos){
        alert("lat:" + pos.coords.latitude
            + ", long:" + pos.coords.longitude)
    }
);
```

Figure 4.9. Example of using geolocation API through a Navigator object by retrieving last cached location.

Furthermore, the draught has the capability of automatically notifying the application when the position of a device is modified.

- WEB WORKERS: Despite the fact that JavaScript within the browser allows for asynchronous communication with servers, the user interface is always drawn and interacted with in a single thread. While computationally expensive operations can be performed on the server without degrading the user interface, there is currently no way to do these processes within a browser. In order to deal with this problem, the Web Workers draught was created. Essentially, the goal behind web workers is to enable for the execution of long-running or computationally demanding operations in the background without interfering with or slowing down the user's interaction with the browser.

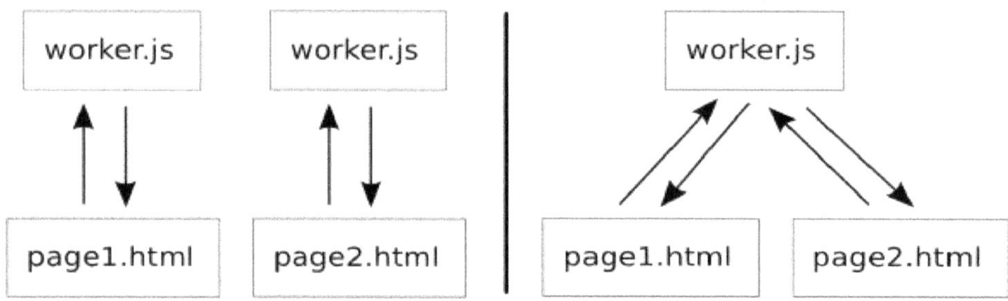

Figure 4.10: Both pages invoke "worker.js" as a Worker (left) which results in separate instances of scripts. The right image represents both pages communicating with a single instance of Shared Worker.

A thread (also known as a worker in web lingo) is formed through the use of the Worker class. It only accepts one parameter, which is the filename of the JavaScript to be executed by the Worker object. In other words, the code that is being performed in a different thread is always contained in a distinct file. Unlike Worker objects, which always create fresh instances of worker objects, Shared Worker objects are shared across scripts that invoke them. In other words, more than one script can connect to the same Shared Worker instance at the same time.

- TWO-WAY COMMUNICATION BETWEEN A WEB BROWSER AND A SERVER-SIDE PROCESS: If you look at the original Web model, a browser will always request a web page or portions of a web page. In accordance with the HTTP 1.1 requirements, browsers can only establish a maximum of two simultaneous connections with a web server, allowing for faster loading and rendering of pages containing numerous images or multimedia content. In the past, a "Comet" model has altered this traditional approach by keeping one of the two connections active at all times for real-time data exchange with the server, rather than the other two. This connection can be used by a web server to push data to a browser without the browser having to expressly ask for it to happen. Sometimes, instead of using two simultaneous connections, a single long-lasting connection might be used in place of both. There have been a number of alternative implementations of this technique, but they all rely on AJAX and the XML Http Request object provided by the technology.

When it comes to pushing data to browser-based clients, the HTML5 Web Socket protocol provides a new, standardised technique. It is a component of the HTML5 specification, and it is designed to be used within scripts in web pages, according to the specification. This allows for a full duplex connection to be established without the requirement for several HTTP connections to be established. It is possible to make an HTTP request from the client that will be upgraded to the Web Socket protocol when a special first handshake is established between the client and the server. The latter creates a persistent HTTP connection, which may be used to transport data in full duplex mode while the former does not. The communication is handled via JavaScript, which necessitates the use of text-based data in order for it to function properly.

The Web Socket protocol relieves a significant amount of strain on web servers, allowing them to handle twice as many simultaneous connections as they could previously. Another significant advantage of the protocol is its ability to pass through firewalls and proxy servers. With an HTTP CONNECT statement, a Web Socket automatically finds a proxy server and immediately constructs a tunnel to allow data to transit across the proxy. It is the latter that demands that the proxy open a TCP/IP connection to a certain host. A similar technique can also be used to build secure connections, which is a good thing (Secure Sockets Layer, SSL).

4.4 CONCLUSION:

The various aspects related to web development tools have been dealt in detail. It is the overall concept of HTML5 and other tools provided in this chapter that the formal specification and construction of consistent solutions for technologies and functionalities that are already in use through various hacks and plug-ins proposed by web developers are being formalised. Modern rich and interactive web designs were built using Adobe Flash technology, which was supported by all of the main browser vendors at the time of publication. The Flash plug-in provided outstanding support for multimedia content, particularly animation and animated interfaces. It was also free. Through the use of native browser support, HTML5 makes it easier to integrate this type of functionality. The aspects of CSS & API are also introduced in this chapter.

The incorporation of semantics into web documents is the most prominent new trend on the Internet right now. The online material is shaped and created primarily to be read and understood by humans; as a result, a computer cannot provide any significant assistance by analysing, searching, and processing the data in any significant way. The incorporation of semantics will eventually lead to the development of the third generation of the Web, known as the Semantic Web. Recent developments in web development practises, rich web content, and the requirement for semantics in web documents are already showing up in the real world. Aside from a few tweaks to HTML syntax and vocabulary, the most significant new features in HTML5 are the introduction of semantics in the form of microdata and ARIA attributes, support for RIA through the introduction of new form widgets, support for multimedia, and dynamic graphic rendering, among other things.

CHAPTER 5

CSS – AN INTRODUCTION

"Websites Promotes You 24/7: No Employees Will Do That."

--Paul Cookson

Chapter Learnings:

After reading this chapter, the reader will have a better grasp of Cascading Style Sheets, how it works, the benefits and limitations of using this tool in the web designing industry, and ultimately the future implementation of CSS in the web designing sector, which will be discussed in the following section.

5.1 INTRODUCTION:

In the past, mark-up elements were responsible for a large portion of the visual formatting of Web pages, resulting in a muddled mixture of the notions of logical and physical mark-up that is known as classic HTML. A clear distinction between the structure provided by mark-up and the appearance dictated by a style sheet written in Cascading Style Sheets (CSS) syntax was made by strict variants of (X)HTML, which deprecated elements and attributes that were primarily concerned with presentation and provided a clear distinction between the structure provided by mark-up and the appearance dictated by a style sheet written in Cascading Style Sheets (CSS) syntax. Having a clear separation of responsibilities between mark-up and style can have significant benefits in terms of production and maintenance, as well as performance, making it a considerably superior presentation solution than simply using mark-up alone.

Cascading Style Sheets (CSS) are a W3C standard for defining the display of documents written in HTML, and in fact, any XML language. Cascading Style Sheets (CSS) are used to define the presentation of documents published in HTML. Presenting the material to the user in any format, whether on a computer screen, a cell phone display, written on paper, or read aloud through the use of a screen reader is known as presentation. With style sheets taking care of the presentation, HTML can get on with the task of defining document structure and meaning, just as it was intended. CSS is a distinct programming language with its own syntax and semantics. This chapter introduces you to CSS vocabulary and key principles that will assist you in gaining a better understanding of the concepts covered in the following chapters.

5.1.1 PRESENTATIONAL HTML:

Traditionally, mark-up has been used to format documents, whether they are correct or incorrect. For example, the *align* attribute is supported by a large number of HTML components, and it provides straightforward text alignment support. When you combine these parts of mark-up with the assumption of visual rendering, such as the opinion that *h1* elements should always make text large, it may appear to some that HTML is intended for formatting, as demonstrated here: HTML is intended for formatting

<h1 align="center">Big Centered Text! </h1>

Although there is a valid case to be made about the semantic significance of the h1 tag establishing a headline, for people who approach HTML simply from the perspective of knowing what a tag does, the assumption that a h1 element creates something significant wins out. Apart from such mistakes that are based on observation rather than the specification's aim, there are elements that are completely presentational in nature, such as font, which is included in the HTML 3.2, HTML 4.01 transitional, and XHTML 1.0 transitional standards:

<font size="7" color=" Red"> I am big and Red! </font>

Even when looking at browser-specific elements, there is a significant amount of presentational mark-up to be uncovered. As an illustration, consider the following mark-up.

<blink> Proprietary HTML Tag Sale: 50% off for users! </blink>

creates blinking text in Firefox, while this mark-up

<marque> Sale! Sale! Sale! </marque>

Text may be animated in practically any browser. The pages of history have already been turned. Whether you like it or not, mark-up has been used to graphically portray Web pages for more than a decade now. The problem with utilising HTML for formatting is that it just isn't very good at it, and it wasn't supposed to be used for this purpose in the first place. For example, if you wanted to create some centred red text on a yellow backdrop, you'd probably resort to utilising mark-up in the following manner:

<table align="center" width="100%">

<tr>

<td bgcolor="yellow" align="center">

<font size="7"

color="red"

face="Arial, Helvetica, sans-serif">

Big Red HTML Text

</font>

</td>

</tr>

</table>

Often, when HTML is used to present a Web page, we notice a significant amount of mark-up being used to design the page, which is often loaded with sophisticated stacked or even nested tables to style the page. It was and continues to be necessary to use layout workarounds such as invisible pixel images, proprietary HTML elements and attributes, text in pictures, and other obscure concepts in order to create high-fidelity design in HTML that is of high quality. Fortunately, there is a better approach for the time being and in the future—style sheets.

5.1.2 THE SLOW RISE OF CSS:

Cascading Style Sheets gives Web designers the power over layouts that they've been asking for years. Surprisingly, CSS has taken a long time to gain popularity. CSS1 was originally published as a standard in late 1996, while CSS2 was released in 1998. Some of the technology was supported by early browsers like Internet Explorer 3 and Netscape 4, but CSS has struggled to acquire mainstream recognition. The usage of CSS has been a lesson in irritation due to inconsistent browser support and numerous flaws, particularly in older versions of Internet Explorer. Consider the Acid2 CSS2 conformance tests, which put many of the most essential aspects of CSS1 and CSS2 to the test. Both Internet Explorer 6 and Firefox 2 fail this test, as seen in Figure 5.1. All major browsers now pass the Acid2 test, thanks to the release of Internet Explorer 8 and Firefox 3, as well as previous conformity of other browsers such as Opera and Safari (Figure 5.2). Given that the test was first introduced in 2005, and that CSS support had been patchy for many years prior, we can now demonstrate that CSS is improving!

Newer browser versions are significantly superior than their predecessors, with excellent support for CSS1 and CSS 2.1, as well as several CSS3 capabilities. Despite the fact that CSS support has become increasingly widespread, there are still serious concerns. Browser flaws still exist, elements of the CSS specification are unsupported, developer education and adoption are behind, and browser makers are increasingly introducing proprietary extensions to style sheets. Regardless of the technology in use, it appears that the more things change, the more they remain the same. In the domain of CSS, HTML experts who have spent time resolving oddities and workarounds will discover plenty of new ones to address.

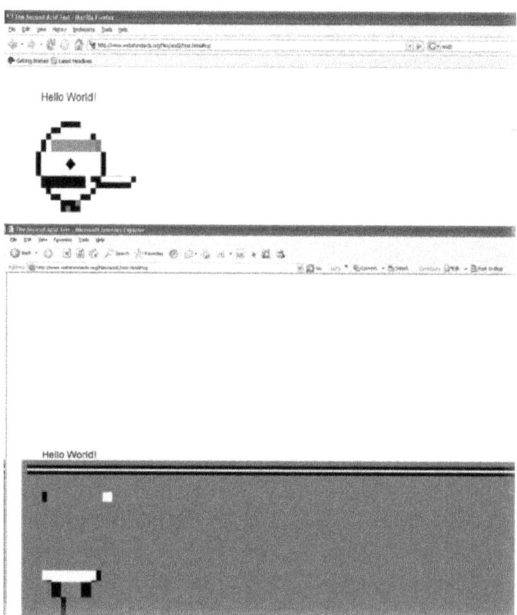

Figure 5.1: Older Browsers Failing Acid2

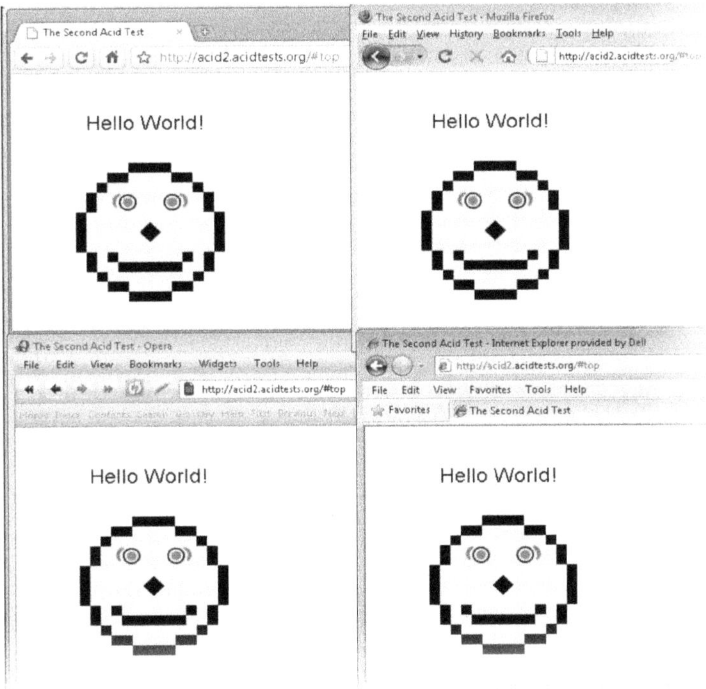

Figure 5.2: Modern Browsers Passing Acid2

5.1.3 HELLO CSS WORLD:

We'll utilise a document-wide style for this demonstration, which is defined by the< style> tag in the <head> element of an HTML document.

```
<!DOCTYPE html>
<html>
<head>
<meta http-equiv="Content-Type" content="text/html; charset=utf-8">
<title>Hello CSS World</title>
<style type="text/css">
/* sample style sheet */
body {background-color: black; color: white;}
h1 {color: red; font-size: xx-large; text-align: center;}
```

```
#heart {color: red; font-size: xx-large;}
.fancy {background-color: orange; color: black; font-weight: bold;}
</style>
</head>
<body>
<h1>Welcome to the World of CSS</h1>
<hr>
<p>CSS <em class="fancy">really</em> isn't so hard either!</p>
<p>Soon you will also <span id="heart">&hearts;</span> using CSS.</p>
<p>You can put lots of text here if you want.
We could go on and on with <span class="fancy">fake</span> text for you
to read, but let's get back to the book.</p>
</body>
</html>
```

The above example makes use of some of the most common CSS features in (X)HTML documents, which results in some minor changes to the page structure, including

- Setting colours with background-color and color
- Sizing text with font-size
- Setting boldness with font-weight
- Setting basic text alignment with text-align
- Using id and class attributes to specify elements to bind style rules to
- Using logical mark-up like as opposed to more physical mark-up like
- Relying on generic tag containers like to style arbitrary portions of text

Apart from the handful we've seen here, there are a slew of other CSS attributes we might use, and we'll go over them later in the book, but for now, this sampling should have plenty to get our first example up and running. The CSS version of the page is shown in Figure 5.3, as opposed to the HTML-only version.

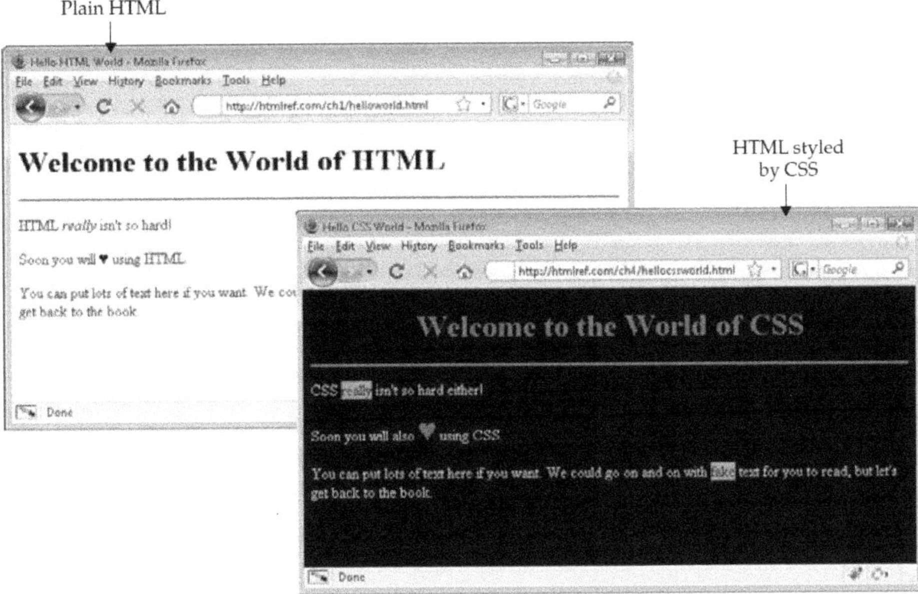

Figure 5.3: Example Hello CSS World Rendering

While the example necessitates the use of two technologies, it's worth noting that CSS, when properly implemented, is both different from and dependent on an HTML text. CSS is not a substitute for mark-up; in fact, it depends on it. If an HTML document is faulty, for example, the tags are not closed properly or other errors are made, the CSS may not attach properly, causing the appearance to be distorted. However, errors can also occur in CSS rules, which are interpreted more rigidly by browsers and can result in a visual rendering problem. CSS and HTML clearly have a symbiotic relationship, but that relationship has evolved through time.

5.2 CSS VERSIONS:

When it comes to the Web, Cascading Style Sheets is a rather ancient technology. The earliest CSS ideas were introduced in 1994, and the CSS1 specification (www.w3.org/TR/REC-CSS1/) was ratified in December 1996. This early version of CSS was supported to varied degrees in browsers including Internet Explorer 3 and Netscape 4. While CSS1's features were significantly superior to those of presentation HTML's font> tags and workarounds, adoption was gradual. CSS1 has many features for changing borders, margins, backgrounds, colours, and a variety of text qualities, but it lacked the much-desired ability to move items directly. CSS-P (www.w3.org/TR/WD-positioning-19970819), an intermediate definition for positioning HTML components, was implemented in Netscape 4 and Internet Explorer 4, and then folded into CSS2 (www.w3.org/TR/1998/REC-CSS2-19980512/), which was released in May 1998. Even in the most contemporary browsers, not all of the functionality introduced by CSS2, such as positioning, media types for style sheets, auditory style sheets, and others, have been implemented. CSS 2.1 (www.w3.org/TR/CSS21/) was released in 2007 as a revision of this specification that deleted a number of unimplemented features and normalised the definition to a more realistic image of what browsers actually do. While CSS3 (www.w3.org/Style/CSS/current-work#CSS3) is definitely the way of the future, with its plethora of modules for dealing with colour, device restrictions, foreign language rendering, enhanced printing, and more, it is unclear when that future will arrive. Select aspects of several CSS3 modules have been implemented in some browsers as of the writing of this edition, but full cross browser support is still inconsistent, save for a few high-value features like the opacity property. The version history of CSS is summarised in Table 5.1.

CSS VERSION	**DESCRIPTION**
CSS1	CSS implementation that introduced the text, list, box, margin, border, colour, and background attributes, as well as the background colour and background image. Although most of the characteristics of CSS1, which was first defined in 1996, are supported by Web browsers, there are still minor quirks that remain around some less-used elements such as white-space, letter-spacing, display, and others. Some CSS1 compatibility issues are particularly severe in earlier browsers, such as those that predate Internet Explorer 7.
CSS2	Specification that is largely renowned for its positioning and media properties, particularly in the context of print style sheets. Many of the features of CSS2, such as aural style sheets, were never widely

	deployed and were eventually deleted from the CSS specification in a subsequent generation of the standard.
CSS 2.1	A modification of the CSS2 specification that makes certain corrections and is normalised to more clearly represent what the majority of browser vendors have implemented is available for download. It should be noted that many of the CSS2 capabilities that were removed from this specification can be found in CSS3 modules instead. This is the CSS specification that is currently recommended for study and application.
CSS3	CSS is a specification that has been modularized. Diverse CSS3 modules extend and improve aspects of previous CSS versions; for example, the CSS3 Color module addresses colour correction, transparency, and other issues, whereas the CSS3 Fonts module addresses features to add effects to fonts while they are displayed, adjust their appearance, and even download custom fonts. Some modules, such as the Transitions and Animations modules, are completely new, while others, such as the Transitions and Animations modules, appear to be rather old and have activity levels that indicate they have been abandoned or are on the verge of being abandoned. Whatever the circumstance, when it comes to CSS3, readers are recommended to carefully examine the CSS3 Website and test support.

Table 5.1 Description of Common CSS Versions

5.2.1 PROPRIETARY CSS:

CSS may be linked with standards and specifications in the minds of some Web developers, but the reality is that it, like mark-up, has proprietary aspects that make it unique. All browser providers have added one or more features to their browsers in order to enhance the functionality of their product. Many of these features are previews of what is likely to be included in the final CSS3 specification, although they are currently only available through the private CSS3 framework.

Unlike (X)HTML, CSS makes it easy for browser vendors to extend the specification, as newly introduced keywords and property names that start with a hyphen "-" or underscore "_" are considered vendor-specific extensions. The syntax is *-vendoridentifier-newproperty* or *_vendoridentifier-newproperty*, though in practice the hyphenated names appear to be the only extensions in use. As an example, *-moz* is used to prefix Mozilla features like *–moz-border-radius.* A list of prefixes that are commonly seen is shown in Table 5.2.

Prefix	**Organization**	**Example**	**Notes**
-ms-	Microsoft	-ms-interpolation-mode	Some older proprietary CSS features found in Internet Explorer are not prefixed in any way
-moz-	Mozilla Foundation	-moz-border-radius	This applies to all Gecko rendering engine–based browsers such as Firefox
-o-	Opera	-o-text-overflow	Opera also supports the -xv- prefix for experimental voice support for aural style sheet properties like -xvvoice-family.
-webkit	WebKit	-webkit-box-shadow	This applies to all WebKit engine–based browsers such as Apple's Safari and Google Chrome.

Table 5.2 CSS Extension Prefixes

There are a variety of different proprietary CSS prefixes that may be encountered, which may or may not follow the appropriate prefixing system, depending on the situation. *-wap-* prefix-based attributes such as *–wap-accesskey*, for example, may be used by wireless phones that enable WAP (Wireless Application Protocol) functionality. Some Microsoft Office implementations may make use of CSS rules with the prefix *-mso-,* such as *-mso-header-data.* Please keep in mind that this syntax does not include the required extension character indicator. In general, it would appear that extensions should be avoided if at all feasible unless their display degrades gracefully. This is especially true given the fact that their compatibility with browsers and future acceptance by standards bodies are both uncertain. Interestingly, many extension properties appear to be CSS3 properties with stems that are simply waiting for the specs to catch up with the latest technology.

5.2.2 CSS RELATIONSHIP WITH MARK-UP:

In light of the fact that CSS is based on mark-up and, in certain situations, overlaps with earlier functionalities given by mark-up elements, it is essential to grasp the relationship between the two technologies. According to the general rule, transitional versions of (X)HTML mark-up include some presentational elements that can be used by Web developers instead of CSS properties, but strict forms of (X)HTML mark-up may delete such elements entirely in favour of CSS properties. As an example, the align attribute may be used to centre a heading tag in the following way:

<h1 align="center">Headline Centered</h1>

CSS should be used in place of the align attribute when using strict markup, however, because the align attribute is deprecated. If you want to do this, you might use an inline style, such as such

<h1 style="text-align: center;">Headline Centered</h1>

or, more appropriately, with some CSS rule applied via class, id, or element selector. Here we use a class rule

h1.centered {text-align: center;}

which would apply to tags with class values containing "centered" like the following:

<h1 class="centered">Centered Headline</h1>

<h1 class="fancy centered">Another Centered Headline</h1>

Some HTML components are simply no longer required in the presence of CSS, as we have discovered in a number of instances. With generic elements like div or span, CSS rules are frequently used in place of HTML tags such as u, sub, and superscript, as well as the font tag (font-weight: bold). Table 5.3 lists the majority of the (X)HTML mark-up elements or attributes that have been deprecated in strict variations, as well as their CSS replacements, in detail.

Additionally, there are other scenarios, such as <sub> and <sup>, <big> and <tiny>, among many others, where we could skip using mark-up and instead apply style. There is no single presentational-like element that has been deprecated by the multiple mark-up specifications, and even if CSS eliminates the necessity for some presentational components, their use persists tenaciously in the wild. For the simple reason that these elements and their counterparts are described in this book, it is necessary. In fact, the continuous inclusion of presentation principles in the emerging HTML5 specification tends to suggest that, despite a desire to shift to a world based solely on semantic mark-up, although definitely desirable, this is unlikely to occur on the Web at large, at least not in the near future.

(X)HTML Tags or Attributes	**CSS Property Equivalent(s)**	**Notes**
<center>	text-align, margin	Values for margin such as auto generally are used when centering blocks with text-align for content.
<font>	font-family, font-size, color	
align attributes	text-align, float	In the case of some elements such as <img>, the CSS float property is more appropriate than text-align.
Color attributes for <body>	color, background-color	To set some of the body attributes like link, vlink, alink, pseudo-classes :link, :visited, :active should be used for <a> tags.
Background image attributes for <body>, <table>, and <td>	background-image	

The type and start attributes on lists and list items	list-style-type, CSS counters	Single CSS properties can't directly substitute some features.
<s>,<strike>	text-decoration: line-through	
<u>	text-decoration: underline;	
<blink>	text-decoration: blink	Not supported in all browsers.

Table 5.3 Common (X)Html Structures Moved to CSS

5.3 HOW CSS WORKS?

The Style Sheet works as follows:

1. Begin with a document that has been marked up using HTML tags.

2. Create a set of style guidelines for how you'd like specific elements to appear.

3. Attach the style rules to the document as a separate attachment. When the browser shows the page, it does so in accordance with the rules for rendering elements in HTML documents. Let's take a closer look at each of these processes in more detail.

5.3.1 MARKING UP THE DOCUMENT:

You are aware that it is critical to select elements that appropriately represent the meaning of the content being presented. The mark-up produces the framework of the page, which is frequently referred to as the structural layer, on top of which the presentation layer can be put to make it visually appealing. Style sheets are unquestionably the way to go when it comes to presentation. The use of CSS allows you to accomplish far more than you could ever accomplish using (X)HTML, such as making text extremely large and transparent, creating backgrounds, carefully manipulating the layout of text, pixel-perfect positioning of page elements, and much more.

5.3.2 WRITING THE RULES:

It is made up of one or more style instructions (also known as rules or rule sets) that govern how an element or group of elements should be displayed on the page. The first step in studying CSS is to become acquainted with the various components of a rule. As you'll see, they're fairly simple to understand and follow. Each rule selects an element and specifies how it should be shown in the document.

Two rules are illustrated in the following example. The first turns all of the *h1* elements in the document green, and the second specifies that the paragraphs should be written in a tiny, sans-serif font throughout the document.

h1 { color: green; }

p { font-size: small; font-family: sans-serif; }

In CSS terminology, the two primary pieces of a rule are the selector, which identifies the element or elements to be impacted, and the declaration, which contains the rendering instructions for the element or items affected. To be more specific, the declaration is composed of a property (such as colour) and its value (green), which are separated by a colon and a space. As seen in Figure 5.4, one or more declarations are enclosed between curly brackets to indicate their importance.

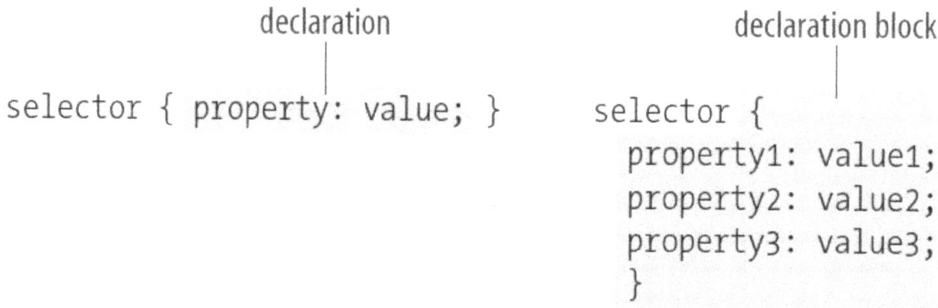

Figure 5.4: The parts of a style sheet rule

SELECTORS: The h1 and p elements are used as selectors in the previous tiny style sheet demonstration. This is referred to as an element type selector, and it is the most basic sort of selector available to programmers. It is possible to define properties for each rule, and these properties will be applied to every h1 and p element in the page. You will learn more advanced selectors, including how to target components that appear in a specific context, as well as how to choose groups of elements and elements that appear only once in a given context. Developing a thorough understanding of selectors—that is, selecting the most appropriate sort of selection and employing it strategically—is a key step in becoming a CSS Jedi Master.

DECLARATIONS: There are two parts to the declaration: a property and a value. There can be many declarations in a single rule; for example, the rule for the p element shown earlier in the code sample has both the font-size and font-family attributes declared in its declaration. Each declaration must be followed by a semicolon in order to be distinguished from the subsequent declaration. It will be ignored if the semicolon is not used, and the declaration and the one that follows it will be ignored. The curly brackets and the declarations contained within them are collectively referred to as the declaration block in programming.

Given that CSS does not recognise whitespace or line returns within the declaration block, authors often write each declaration in the block on a separate line, as illustrated in the accompanying example. This makes it easy to identify the characteristics that have been applied to the selector and to determine when the style rule has been applied.

```
p {
font-size: small;
font-family: sans-serif;
}
```

It is important to note that nothing has really changed in this code—there is still only one set of curly brackets, semicolons after each declaration, and so on. Adding line returns and a few character spaces for alignment are the only differences between the two versions. In style sheets, the collection of standard properties that may be applied to selected elements is at the heart of the design. There are dozens of attributes defined in the whole CSS specification for everything from text indents to how table headers should be read aloud. This book covers the most often encountered and best-supported characteristics, which you can put to use straight immediately. The value of a property is determined by the property. Some attributes require length measurements, while others require colour values, and still others require a predetermined list of keywords to be entered. However, in many circumstances plain common sense will suffice when dealing with a property. When dealing with a property it is vital to understand which values it accepts.

5.3.3 ATTACHING THE STYLES TO THE DOCUMENT:

There are three types of style sheets included. They are: External Style Sheets; Embedded Style Sheets and Inline style sheets.

EXTERNAL STYLE SHEETS: An external style sheet is a distinct, text-only document that contains a set of style rules that are independent of the main content. It is necessary to use the.css suffix when naming the file. It is then necessary to link or import the CSS document into one or more HTML documents. As a result, all of the files on a website may use the same style sheet as one another. When it comes to attaching style sheets to content, this is the most powerful and favoured way.

EMBEDDED STYLE SHEETS: This is the type of style sheet we worked with in the exercise. It is placed in a document using the style element, and its rules apply only to that document. The style element must be placed in the head of the document.

```
<head>
 <title>Required document title here</title>
 <style>
 /* style rules go here */
 </style>
</head>
```

INLINE STYLES: You can apply properties and values to a single element using the style attribute in the element itself, as shown here:

```
<h1 style="color: red">Introduction</h1>
```

To add multiple properties, just separate them with semicolons, like this:

```
<h1 style="color: red; margin-top: 2em">Introduction</h1>
```

Inline styles are only applied to the specific element in which they are contained. Inline styles should be avoided unless it is absolutely necessary to override styles from an embedded or external style sheet, in which case they should be used. Inline styles are problematic because they intersperse presentation information into the structural mark-up, making it difficult to read. Because every style attribute must be tracked down in the source code, they also make it more difficult to make modifications to your website.

5.4 BENEFITS OF CSS:

Although it is unlikely that you require any additional convincing that style sheets are the way to go, here is a quick summary of the advantages of utilising style sheets.

- *Precise type and layout controls:* CSS may be used to attain precision similar to that of printing. There is even a collection of characteristics that are designed expressly for use on a printed document.
- *Less work:* By altering a single style sheet, you can completely transform the appearance of a website.
- *More accessible sites:* When CSS is in charge of all aspects of presentation, you have the freedom to mark up your information in a meaningful way, making it more accessible for non-visual or mobile devices.
- *Reliable browser support:* Every browser currently in use supports CSS Level 2 as well as several of the more interesting features of CSS Level 3.
- *Improves website presentation:* In web development, the most notable advantage of CSS is the increased design flexibility and interactivity it provides. Developers have better control over the layout, allowing them to make fine-grained adjustments to individual sections. Because CSS customisation is considerably easier than plain HTML customization, web developers are able to generate unique designs for each website they design. CSS makes it possible to create complex websites with pages that are uniquely presented.
- *Makes updates easier and smoother:* CSS operates through the creation of rules. These rules are applied to a number of different items on the website at the same time. By eliminating the repetitive coding style of HTML, development work may be completed more quickly and with less monotony. Errors are also significantly decreased as a result of this. The fact that the

content and the design are fully distinct means that updates may be deployed across the entire website at the same time. This shortens the delivery time and lowers the cost of future revisions.

- *Helps web pages to load fast:* `The value of faster page loading often underappreciated, but it is quite crucial. Browsers download the CSS rules only once and keep them cached so that they can be used to load all of the pages on a website. Because of this, navigating the website becomes faster, and the entire user experience is improved. This feature is useful for ensuring that websites run smoothly even when internet speeds are limited. Improved loading speeds on low-end devices also result in improved accessibility for these devices.

5.5 LIMITATIONS OF CSS:

The limitations are as follows:

- *Browser Dependent:* The only major drawback of CSS is that its performance depends largely on browser support. Besides compatibility, all browsers (and their various versions) behave differently. So your CSS needs to account for all these variations. However, in case your CSS styling isn't fully supported by a browser, visitors will still be able to experience the HTML functions. Therefore, you should always have a well-structured HTML together with good CSS.

- *Difficult to retrofit in old websites:* After learning about the numerous advantages of CSS, your first intuitive reaction is to include it into your existing website. Unfortunately, this is not a straightforward procedure. CSS style sheets, particularly the most recent versions, must be integrated into the HTML code at the root level and must also be compatible with previous HTML versions in order to function properly. Retrofitting CSS into outdated websites is a time-consuming and labour-intensive operation. There is also the possibility of completely destroying the existing HTML code and therefore rendering the site inoperable. It is preferable to wait until you have completely redesigned your website.

5.6 MOVING FORWARD WITH CSS:

CSS, like mark-up, is riddled with misunderstandings. CSS is without a doubt the way to go, according to the author. However, several of the claims made by CSS fanatics regarding the technology have been called into question. A handful of the more prevalent claims are offered here, along with some discussion of why readers should avoid making fast decisions regarding CSS's power. However, like with many things in life, there are other interpretations, therefore if this part causes you to consider both sides, the argument has been made successfully, regardless of your final point of view.

There are a lot of Web professionals who long for the day when all browsers would support W3C Web standards on an equal basis. It may sound cynical, but they are going to be waiting for a long time at the very least. The implementation of a specification, even if it is broadly agreed upon, will always leave opportunity for interpretation on the part of the implementers. There may be some ambiguity about the extent to which a specific property can be used in terms of its potential applications. Even if this were not the case, if characteristics are utilised in conjunction with one another, some issues that have not been addressed may arise. It is also possible that, despite the existence of a thorough specification, a given standard feature will not be correctly implemented by a web browser. Even in a world where rigid standards are enforced, browser flaws will continue to exist. Given market pressures to gain user and developer loyalty, it is even more likely that innovation will continue to emerge, and variability will exist regardless of specification quality.

The use of simple CSS examples makes executing basic layout chores appear lot easier than it would be in HTML. However, in fact, some layouts are quite difficult to implement, particularly in light of browser compatibility issues. This is not to argue that you will not be able to accomplish a desired design; you will be able to do so and perhaps much more. Despite this, some designers will determine that CSS isn't worth the effort because of the numerous tiny hacks and workarounds. He disagrees, believing that dealing with the devil you know is more likely to result in a favourable outcome compared to dealing with the devil you don't know at all. However, it is also possible that the notion that CSS is inherently easier to use than mark-up-based layout is a myth that has little basis in fact. Most likely, they are equally tough in a variety of ways and under a variety of conditions.

It doesn't matter which browser you use or which vendor you like; the stark reality is that proprietary features and customization are at the heart of all browser makers' business models. All manufacturers want to be innovative, and even those who actively support the cause of standards have a slew of features that other browser suppliers may be unable to provide. That any vendor has a nefarious purpose to co-opt the Web standards process is untrue; rather, it is simply the commercial reality of wanting to attract Web developers to their platform or keep those who are currently using it. Consider a future in which all implementations are perfectly standard; what would be left for browser providers to innovate with in such an environment? If your answer is "end-user features," keep in mind that such end-user features must frequently be expressed in mark-up, style, or script in order to function properly. After more than a decade of waiting for the dust to settle in the world of mark-up and style requirements, the trends just do not support this assumption any longer.

While it is true that table-heavy Web pages can become rather bulky and that CSS rules can better define such layouts, this isn't always the case, especially given how CSS is frequently used by Web professionals. <Table>, <tr>, and <td> elements are frequently substituted by nested <div> tags, transforming a table less design into a <div>-heavy design. When you combine this with the overuse of long class and id names, especially in the absence of shorthand CSS attributes, CSS designs can become far larger than similar HTML-focused designs. The speed advantage of CSS over HTML is nearly gone when these styles are applied inline or in a style> block. If caching is properly employed in the case of an external style sheet, download benefits may occur on subsequent page views since the style information cached in the external style sheet is no longer needed. Of course, assuming that caching is handled correctly is not a given, and claiming that CSS results in more download-friendly pages is inaccurate and ignores the complexities of page delivery optimization. Of course, it should be highlighted that even if CSS were always larger, which it isn't, the technology offers a more comprehensive and appropriate feature set than presentational mark-up.

Redesigning a website, according to popular belief in the Web development world, is simply a matter of changing styles. In the author's experience, however, nothing could be further from the truth. A significant redesign generally entails modifying the site's navigation, content, and even its purpose. A style sheet will not necessarily apply to pages with fundamentally different structure and content. This isn't to say that style sheets aren't useful; rather, it should serve to correct expectations about the ease with which a site's look may be changed throughout a redesign. If the goal is just to give an existing site a new skin, CSS can definitely deliver on the promise of a speedy makeover.

Rollovers and menus, which were formerly implemented in JavaScript, are now implemented in CSS using simple pseudo-property selectors like: hover. Some browsers, such as Internet Explorer, have included proprietary capabilities called behaviours that link appearance to interactivity. HTML5 continues the trend of blurring the line between presentation and interaction. The problem is that there is no difference between generating a mess by combining content, structure, and appearance with a disaster created by combining style and interaction. For the same updating and separation of concerns goal described so many times before, a decoupled or, more accurately, loosely coupled connection is the way to go. Unfortunately, we often have to relearn difficult lessons in new environments, as we do with many technologies.

5.7 CSS PREPROCESSORS:

CSS (Cascading Style Sheets) is a standard language for defining the look and feel of structured documents, such as HTML and XML documents. According to surveys, more than 90% of web developers utilise CSS in their daily development duties, and more than 90% of websites include CSS in their technology portfolio. CSS has lately begun to be used in the design of desktop programmes (e.g., using WinJS) and mobile applications (e.g., using Phone Gap), extending its use across a broad range of application domains.

CSS code is applied to a variety of target documents, the most common of which are HTML documents. CSS has a fairly simple syntax, as shown in the diagram below. A list of CSS rules in the form of one or more CSS selectors can be found in every CSS file (i.e., Style Sheet). A selector tells the styler which elements of the target page should be styled (e.g., selector p selects all paragraphs in an HTML document). There are one or more style declarations inside the body of a selector that apply some style values (e.g., red) to some style attributes (e.g., colour) of the selected items.

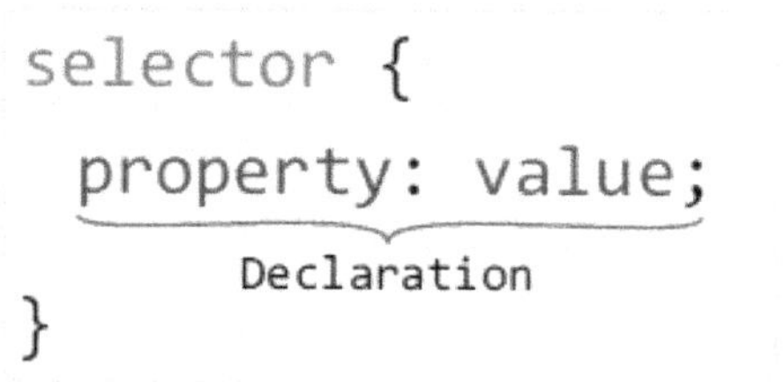

```
selector {
  property: value;
       Declaration
}
```

Figure 5.5 CSS Syntax

The CSS syntax's simplicity has historical antecedents. CSS was created with web designers with little programming knowledge in mind. As a result, it lacks many of the essential programming constructs that enable code reuse and structured programming, such as variables, functions, loops, and conditionals. As a result, CSS code maintenance can be a demanding undertaking. CSS developers are prone to duplicate style declarations from one selector to another as a result of this lack of programming features (i.e., code cloning). Although there is some built-in CSS help for avoiding duplication (such as grouping selectors that share common declarations), the CSS code delivered to website end-users still contains a significant amount of duplicated code.

CSS pre-processor languages were created by the industry in reaction to CSS's shortcomings. Variable and function declarations can be included in CSS pre-processor code, which can then be utilised inside CSS selectors. The pre-processor compiler basically transpires the function calls and variable uses to pure CSS. There is already a big list of CSS pre-processors (e.g., HSS, SASS, LESS, Google Closure Stylesheets) that offer very comparable functionality with different syntax, and their adoption is becoming a fast-growing trend in the industry. According to an online study of over 13,000 web professionals done by a well-known website specialising on CSS development, roughly 54% of web developers use a CSS pre-processor in their development work. Front-end web developers working on government websites are encouraged to utilise SASS as their Style Sheet development language since it provides "resources such as frameworks, libraries, courses, and a thorough style guide as support."

In spite of the fact that CSS pre-processors are widely used among developers and contain a number of valuable features, we do not have a sufficient understanding of how developers use these features in real-world web applications. Having this type of information can be beneficial for a variety of reasons, including:

- A significant proportion of web professionals are still coding in pure CSS, which is a legacy language. Because of this, moving existing CSS code to take advantage of pre-processor features (e.g., extracting duplicated declarations to a CSS pre-processor function) is highly sought after in the business. It is likely that understanding the best techniques used by web developers while writing in pre-processors will aid in the development of more effective and efficient migration strategies in the future.
- CSS pre-processor may be utilised in an inefficient manner because web developers fail to take advantage of chances to further minimise existing redundant code and other poor practises. Refactoring recommendation tools are therefore required to assist developers in enhancing the overall quality of their CSS pre-processor code, which is currently lacking. Knowing the practises of developers will assist in selecting refactoring possibilities that will lead to the most often used solutions/patterns in the future.
- Finally, understanding developers' practises can assist CSS pre-processor language designers in revising the design of these languages, for example, by adding support for new features (which are currently implemented by developers in an ad hoc manner), making existing features easier to use, or eliminating features that are not used by developers, among other things.

5.8 STYLE SHEETS IN WEB PUBLISHING:

In contrast to structured documents, style sheets define how documents should be presented. Structured documents contain content and structure, but style sheets describe how documents should be presented. This separation is required for device-independent publications (all device-specific information is left to the style sheet), and it facilitates document management because a style sheet can define a large number of documents at the same time.

For example, if an XML document uses element names, such as “author,” “name,” and “email” (see code below), there is no hint as to how to present the content on, say, A4 paper.

Markup:

```
<author>
<name>Janne Saarela</name>
<email>Jsaarela@w3.org</email>
</author>
```

Style sheet:

```
author { font: 12pt Times }
name { font-weight: bold }
email { font-style: italic }
```

CSS development began at CERN in 1994 with the intention of creating a style-sheet language for the Web that would allow authors to exercise more stylistic control than was previously possible with HTML. It was recommended by the World Wide Web Consortium (W3C) in 1996, and it was implemented by major browsers such as Netscape Navigator 4 and Microsoft Internet Explorer 4, as well as numerous writing tools, starting in 1997. CSS applies style to elements through the use of declarative rules. A straightforward rule can state that any P components belonging to the class "danger" should be displayed in red text on a white background:

```
P.warning {
color: red;
background: white;
}
```

CSS1 provides functionality for screen-based formatting, such as fonts, colours, and layouts (see Figure below). Before the advent of style sheets, web authors were forced to create images of text in order to express colour and font information. Thus, instead of text, the majority of the network bandwidth is now consumed by pictures of text on the World Wide Web. In order to achieve this, style sheets can significantly improve network performance, as demonstrated by a recent study of how new Web technologies affect network performance, which concluded that "To our surprise, style sheets promise to be the most promising source of significant network bandwidth improvements, whether deployed with HTTP/1.0 or HTTP/1.1, by significantly reducing the need for in-lined images to provide graphic elements, and the resulting network traffic."

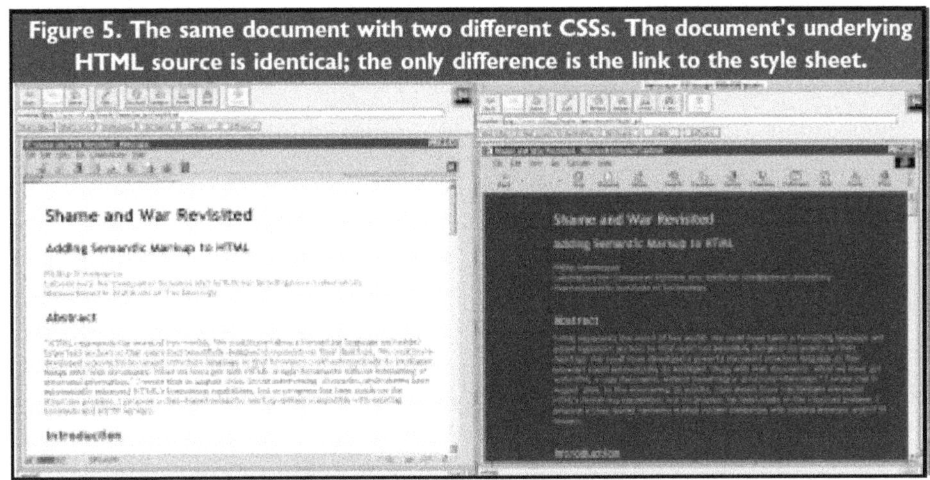

Figure 5.6 Same document with different CSS

The use of style sheets rather than images increases the accessibility of the Web. Using a speech synthesiser, a blind person can hear HTML-encoded text read to them; the text can also be displayed to them through a braille tactile feedback device. Images, on the other hand, prohibit access to those who are not visually impaired. Media-specific style sheets (CSS2), the second level of CSS (which became a W3C Recommendation in May 1998), improves Web accessibility by introducing the concept of media-specific style sheets. Example: A style sheet can indicate how a document is rendered audibly, like in the following sentence:

```
@media speech {
BODY { voice-family: female }
H1 { volume: loud }
}
```

It is applicable to any Web device that has the capability of generating speech output. Media-specific style sheets allow designers to precisely characterise presentations for a variety of devices while the underlying texts remain device-independent, as shown in the following example. Because of their small display area, handheld Web devices necessitate the use of style sheets that are tailored specifically for them. In some cases, there may not be enough space for photos, and just a condensed version of the paper should be displayed instead. The following style sheet disables the display of images and normal paragraphs, resulting in only paragraphs with the class "ingress" being displayed:

```
@media handheld {
IMG { display: none }
P { display: none }
P.ingress { display: block }
}
```

A CSS style file is normally processed by the Web browser on the client computer. While processing the style sheet on a stationary proxy server may be more efficient for mobile handheld devices, it may be more efficient for mobile handheld devices. The style sheet in the "ingress" example above prevents images from being shown, allowing the proxy server to prevent images from being downloaded by the mobile device. This conserves valuable bandwidth while simultaneously improving the perceived performance of the Web.

The Extensible Stylesheet Language (XSL), which is currently being developed by a W3C working group, extends the concept of style sheets by allowing them to modify the structure of a document. For example, an XSL sheet can build a table of contents by extracting all chapter names from a document and putting them together in one place. It is expected that using XSL to transform XML data into structured documents, like as HTML, would continue to play a significant role in multifunctional publishing for many years to come. But is it possible to go too far in terms of fashion? Forms, which allow users to interact with pages by filling in text fields and hitting buttons, were among the first improvements to HTML when it escaped from CERN. Later, with the development of scripts (such as JavaScript, which is now standardised as ECMAScript) and Java applets, it became possible to distribute applications through the World Wide Web.

Many Websites combine declarative data (such as HTML, XML, and CSS) with executable programmes (such as Java and PHP) (such as scripts and applets). It is common for content providers to be driven to employ programmes in order to generate particular presentational effects (for example, an animated title or a pop-up menu). The costs and benefits of relying solely on scripts and applets to provide information should be carefully considered when seeking to achieve multifunctional publishing. The following expenses are incurred:

Accessibility: Content embedded in a program is hidden from Web search engines, and it's difficult or even impossible to convert that content to other formats.

Maintainability: In 20 years, will machines be able to decode HTML files? Probably. Will machines be able to run current scripts and applets? Maybe. Declarative data is generally easier to maintain and lives longer than programs.

Device independence: Many scripts assume a graphical Web device and will not work on, say, a textonly browser.

We anticipate that as the development of style sheets develops, the most popular presentational effects produced through programming will make their way into declarative style rules. Using the above example, CSS2 offers capabilities for highlighting an element when the mouse is moved over it; previously, this type of highlighting could only be achieved through the use of scripts.

The World Wide Web Consortium (W3C) launched a project in 1997 called Document Object Model (DOM) to explain the interface between programmes and documents. With this specification, the purpose is to establish an application programming interface (API) that is independent of the programming language in which it is used. This API will allow programmes to read, change, and create new HTML and XML documents.

Structured documents combined with style sheets enable the same document to be displayed on a range of Web-enabled devices at the same time. Indeed, the goal of multifunctional publishing is to require only a single source text that is flexible enough to be used in a variety of different settings. On the other hand, it may be essential to convert a document from one representation type to another before it can be published on the Web in some cases. However, there are difficulties in handling content in a different representation than the one that is actually delivered. It is our primary assertion that HTML, in conjunction with style sheets, should be rich enough to serve as a master document format for a large number of publications. In addition to traditional papers, XML-based data formats such as spreadsheets and databases can also record semantic information.

Capturing semantics for future applications: When discussing how to translate documents from one format to another, the terms "down-translation" and "up-translation" are sometimes used interchangeably with one another. Down-translation is a procedure in which the final document has less semantically significant markup available than the original source document, as opposed to up-translation. A reversed procedure in which the source document can be in any format and specific rules are employed to remove presentation-oriented, typically proprietary markup from the output document is referred to as up-translation. Ultimately, the goal is to create a higher-level representation with abstract markup components that may be used for a document description that is independent of platform and device. In this context, up-translation can be seen of as a preparation process for multifunctional publication, in which the value of information material is leveraged to the point where new applications can be applied. The real down translation is frequently an easy process that is fine-tuned using in-house criteria to do the actual translation to other document formats, such as Word or Excel. In addition, the down-translation process must be able to accommodate the real-world constraints of the publication schedule. For example, in the context of an encyclopaedia, this procedure may occur once a year, whereas it may occur 50 times a second in the context of an interactive online service. Up-translation of current material, as well as learning to utilise new writing tools or existing tools in new ways, will constitute an investment that will be justified by the long-term worth of the information if it is done properly. Several scenarios demonstrate the kind of applications that could be made viable by using more semantic mark-up and metadata, including the following:

Structured queries: Locating documents through URLs or search engines is standard practice on the Web today. Structured queries would extend the range of search options by allowing queries for, say, a given author or location

Alternate user interface metaphors: Web devices typically arrange visited documents in a linear list as they are traversed. An alternative user interface could create a virtual landscape of traversed links whereby, say, the location and political bias of authors are visualized.

Intelligent agents: Users place an offer for some merchandise, then have their agent find the best vendor on the Web. Users indicate interest in buying an item, and their agents search for and identify a maximum price and negotiation strategy. Then, without user intervention, these agents use the item description to find, say, all potential resellers and commits a financial transaction to inform the user of a shipment arriving tomorrow at 7:00 A.M.

These scenarios demonstrate there is room for improvement in the way information is represented and reused on the Web. An important catalyst for new Web applications will be the incorporation of additional semantics in machine-understandable form.

5.9 CONCLUSION:

In terms of the appearance and feel of Websites, CSS gives you more control. Style sheets aren't just for making pages seem nice; they're also handy for a variety of other things. They can simplify the creation of documents and make them easier to manipulate by separating the structure from the style. CSS provides a plethora of useful layout attributes that allow designers to create a more diverse range of designs than they could possibly achieve with presentation mark-up alone. CSS, on the other hand, should not be considered a substitute for mark-up because it is heavily reliant on precise (X)HTML mark-up as well as proper tag naming conventions. While the promise of CSS has been enticing to developers, the implementation of accurate style sheets in browsers has proven to be a significant challenge. With the introduction of CSS, cross-browser rendering issues reappeared with a fury, and we discovered that the erroneous methods of tinkering around for filtering and selecting demonstrates the necessity of client-side scripting.

CHAPTER 6

CSS TRANSITIONS, TRANSFORMS AND ANIMATIONS

"Animation is not the art of drawings that move but the art of movements that are drawn."

-Norman McLaren

Chapter Learnings:

The reader will have a better understanding of CSS Transforms, Transitions, and Animations after reading this chapter. We'll start with CSS Transitions, which are a handy technique to make style changes fade in and out gracefully. Then, users will learn how to use CSS Transforms to animate items by moving, scaling, rotating, and skewing them. 3D Transforms and CSS Animation will be briefly introduced towards the end of this chapter.

6.1 INTRODUCTION:

CSS transforms, CSS transitions, and CSS animations are all different CSS specifications that can be used in conjunction with one another. While the three names sound like they all achieve the same thing—make something move—CSS transitions and animations are more about making things move over time than they are about making anything move immediately. Transitions and animations allow users to specify the transition between two or more states of an element. Transitions and animations are used in web design.

Transforms alter the appearance of an element by translating, rotating, scaling, and skewing it; however, they do not have a temporal component to them. CSS transform property can be used to modify the location of an element's coordinate space in the CSS visual for matting model, but transitions or animation are required to make that change appear to occur over time. The transform property is addressed in detail in the CSS Transforms section.

However, while animation is doable using JavaScript, becoming familiar with CSS3 transitions and animations will save users a lot of time and effort if users ever need to animate anything on the Web. In general, when compared to JavaScript, it will save users users' CPU and battery life as well. CSS animations and transitions, when used effectively, can breathe life and depth into user's web apps. The purpose of this chapter is to teach users how to transition and animate elements in user's documents. However, understanding when to utilise animation can help users improve users experience (UX). Animating user interface can help users UX communicate on a deeper level by adding the sense of time.

6.2 BASIC PRINCIPLES OF ANIMATION:

Disney animators devised 12 principles for cartoon animation long before the Internet was invented. Some of these ideas also apply to CSS animation. There are 12 basic principles for animation, according to Frank Thomas and Ollie Johnston's "bible of animation," The Illusion of Life: Disney Animation.

- ✓ **Squash and stretch:**

Objects deform under motion depending on their composition. As an object or character bounces or moves, squashing and stretching gives the sensation of weight and volume. When a ball bounces, for example, it is squished when it touches the ground and extends as it rises.

- ✓ **Anticipation:**

Users may struggle to grasp an animation unless it follows a clear path from one activity to the next. They must foresee or predict a change before it occurs. It's a movement in cartoons that prepares the spectator for a major action the character is about to make, such as bending the knees before jumping. It might be a button depression on the web before the commencement of a longer animation that begins when the button is selected. Before starting the main effect, mentally direct user's customers to where they should concentrate, especially if the commencement of the animation is critical.

- ✓ **Staging:**

Staging is the presenting of an idea in a cartoon so that it is obviously clear. Staging on the Web is the process of drawing a user's attention to a certain activity, such as a little jiggle of a call-to-action button. Staging assists users in following the story or idea being presented, such as the steps of a check-out procedure.

✓ **Straight ahead action and pose to pose:**

On the large screen, there are two main ways to animation. In the straight ahead action style, the animator begins with the initial drawing and progresses through the scenario drawing by drawing. The animator sketches the primary points of an animation in pose to pose and then creates (or has an assistant make) the points in between later. While this theory appears to be limited to storyboarding, it also applies to sketching key frames and how the animation fills in the space or time between them.

We emulate the Straight Ahead technique with CSS animations when we animate image sprites to produce motion. We let the browser be our assistance in most animation circumstances, defining precise positions, or poses, inside the animation and letting the browser interpolate property values as it animates from pose to pose, or key frame definition to key frame definition.

✓ **Follow-through and overlapping action:**

The insertion of additional motion after the main animation has finished is referred to as follow-through. A character sprinting and stopping, for example, will likely have her hair and garments bouncing and falling back into place once her legs and body stop moving, catching up with the main mass of the character. Nothing comes to a complete halt at once. While an example, the way Wile E. Coyote's legs continue to go forward as he falls down a cliff is an example of overlapping action: some components are somewhat delayed after other components change direction. It takes a time for his ears to catch up. In the event that users CSS animations develop complicated enough to necessitate follow-through and overlapping action, timing will be important to ensuring that users effects are effective.

✓ **Slow in and slow out:**

Slow ins and slow outs make animation more lifelike and soften the action, just how cars don't start and stop at full speed—rather, they accelerate from a stop to full speed and then decelerate back to zero. Only mechanical animations will run in a straight line. The slow in and slow out concept asserts that the beginning and end of an animation are more engaging than the middle; so, unless the animation is mechanical, the animation should move at its fastest in the middle, with a slower start and end. The effect is achieved in cartoon animation by having more cells at the endpoints and fewer in the midst of the motion. This effect is achieved using CSS by changing the linearity of cubic Bézier timing functions.

✓ **Arcs:**

Almost all activities, according to the arcs principle, take an arc or a somewhat round course. Consider how users hand moves back and forth as users walk: it arcs back and forth rather than remaining at a constant distance from the ground. Linear animations have a mechanical feel to them. Within a key frame animation, granular control can be used to create arcs. CSS developers frequently employ CSS animations rather than transitions because animations allow for more detail in the creation of an arced route, whereas CSS transitions merely allow for movement between two states. Creating an arc with CSS transitions is not only doable, but also pretty simple, thanks to some cubic Bézier timing methods.

✓ **Secondary action:**

Secondary actions can give dimension to a major action by supplementing or reinforcing it, as well as giving the scene more life. If supplementary actions are included, the animations should work together to support one another. If user's main animation drops a module onto a page, for example, a secondary action may be the main call-to-action button within the module dropping into place, then performing its action once the main module has done animating in. The main action should be reinforced by a secondary action. It's quite OK to "think outside the box" and animate a child element in a way that differs from its parent.

✓ **Timing:**

When it comes to animation, timing is probably the most crucial of the principles on this list. While traditional animation is dependent on the number of frames, CSS animation is primarily concerned with providing the right length of time for the user to read the motion without making the site appear slow. The duration of the animation, as well as the delay and timing function, are all included in the timing. When it comes to time, there are no right or wrong solutions. If it occurs at all, timing expertise comes with practise and experimenting. Here, recommend utilising trial and error to fine-tune user's animation's timing before cutting it in half: While users may want user's animation to go slowly enough for users to understand the difference in timeframes and figure out what the optimal combination of duration, delay, and progression is, users don't want users site to appear slow.

- ✓ **Exaggeration:**

In order to draw the user's attention to what users want them to focus on, exaggeration is used to highlight movements that are beyond their normal condition. The use of a small amount of exaggeration may breathe new life into an animation and even make it appear more lifelike. Make use of good taste and common sense: exaggeration is not an extreme distortion, but rather a little distortion that emphasises a point without being so overdone as to be visually warped for user's audience.

- ✓ **Solid drawing:**

The solid drawing principle encompasses the principles of drawing or coding forms that provide the sense of three dimensions, such as weight and solid form, while maintaining the illusion of two dimensions. In CSS, this includes the use of box shadows, gradients, and transforms, which provide the appearance of three-dimensionality to user's website's content. In the absence of 3D animation, this principle is only distantly connected to online animation, because we're drawing with CSS in a two-dimensional environment on the web, not in three dimensions.

- ✓ **Appeal:**

The appeal concept is concerned with the characteristics of charm, believability, and interest. An appealing design on the Web contains an easy-to-read lauder, a clear drawing, and motion that will attract and engage the visitor's attention and participation. The animation must be appealing to the mind as well as the eye in order to be successful.

6.3 CSS TRANSITIONS:

In order to animate CSS properties from an original value to a new value over time when the value of a property changes, we can use transitions in CSS. It is customary for CSS property values to change in response to "style change events," such that the change is instantaneous. It only takes milliseconds to repaint (or reflow and repaint, if necessary) the impacted content before the new property value takes over and overrides the old property value. The majority of value changes appear to be instantaneous, requiring less than 16 milliseconds to show. While it may take longer to make changes, it is only a single step from one value to the next. For example, when changing a backdrop colour on hover, the background shifts from one colour to the next with no gentle transition between the two colours. When we use CSS transitions, we can smoothly animate CSS properties from their original value to their new value over time as the style computation process progresses: The appeal principle has to do with charisma, credibility, and interest, among other things. An appealing design on the Web contains an easy-to-read lauder, a clear drawing, and motion that will attract and engage the visitor's attention and participation. The animation must be appealing to the mind as well as the eye in order to be successful.

```
button {
 color: magenta;
 transition: color 200ms ease-in 50ms;
}
button:hover {
 color: rebeccapurple;
 transition: color 200ms ease-out 50ms;
}
```

In CSS animatable properties, transitions allow the values of the properties to vary over time, allowing for simple animations. In contrast to instantly changing the colour of a button on hover, CSS transitions allow the button to gently fade from magenta to Rebecca purple over 200 milliseconds, with the option of adding a 50-millisecond wait before transitioning to Rebecca purple. A transition occurs whenever a colour is changed, no matter how long it takes. The CSS transition attribute, on the other hand, allows for a more progressive colour change. CSS transitions are currently supported by all browsers, including Internet Explorer 9 and older versions. If a browser does not support CSS transition attributes, the shift will be immediate rather than gradual, which is good and easily accessible in most cases. If the stated property or property values are not animatable, the change will be immediate rather than gradual, as it has been in the past. Given that transitions are merely progressive enhancements, there is no reason why they should not be used now.

CSS transitions allow users to control how a property moves from one value to another throughout the course of a page's life. In order to create pleasant and, ideally, subtle effects on the property value, we can make the value vary gradually. After an optional delay, the CSS transition properties can be used to animate CSS property values from a previous value to a new value over a set period of time, following an acceleration curve and a specified duration of time. It is possible to control which attributes are animated, how long the animation should last before it begins, how long the transition should take, and the manner in which the transition will progress using CSS transitions. All of these options are completely configurable.

Sometimes users require instantaneous changes in the value of a variable. The preceding section utilised link colours as an example, but link colours should change quickly on hover to alert sighted users that an interaction is taking place and that the hovered item contains a link. Additionally, options in an autocomplete list box should not fade in: users want the alternatives to appear immediately rather than fading in more slowly as the user types. Instantaneous value changes provide the optimum user experience in many situations. At other times, users might want to create a gradual shift in the value of a property to draw attention to what is taking place in the market.

For example, users might want to make a card game more realistic by animating the flipping of a card for 200 milliseconds, as the user might not notice what happened if there is no animation. For instance, users might want user's site's drop-down menus to expand or become visible over 200 milliseconds (rather than instantly), which could be distracting. Users can make a drop-down menu appear slowly using CSS transitions. We're changing the height and opacity of the submenu in Figure 6.1 over 200 milliseconds. The hidden menu becomes entirely opaque and extended.

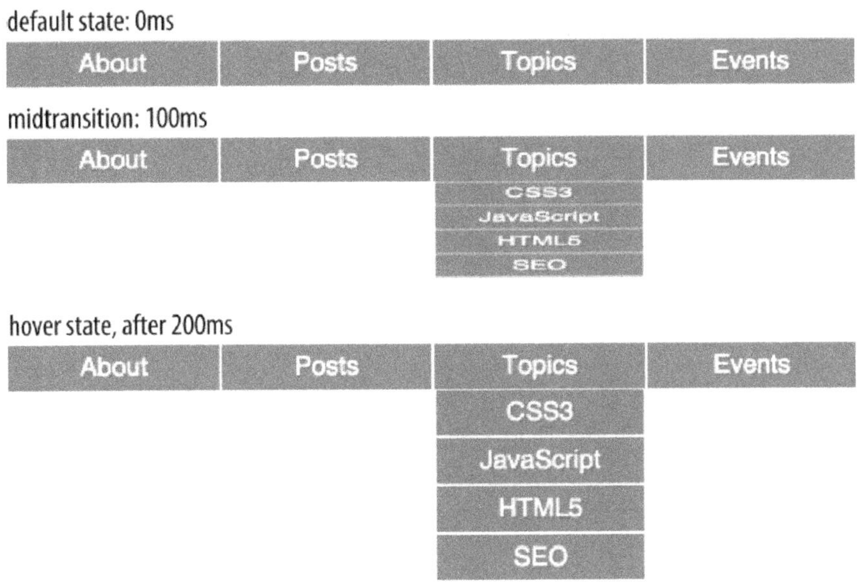

Figure 6.1. Transition initial, midtransition, and final state

We'll go over the four transition attributes as well as the transition shorthand in this chapter, which not only make our transition viable but also incredibly simple to execute.

6.3.1 TRANSITION PROPERTIES:

Transitions are written in CSS using the transition property, transition-duration, transition-timing-function, and transition delay properties, as well as the transition property as a shorthand for the four longhand attributes.

We used all four CSS transition attributes to generate the drop-down navigation in the below example:

```
nav li ul {
 transition-property: transform;
 transition-duration: 200ms;
 transition-timing-function: ease-in;
 transition-delay: 50ms;
 transform: scale(1, 0);
```

```
 transform-origin: top center;
}
nav li:hover ul {
 transform: scale(1, 1);
}
```

The transition for our drop-down navigation example is defined by this example. Hovering over navigational elements causes the style change in this example. The starting state of the nested lists in the navigation shown is transform: scale (1, 0) with a transform-origin: top centre. The final state is transform: scale (1, 1), with the same transform-origin.

- ✓ **The transition-property Property:**

The names of the CSS properties users want to transition are specified by the transition-property property. Yes, saying "the transition-property property" is strange. The transition-property value can be a comma-separated list of properties, the keyword none if no properties should be transitioned, or the default all, which means "transition all transitional properties." Users can also provide a comma-separated list of properties to contain the key phrase. All the transitional properties will transition in unison if all is the lone key term—or if all is the default. Assume users wish to change the appearance of a box on hover:

```
div {
 color: #ff0000;
 border: 1px solid #00ff00;
 border-radius: 0;
 transform: scale(1) rotate(0deg);
 opacity: 1;
 box-shadow: 3px 3px rgba(0, 0, 0, 0.1);
 width: 50px;
 padding: 100px;
```

```
}
div:hover {
 color: #000000;
 border: 5px dashed #000000;
 border-radius: 50%;
 transform: scale(2) rotate(-10deg);
 opacity: 0.5;
 box-shadow: -3px -3px rgba(255, 0, 0, 0.5);
 width: 100px;
 padding: 20px;
}
```

Every property that has a different value in the default state versus the hovered state will change to the hover-state values when the user hovers over the div. The transition-property property is used to specify which of the properties should be animated over time (versus instantly). On hover, all of the properties change from their default values to the hovered values, but only the animatable properties in the transition-property will transition over time. Border-style and other non-animateable properties will shift from one value to the next instantly.

Use all to define all of the properties for a transition at the same time, speed, and pace. All the animatable properties will transition in unison if all is the lone value or the last value in the comma-separated value for transition-property. The following phrases are nearly comparable if we wish to transition all of the properties:

```
div {
 color: #ff0000;
 border: 1px solid #00ff00;
 border-radius: 0;
 transform: scale(1) rotate(0deg);
```

```
 opacity: 1;
 box-shadow: 3px 3px rgba(0, 0, 0, 0.1);
 width: 50px;
 padding: 100px;
 transition-property: color, border, border-radius, transform, opacity,
 box-shadow, width, padding;
 transition-duration: 1s;
}
```

and

```
div {
 color: #ff0000;
 border: 1px solid #00ff00;
 border-radius: 0;
 transform: scale(1) rotate(0deg);
 opacity: 1;
 box-shadow: 3px 3px rgba(0, 0, 0, 0.1);
 width: 50px;
 padding: 100px;
 transition-property: all;
 transition-duration: 1s;
}
```

Both transition-property property declarations will transition all of the properties listed—however, the former will transition only the eight properties that may change, based on property declarations that may be included in other rule blocks—whereas the latter will transition all of the properties listed. However, it is not required that those eight property values be provided in the same rule block. It is ensured that all animatable property values that would change as a result of any style change event—no matter which CSS rule block includes the new property value—transitions over a one-second period by using the all keyword in the later example. The transition applies to all animatable attributes of all elements that are matched by the selector, not just those that are specified in the same style block as the rest of the elements in the selection.

Declaring individual properties means that when the value of the transition-property transition is changed, only the properties that were specifically defined in the value of the transition-property transition are affected, regardless of whether the property values were inherited, declared in the same rule block, or applied to the element through a different CSS rule block. In this situation, the initial version restricts the transition to only the eight attributes provided, but it allows us to provide more flexibility over how each property transitions in the subsequent versions. Declaring the properties independently allows us to provide varied speeds, delays, and/or durations to the transitions of each property if we define those transition properties separately.

```
<div class="foo">Hello</div>
div {
 color: #ff0000;
 border: 1px solid #0f0;
 border-radius: 0;
 transform: scale(1) rotate(0deg);
 opacity: 1;
 box-shadow: 3px 3px rgba(0, 0, 0, 0.1);
 width: 50px;
 padding: 100px;
}
.foo {
 color: #00ff00;
 transition-property: color, border, border-radius, transform, opacity,
```

```
box-shadow, width, padding;
transition-duration: 1s;
}
```

The transition-property property does not have to be in the same rule block as the properties that make up its value in order for it to have any effect. To define the transitions for each property individually, write them out in their entirety, separating each of the properties with a comma between them. With a few exceptions, if users wish to animate practically all of the properties at the same time, delay, and pace, users can use a combination of all and the specific properties users want to transition at various times, speeds, or pace. Make sure to use all as the first value in the expression:

```
div {
color: #f00;
border: 1px solid #00ff00;
border-radius: 0;
transform:
scale(1) rotate(0deg);
opacity: 1;
box-shadow: 3px 3px rgba(0, 0, 0, 0.1);
width: 50px;
padding: 100px;
transition-property: all, border-radius,
opacity; transition-duration: 1s, 2s, 3s;
}
```

When users use the comma-separated value, it includes all of the properties stated in the preceding example, as well as all of the inherited CSS properties, and all of the properties declared in any other CSS rule block that matches or is inherited by the element in question. Except for border-radius and opacity, which were expressly added individually, all of the properties receiving new values will transition at the same duration, delay, and timing function as the properties that are receiving new values in the preceding example. Because we included them as part of a comma-separated list after the rest of the properties, we can transition them at the same time, delay, and timing function as the rest of the properties, or we can provide different times, delays, and timing functions for these two properties, depending on our needs. This time, we transition every property over one second, with the exception of border-radius and opacity, which transition over two and three seconds, respectively, in this example. Following that, we'll talk about transition duration.

✓ The transition-duration Property:

The transition-duration property accepts as a value a comma-separated list of lengths of time, in seconds (s) or milliseconds (ms), that should be required to transition from the original property values to the final property values, with the lengths in seconds (s) or milliseconds (ms) being the shortest. The transition-duration property specifies how long it should take for each property to migrate from its original value to its new value, and it is used in conjunction with the transition-duration property. It will take the following amount of time to transition between two states if the duration is only declared in one of those states: If the transition is between two states and the duration is only declared in one of those states, the transition will take the following amount of time to transition to the previous state:

```
input:invalid {
 transition-duration: 1s;
 background-color: red;
}
input:valid {
 transition-duration: 0.2s;
 background-color: green;
}
```

It is important to note that if different values for the transition-duration are declared in two different rule blocks, the transition-duration value declared in the rule block it is migrating to will determine the duration of the transition. When a valid input is entered into the input box, it will take one second for the input to change to a red backdrop. When an invalid input is entered into the input box, it will take only 200 milliseconds for it to convert to a green background. A positive number in seconds (s) or milliseconds (ms) should be stated for the transition-duration property, with the latter being the preferred unit (ms). Even if the duration is set to zero seconds, the standard requires a time unit of milliseconds or seconds. When left to their own devices, properties simply change from one value to another quickly. Following this logic, the default value for the duration of a transition is 0s, which indicates that the transition is immediate and does not display any animation.

If transition-duration is omitted from a property declaration, it is treated as if no transition-property declaration had been applied, and no transitioned event occurs unless a positive value for transition-delay has been specified on the property. A transition will be applied as long as the total time set for the transition to occur is greater than 0s (which can happen when the transition-duration is omitted and the transition-duration value defaults to 0s, if there is a positive transition-delay value), and a transitioned event will occur if the transition is completed. Negative values for transition-duration are invalid, and if they are included in the calculation, the entire property value will be invalidated. The same super-long transition property declaration can be used to declare a single duration for all of the properties or distinct durations for each property, or we can make alternate properties animate for the same length of time using the same super-long transition property declaration. By providing a single transition-duration value, we can declare a single duration that applies to all properties throughout the transition:

```
div {
 color: #ff0000;
 ...
 transition-property: color, border, border-radius, transform, opacity,
 box-shadow, width, padding;
 transition-duration: 200ms;
}
```

Instead, we could have specified the same number of comma-separated time values for the transition-duration property value as the number of CSS properties we enumerated in the transition-property property value for the transition-duration. To allow each property to transition over a distinct amount of time, we must provide a different comma-separated value for each property name stated. For example:

```
div {
 color: #ff0000;
 ...
 transition-property: color, border, border-radius, transform, opacity,
 box-shadow, width, padding;
 transition-duration: 200ms, 180ms, 160ms, 140ms, 120ms, 100ms, 1s, 2s;
}
```

If the number of properties declared does not equal the number of durations declared, the browser has specific rules on how to deal with the discrepancy in the number of properties declared and durations declared. If there are more durations than there are properties, the extra durations are not taken into consideration. If there are more properties than there are durations, the durations are repeated until all properties have been exhausted. Colour, border-radius, opacity, and width will all have a duration of 100 milliseconds; border, transform, box-shadow, and padding will all have a period of 200 milliseconds.

```
div {
 ...
 transition-property: color, border, border-radius, transform, opacity,
 box-shadow, width, padding;
 transition-duration: 100ms, 200ms;
}
```

Assuming we declare exactly two time values separated by commas, any odd properties will transition over the first time value declared, and any even properties will transition over the second time value declared. Because of the slowness of a transition, the website will appear to be slow or unresponsive, pulling attention away from what should be a subtle effect. If a change is made too quickly, it may be too subtle to be detected by the audience. While users can specify any positive duration for users transitions that users wish, users goal is likely to be to give an enhanced rather than an irritating user experience for user's users. Effects should be visible for a long enough period of time to be noticeable, but not for an inordinate amount of time. Generally speaking, the optimum transition effects occur between 100 and 200 milliseconds, resulting in a perceptible, but not disturbing, transition between two images. We want a good user experience for our drop-down menu, so we set both properties to transition over 200 milliseconds:

```
nav li ul {
 transition-property: transform, opacity;
 transition-duration: 200ms;
 ...
}
```

✓ **The transition-timing-function Property:**

Do users want users transition to begin slowly and progress to a quicker pace, begin quickly and progress to a slower pace, progress on an even keel, jump through various levels, or even bounce? The transition-timing-function gives a means of regulating the speed at which the transition occurs. During the execution of the transition, the transition-timing-function property explains how the transition will progress.

The transition-timing-function values include ease, linear, ease-in, ease-out, ease-in-out, step-start, step-end, steps (n, start)—where n is the number of steps—steps (n, end), and cubic-bezier (x1, y1, x2, y2).

The non-step term refers to smoothing timing functions that use cubic Bézier mathematical functions. The specification includes five predefined easing functions, but users can define users own cubic-bezier () function, as shown in Table 6.1, to describe users own precise timing function.

Timing Function	Definition	Cubic-Bezier Value
ease	Starts slow, then speeds up, then ends very slowly	cubic-bezier (0.25, 0.1, 0.25, 1)
linear	Proceeds at the same speed throughout transition	cubic-bezier (0, 0, 1, 1)
ease-in	Starts slow, then speeds up	cubic-bezier (0.42, 0, 1, 1)
ease-out	Starts fast, then slows down	cubic-bezier (0, 0, 0.58, 1)
ease-in-out	Similar to ease; faster in the middle, with a slow start but not as slow at the end	cubic-bezier(0.42, 0, 0.58, 1)
cubic-bezier()	Specifies a cubic-bezier curve	cubic-bezier(x1, y1, x2, y2)

Table 6.:. Supported key terms for cubic Bezier timing functions

Cubic Bézier curves include four numeric parameters, including the underlying curves that define the five named easing functions listed in Table 6.1 and shown in Figure 6.2. For example, linear and cubic-bezier are the same thing (0, 0, 1, 1). The values for the first and third cubic Bézier function parameters must be between 0 and 1.

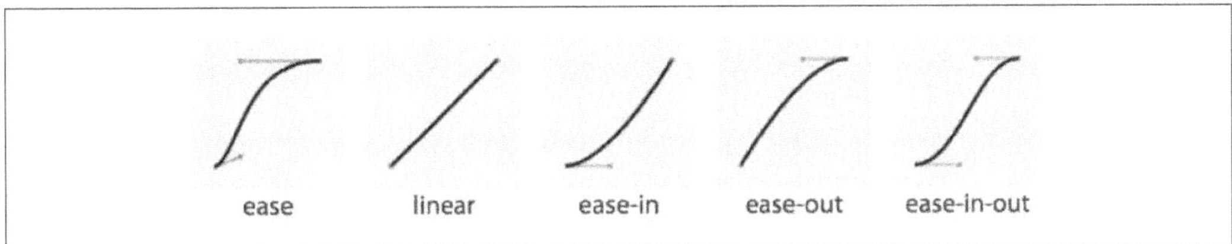

Figure 6.2. Supported cubic Bezier named functions include ease, linear, ease-in, ease-out, and ease-in-out

✓ The transition-delay Property:

Users can use the transition-delay property to add a time delay between when the transition-initiating modification is applied to an element and when the transition starts. Hovering over an element with a colour change on hover without a transition causes the colour to change quickly. A transition-delay of 0s (the default) signifies that the transition will begin immediately—it will begin executing as soon as the element's state changes. Otherwise, the transition-time delay's value specifies the time interval between when the property values would have changed (if no transition or transition-property had been applied) and when the property values declared in the transition or transition-property value begin animating to the next value.

Including a transition-delay with a positive number of milliseconds (ms) or seconds (s) to delay the transition will delay the onset of the transition effect. The time unit, as s or ms, is required. Negative values of time are valid.

We make every odd-numbered property begin its transition immediately by specifying transition-delay: 0s, 200ms on a set of properties that each take 200 milliseconds to transition; all even-numbered transitions begin their transitions as soon as the odd transitions have completed.

When the number of comma-separated transition-delay values exceeds the number of comma-separated transition-property values, the excess delay values are disregarded, just as they are with transition-duration and transition-timing-function. The delay values are repeated when the number of comma-separated transition-property values exceeds the number of comma-separated transition-delay values. With only two values, the first (0s) is applied to each odd property, resulting in no delay, while the second (0s) is applied to each even property, resulting in a 200-millisecond delay. Because we set the transition-duration to 200 milliseconds in this instance, every even-numbered property will start transitioning after the odd-numbered properties have done transitioning:

```
div {
...
transition-property: color, border-width, border-color, border-radius,
transform, opacity, box-shadow, width, padding;
transition-duration: 200ms;
transition-timing-function: linear;
```

```
transition-delay: 0s, 0.2s, 0.4s, 0.6s, 0.8s, 1s, 1.2s, 1.4s, 1.6s;
}
```

We can even set nine separate transition-delay values, so that each property transitions after the one before it. The transition-duration attribute was used in this example to set the duration of each transition to 200 milliseconds. Then, for each property, we create a transition-delay that gives comma-separated delay values that increment by 200 milliseconds, or 0.2 seconds—the same time as the transition's duration. That implies we can start converting each property as soon as the preceding one is finished. We may use math to assign distinct durations and delays to each transitional property, guaranteeing that they all transition at the same time:

```
div {
 ...
 transition-property: color, border-width, border-color, border-radius,
 transform, opacity, box-shadow, width, padding;
 transition-duration: 1.8s, 1.6s, 1.4s, 1.2s, 1s, 0.8s, 0.6s, 0.4s, 0.2s;
 transition-timing-function: linear;
 transition-delay: 0s, 0.2s, 0.4s, 0.6s, 0.8s, 1s, 1.2s, 1.4s, 1.6s;
}
```

Each property in this sample transitions at the 1.8-second mark, but with a distinct length and delay. The sum of the transition duration and transition-delay values for each attribute is 1.8 seconds:

```
div {
 ...
 transition-property: color, border-width, border-color, border-radius,
 transform, opacity, box-shadow, width, padding;
 transition-duration: 200ms;
 transition-timing-function: linear;
 transition-delay: 50ms;
}
```

In general, all transitions should start at the same time. This can be accomplished by using a single transition-delay value that is applied to all properties. A delay of 50 milliseconds is included in our drop-down menu in Figure 6.1. This delay is not lengthy enough for the user to notice, and the application will not appear slow as a result. Instead, a 50-millisecond delay can assist prevent the navigation from opening unintentionally as the user moves the pointer from one portion of the page or app to another and accidently passes over or hovers over the menu items.

✓ **The transition Shorthand Property:**

The transition shorthand property combines the four attributes discussed above into a single property: transition-property, transition-duration, transition-timing-function, and transition-delay.

The transition attribute can be set to none or any number of discrete transitions separated by commas. A single transition contains a single property to transition, or the keyword all to transition all the properties, ideally the transition's duration, as well as the timing function and delay, if applicable.

If the property to transition (or the keyword all) is omitted from a single transition within the transition shorthand, the single transition will default to all. If the transition timing-function value is left blank, easy will be used. If only one-time value is specified, the duration will be that value, with no delay, as if transition-delay was set to 0s. The first time value is the transition-duration, and the second is the transition-delay if two time values are present. Within each single transition, the order of the duration versus the delay is important: the first value that can be parsed as a time will be set as a duration. If an additional time value is found before the comma or the end of the statement, that will be set as the delay.

```
nav li ul {
 transition: transform 200ms ease-in 50ms,
 opacity 200ms ease-in 50ms;
 ...
}
nav li ul {
```

```
transition: all 200ms ease-in 50ms;
...
}
nav li ul {
 transition: 200ms ease-in 50ms;
 ...
}
```

There are three methods to write the shorthand for our drop-down menu. We used shorthand for each of the two properties in the first example. We might use the term all to transition all the attributes that change on hover, as seen in the second example. We could write the shorthand with simply the duration, timing-function, and delay because all is the default value. We could have skipped the timing function if we had chosen ease instead of ease-in, because ease is the default.

Without the time, there would be no noticeable transition. In other words, transition-duration is the only part of the transition property that may be regarded mandatory. We'd still need to provide a duration of 0s if we just wanted to delay the move from closed to open menu without a progressive transition. Remember that the length will be set as the first number parsable as time, and the delay will be set as the second:

```
nav li ul {
 transition: 0s 200ms; ...
```

If there is a comma-separated list of transitions (versus just a single declaration) and the word none is included, the entire transition declaration is invalid and will be ignored:

```
div {
 ...
 transition-property: color, border-width, border-color, border-radius,
 transform, opacity, box-shadow, width, padding;
```

```
 transition-duration: 200ms, 180ms, 160ms, 140ms, 120ms, 100ms, 1s, 2s, 3s;
 transition-timing-function: ease, ease-in, ease-out, ease-in-out, linear,
 step-end, step-start, steps(5, start), steps(3, end);
 transition-delay: 0s, 0.2s, 0.4s, 0.6s, 0.8s, 1s, 1.2s, 1.4s, 1.6s;
}
div {
 ...
 transition:
 color 200ms,
 border-width 180ms ease-in 200ms,
 border-color 160ms ease-out 400ms,
 border-radius 140ms ease-in-out 600ms,
 transform 120ms linear 800ms,
 opacity 100ms step-end 1s,
 box-shadow 1s step-start 1.2s,
 width 2s steps(5, start) 1.4s,
 padding 3s steps(3, end) 1.6s;
}
```

Users can declare comma-separated values for the four longhand transition properties, or users can include a comma-separated list of single transitions in the two preceding CSS rule blocks. However, users cannot combine the two: transition: transform, opacity 200ms ease-in 50ms will gradually increase the opacity over 200 milliseconds after a 50 millisecond wait, however the transform change will be instantaneous and without a transition. In all single transitions, the duration comes before the delay. Also, the delay and timing-function aren't included in the first single transition because the values they're mapped to in the longhand syntax version are the properties' default values.

6.4 CSS TRANSFORMS:

Users can rotate, move, resize, and skew HTML elements in two- and three-dimensional space using the CSS3 Transforms module. This section, on the other hand, focuses on the 2-D forms, which have more practical applications. With vendor prefixes, transforms are supported on all major browser versions. IE8 and earlier, Firefox 3 and earlier, and Opera 10.1 and earlier do not support them at all. When the page loads, users can apply a transform on an element's normal state, and it will display in its altered state. Just make sure that browsers that don't support transforms may still use the page. When users interact with an element via a rollover or JavaScript event, it's typical to hide the transforms. Transforms are a strong option for progressive enhancement in either case—if an IE8 user sees an element straight rather than on a jaunty angle, it's probably not a significant deal.

The diagram below depicts four different types of two-dimensional transforms: rotate, translate, scale, and skew. The element's original position is indicated by the dashed outline.

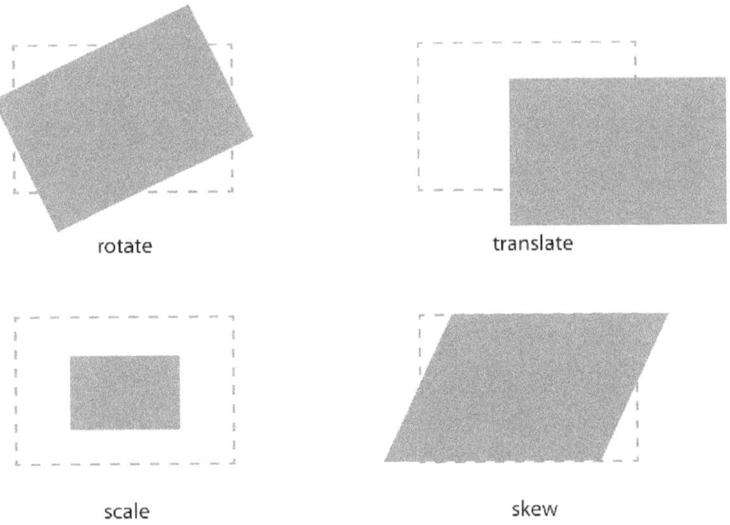

Figure 6.3: Four types of transforms: rotate, translate, scale, and skew

When an element transforms, its element box retains its original position and has an impact on the lauders surrounding it, in the same way that space is left behind by an element that is relatively positioned in the lauders. It's as if the transformation miraculously scoops up the pixels of the rendered element, plays with them, and then magically drops them back onto the top of the page. As a result, when users transform an element, users' really just moving a picture of that element. The surrounding arrangement is unaffected by the image in question. Let's go over each of the transform functions one by one, starting with the rotate function.

✓ **Transforming the angle (rotate):**

In order to create an element that appears at a slight angle, users must utilise the rotate transform function. The value of the rotate function is an angle in degrees that can be either positive or negative in value. By employing the following style rule, the image in Figure 6.4 has been rotated –10 degrees (350 degrees) to the right. The element's original position is depicted in a coloured image for the sake of reference.

```
img {
 width: 300px;
 height: 400px;
 transform: rotate(-10deg);
}
```

Figure 6.4: Rotating an img element using transform: rotate ().

Take note of the fact that the image rotates around its centre point, which serves as the default point around which all modifications occur. The transform-origin attribute, on the other hand, allows users to quickly change that.

The value for transform-origin might be either two keywords, length measurements, or percentage values, depending on the context. Both the horizontal and vertical offsets are represented by the first and second values, respectively. In the event that just one value is provided, it will be utilised for both purposes. This is how we would write it if we wanted to rotate the redwood forest image around a point in the centre of its upper edge:

transform-origin: center top;

transform-origin: 50%, 0%;

transform-origin: 150px, 0;

The images in Figure 6.5 have all been rotated 25 degrees, although they come from a variety of distinct locations of origin.

Figure 6.5: Changing the point around which the image rotates using transform origin.

Even though it is simple to show the origin point using the rotate function, it is important to remember that users may set an origin point for any of the transform functions.

✓ Transforming the position (translate):

Another thing user can do with the transform property is give the element's rendering a new location on the page using one of three translate functions, as shown in the examples in Figure 6.7. The translate X function allows users to move an element on a horizontal axis; translate Y is for moving along the vertical axis, and translate is a shorthand for combining both X and Y values (translate (translate X, translate Y)).

transform: translateX(50px);

transform: translateY(25px);

transform: translate(50px, 25px);

Figure 6.6: Moving an element around with the translate function.

Users can specify a length value in any of the CSS units or as a percentage of the total length of the document. For the purposes of this transformation, percentages are computed based on the width of the bounding box, which is from border-edge to border-edge. This is similar to how percentages are calculated in SVG, from which transformations were adapted. As illustrated in Figure 6.8, users have the option of providing either positive or negative numbers. If users provide only one value for the shorthand translate function, it will be presumed to be the translateX value, and translateY will be set to zero. So translate(20px) would be equivalent to applying both translateX(20px) and translateY(0).

Figure 6.7: Moving an element around with the translate function.

✓ **Transforming the size (scale):**

Using one of three scale functions, users can make an element appear larger or smaller: scaleX (horizontal), scaleY (vertical), and the shorthand scale. An integer with no units that provides a size ratio is represented by the value. In this example, the image is stretched to 150 percent of its original width:

```
a img {
 transform: scaleX(1.5);
}
```

There are two values listed in the scale shorthand: one for scaleX and another for scaleY. This example produces an element twice as broad as the original, but only half as tall as it was before.

```
a img {
 transform: scale(2, .5);
}
```

Unlike translate, however, if users provide only one value for scale, it will be used as the scaling factor in both directions. So specifying scale(2) is the same as applying scaleX(2) and scaleY(2), which is intuitively the way users' want it to be.

✓ **Making it slanty (skew):**

The skew properties (skewX, skewY, and the shorthand skew) are a quirky collection of characteristics that vary the angle of either the horizontal or vertical axis (or both axes) by a specified amount of degrees. When it comes to translate, if users only provide one value, it will be utilised for skewX, and skewY will be set to zero as well. The best way to get an idea of how skewing works is to take a look at some examples (Figure 6.9).

```
a img {
 transform: skewX(15deg);
}
a img {
 transform: skewY(30deg);
}
a img {
 transform: skew(15deg, 30deg);
}
```

Figure 6.8: Slanting an element using the skew function.

✓ **Applying multiple transforms:**

Of course, a single element can have several transforms applied to it. Simply list the functions and their values in the following format, separated by spaces:

```
transform: function(value) function(value);
```

When the mouse is over the forest image in Figure 6.10, it grows larger, tilts slightly, and moves down and to the right.

```
img:hover, img:focus {
 transform: scale(1.5) rotate(-5deg) translate(50px,30px);
```

Figure 6.9. Applying scale, rotate, and translate to a single element.

It's worth noting that transformations are applied in the order that they're listed. A rotate and then a translate, for example, yields a different result than a rotate and then a translate. Another thing to keep in mind is that if users wish to apply an extra transform to an element in a different state (such as hover, focus, or active), users will have to redo all of the previous transforms. In its natural condition, this element, for example, is rotated 45 degrees. I'd lose the rotation if I applied a scale transform on the hover state until I specifically declared it again.

```
a {
 transform: rotate(45deg);
}
a:hover {
 transform: scale(1.25); /* rotate on a element would be lost */
}
```

To achieve both the rotation and the scale, provide both transform values:

```
a:hover {
 transform: rotate(45deg) scale(1.25); /* rotates and scales */
}
```

✓ 3-D transforms:

The CSS Transforms specification also provides a mechanism for producing a feeling of space and perspective, in addition to two-dimensional transform operations. Users can utilise 3-D transforms in conjunction with transitions to create complex interactive interfaces like picture carousels, flappable cards, and spinning cubes! (There are plenty of CSS cubes on the web right now; it must be a nice learning project.) Figure 6.11 depicts a few instances of 3-D transform-based interfaces. In the past, 3-D interfaces like these were assumed to be Flash-based. Now it's all about native browser features and plain old CSS3.

Paul Hayes' 3D cube
(www.paulhayes.com/experiments/cube-3d/touch.html)

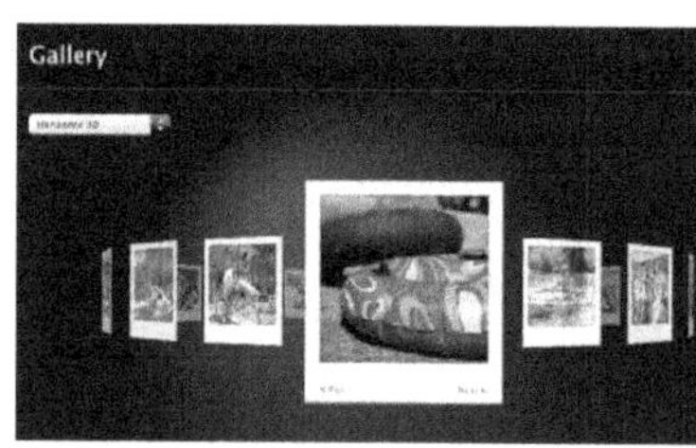

Safari Technology Demos: Web Gallery
(developer.apple.com/safaridemos/showcase/gallery/)

Snow Stack by Charles Ying
(www.satine.org/research/webkit/snowleopard/snowstack.html)

Figure 6.10: Some examples of 3-D transforms.

To give users a simple example, I'm going to arrange the photographs as if they were in a 3-D carousel-style gallery.

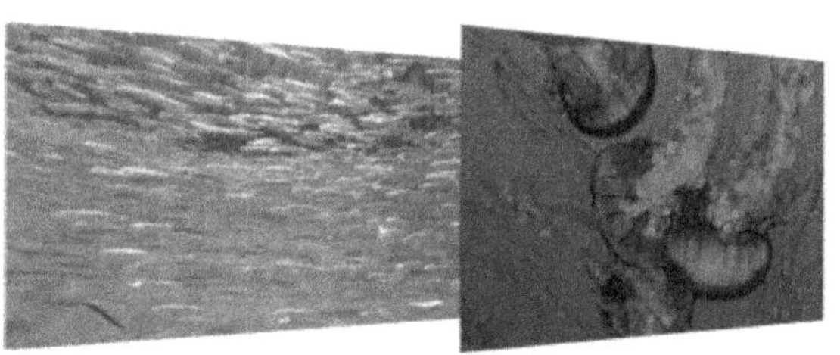
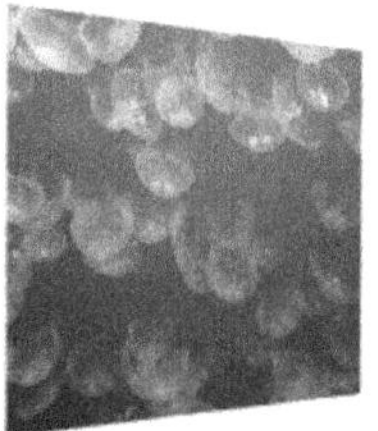
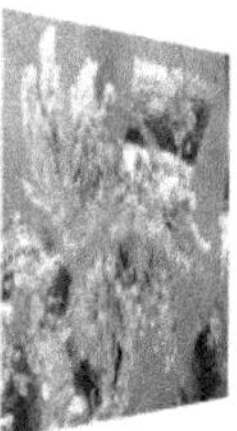

Figure 6.11. Example of 3D transform

The mark-up is the same unordered list used in the previous exercise.

```
<ul>
 <li><a href=""><img src="anchovies.jpg" id="img1" alt=""></a></li>
 <li><a href=""><img src="jellyfish1.jpg" id="img2" alt=""></a></li>
```

```
<li><a href=""><img src="bluejellyfish.jpg" id="img3" alt=""></a>
</li>
<li><a href=""><img src="seadragon.jpg" id="img4"alt=""></a></li>
</ul>
```

The first step is to use the perspective property to give the contained element some "perspective." This instructs the browser to treat the child elements as though they were in 3-D space. The perspective attribute defines a distance from the element's origin on the z-axis and has a value greater than zero. The more extreme the perspective, the lower the value. I've found that values between 300 and 1500 are reasonable, but users will have to experiment until users achieve the desired impact.

```
ul {
 width: 1000px;
 height: 100px;
 list-style-type: none;
 padding: 0;
 margin: 0;
 -webkit-perspective: 600;
 -moz-perspective: 600;
 perspective: 600;
}
```

The perspective-origin property (not shown) describes the position of users eyes relative to the transformed items. The values are a horizontal position (left, center, right, or a length or percentage) and a vertical position (top, bottom, center, or a length or percentage value). The default (shown in Figure 6.12) is centred vertically and horizontally (perspective-origin: 50% 50%). The final transform-related property is backface-visibility, which controls whether the reverse side of the element is visible when it spins around.

With the 3-D space established, apply one of the 3-D transform functions to each li within the ul. The 3-D functions include: translate3d, translateZ, scale3d, scaleZ, rotate3d, rotateX, rotateY, rotateZ, and matrix3d. Users should recognize some terms in there. The *Z functions define the object's orientation relative to the z-axis (picture it running from users nose to this page, where the x- and y-axes lie flat on the page).

In our example in Figure 6.12, each li is rotated 45 degrees around its y-axis (vertical axis) using the rotateY function. Compare the result to Figure 6.13 in which each li is rotated on its x-axis (horizontal axis) using rotateX.

```
li {
float: left;
margin-right: 10px;
-webkit-transform: rotateX(45deg);
-moz-transform: rotateX(45deg);
transform: rotateX(45deg);
}
```

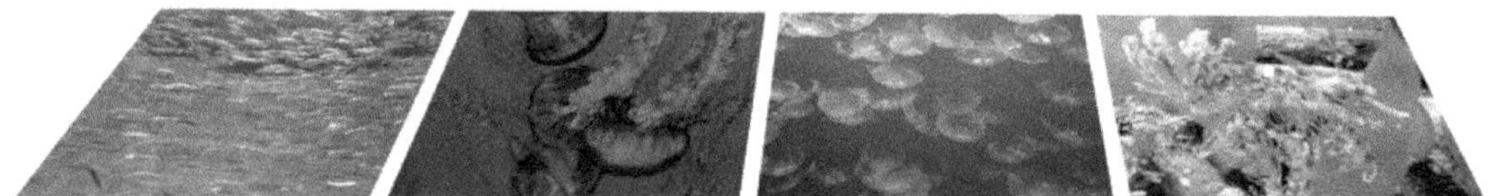

Figure 6.12. The same list of images rotated on their horizontal axes with rotateX.

6.5 CSS ANIMATION:

Simple animations were made possible using CSS transitions, which were discussed in the previous chapter. The properties of an element shift from the values set in one style block to the values set in another style block as the element changes state over time rather than instantly with transitions. With CSS transitions, existing property values dictate the start and end states of property values, giving users minimal control over how the interpolation progresses over time.

Transitions and CSS animations are similar in that the values of CSS properties change over time. Transitions, on the other hand, simply allow us to animate from one value to another. CSS key frame animations allow us to control whether and how an animation repeats, as well as what happens during the animation. CSS animation uses key frames to animate the values of CSS properties over time. Animation, like transitions, gives us control over the delay and duration. We can manage the number of iterations, the behaviour of iterations, what happens before the first animation starts, and the state of animated properties after the last animation iteration with CSS animations. We may utilise CSS animation properties to modify time and even pause an animation in the middle of it.

When animation key frame properties are applied, animations are explicitly executed, whereas transitions cause implicit property value changes. CSS animations allow users to change property values that aren't part of the element's set before or post state. The animation progression does not have to include the property values set on the animated element. Transitioning from black to white, for example, will only show different degrees of grey. During animation, the same element does not have to be black or white, or even in between shades of grey. Instead of transitioning through shades of grey, users might make the element yellow and then animate it from yellow to orange.

Users could also animate between other colours, starting with black and ending with white, but moving through the complete rainbow if desired. With animations, users may build users desired effect by using as many key frames as users need to granularly manage an element's property values. The first step in using CSS animations is to construct a key frame animation, which is a reusable @key frames at-rule that specifies which properties will be animated and how they will be animated. The second step is to apply the keyframe animation to one or more elements in users document or application, defining how it will advance through the key frames using various animation attributes.

6.5.1 KEYFRAMES:

We need to name a keyframe animation in order to animate an element; to do so, we require a named keyframe animation. The @key frames at-rule will be used to define this reusable CSS keyframe animation. To create a CSS animation, we use the @key frames rule to create a reusable keyframe animation and give it a name. The name we come up with will be used in the code block of a CSS selector to link this animation to the element(s) and/or pseudo-element(s) defined by the selector (s).

The animation identification, or name, and one or more keyframe blocks are included in the @key frames at-rule. One or more keyframe selectors are included in each keyframe block, along with declaration blocks containing zero or more property/value pairs. The complete @key frames at rule defines the animation's behaviour for one full iteration. The animation can iterate zero or more times, based on the value of the animation-iteration-count parameter.

The animation identifier (the name users give users animation for future reference) is followed by curly braces that encompass the series of keyframe blocks, then the @key frames at-rule key term. One or more keyframe selectors are included in each keyframe block. The keyframe selectors are percentage-of-time positions along the animation's runtime; they're expressed as percentages or as key terms from and to:

```
@key frames animation_identifier {
 keyframe_selectorA {
 property1: value1a;
 property2: value2b;
 }
keyframe_selectorB {
 property1: value1b;
 property2: value2b;
 }
}
```

6.5.2 KEYFRAME SELECTORS:

The values of the properties we wish to animate are set at keyframe selections during our animation. When we define animations, we specify the values we want attributes to have at a given point in the animation. Users define a value at the 0 percent mark if users want it at the start of the animation. Users specify the property value at the 100% point if users want a different value at the end of the animation. Users specify a value at the 33 percent mark if users want it a third of the way through the animation. Keyframe selectors are used to define these markers. A comma-separated list of one or more percentage values or the keywords from or to makes up a keyframe selector. The keyword from has a value of 0%. To equate 100 percent is the keyword. The keyframe selectors are used to define the percentage of the animation that each keyframe represents. The block of property values declared on the selector defines the keyframe itself. On percentage values, the percent unit must be utilised; in other words, 0 is not a valid keyframe selector:

```
@key frames W {
from {
left: 0;
top: 0;
}
25%, 75% {
top: 100%;
}
50% {
top: 50%;
}
to {
left: 100%;
top: 0;
}
}
```

When coupled to a non-statically positioned element, this @key frames animation named W would move that element along a W-shaped path. At the 0 percent, 25 percent, 50 percent, 75 percent, and 100 percent markers, W contains five key frames. The 0 percent mark is the starting point. This represents the hundred percent milestone.

We put two keyframe selectors together as a comma-separated list because the property values we provided for the 25% and 75% marks are the same. We can use many comma-separated keyframe selectors in front of a single CSS block, just as conventional CSS selectors. Users CSS style rules will determine whether users maintain the selectors on one line (as in the example) or place each selection on its own line:

25%,

75% {

top: 100%;}

It's worth noting that selectors don't necessarily have to be presented in ascending order. The 25 percent and 75 percent marks are on the same line in the preceding example, with the 50 percent mark appearing after that declaration. It is highly recommended that users advance from 0% to 100% legibility. It is not, however, needed, as seen by the 75 percent keyframe in this example, which is "out of order."

6.5.3 ANIMATED ELEMENTS:

Users must apply the keyframe animation to components and/or pseudo-elements in order for anything to really motion after users have completed the creation of the animation. HTML5 animation provides us with several animation characteristics that allow us to connect a keyframe animation to an element and control the advancement of the keyframe animation over time. We must at the very least provide the name of the animation in order for the element to animate, as well as the duration of the animation if we want the animation to be visible.

A total of three animation events are defined: the animation start event at the beginning of an animation, the animation end event at the end of an animation, and the animation iteration event at the end of an iteration and the start of a following iteration. Start and finish events will be generated for any animation for which a valid keyframe rule has been set; this includes animations with no keyframe rules defined at all. The animation iteration event is only triggered when an animation has more than one iteration, as the animation iteration event does not fire if the animation end event is triggered at the same time as the animation iteration event does.

The animation shorthand property (or a combination of shorthand and longhand properties) can be used to attach animation properties to an element in two ways: users can include each animation property individually, or users can declare all of the properties in a single line using the animation shorthand property (or a combination of shorthand and longhand properties). Our initial step will be to become familiar with all of the longhand attributes. With the animation shorthand property, we'll be able to condense all of the declarations into a single line later on in this chapter. Let's have a look at the individual characteristics:

✓ **The animation-name Property:**

The animation-name property accepts as a value either the name of the keyframe animation users want to apply to an element or a comma-separated list of names of the keyframe animation users want to apply to a group of elements. It is the names of the unquoted identifiers that users defined in users @key frames rule that are used. The default value is none, which means that there will be no animation when the button is pressed. It is possible to use the none value to override any animation that has been applied elsewhere in the CSS cascade. To apply an animation, include the @keyframe identifier, which is also the name of the animation, in the code for the animation.

```
div {
 animation-name: change_bgcolor;
}
```

More than one comma-separated @keyframe identifier can be used to apply more than one animation. For example:

```
div {
 animation-name: change_bgcolor, round, W;
}
```

Rather than failing because one of the keyframe identifiers provided in the sequence does not exist, the series of animations will be discarded and the valid animations will be applied instead. While initially ignored, the failed animation will be implemented if and when the identifier for that failed animation is discovered to be a legitimate animation:

```
div {
 animation-name: change_bgcolor, spin, round, W;
}
```

In this example, there is no keyframe animation for the spin movement. The spin motion will be ignored, and instead, the change bgcolor, round, and W animations will be used in their place. If and when a spin keyframe animation is created, it will be applied to the element at the moment the animation is created. For the purpose of include more than one animation, we've included the identifiers for each @keyframe animation in our list of comma-separated values for the animation-name property. If more than one animation is applied to an element, and those animations have repeated properties, the property values in the subsequent animations take precedence over the property values in the preceding animations. When two different keyframe animations with more than two background colour changes are applied simultaneously, the background property declarations of the latter animation will override the background property declarations of the preceding animation, but only if the background colours were both set to change at the same time.

✓ **The animation-duration Property:**

Using the animation-duration property, users can specify how long a single animation iteration should take, either in seconds (s) or milliseconds (ms). The animation-duration property accepts as a value the amount of time, measured in seconds (s) or milliseconds (ms), that should be required to complete one cycle through all of the key frames in the animation. If this parameter is missing, the animation will still be applied with a duration of 0s, with the animation start and animation end events still being called, despite the fact that the animation, with a duration of 0s, is barely noticeable. Numerical numbers that are negative are invalid. When including a duration, users must include the second (s) or millisecond (ms) unit:

```
div {
 animation-name: change_bgcolor;
 animation-duration: 200ms;
}
```

if users have more than one animation, users can include a distinct animation duration for each animation by including more than one comma-separated time duration: comma-separated time duration for each animation.

```
div {
 animation-name: change_bgcolor, round, W;
 animation-duration: 200ms, 100ms, 0.5s;
}
```

If users include an erroneous value in user's comma-separated list of durations, such as animation-duration: 200ms, 0, 0.5s, the entire declaration will fail, and the animation will behave as if animation-duration: 0s had been declared instead of animation-duration: 0s. The time value 0 is not a valid time value.

Users should generally include an animation-duration value for each animation-name that is provided. The animations will all last the same length of time if users merely specify a single duration for them. There will not be a failure if users have less animation-duration values than animation name values in user's comma-separated property value list; rather, the values that are included will be repeated many times. Extra values for animation duration will be discarded if users have a greater number of animation duration values than animation-name values in user's script. There will be no failure in the series of animations and animation durations if one of the included animations does not exist: both the failed animation and the length of the failed animation will be ignored:

```
div {
 animation-name: change_bgcolor, spin, round, W;
 animation-duration: 200ms, 5s, 100ms, 0.5s;
}
```

In this example, the 5s, or 5 seconds, is associated with spin. As there is no spin @key frames declaration, spin doesn't exist, and the 5s and spin are ignored.

✓ **The animation-iteration-count Property:**

It is sufficient to provide the required animation-name in the script to have the animation play once. If users want to iterate over the animation more or less than the default one time, users should provide the animation-iteration-count attribute in user's code. In the default configuration, the animation will only play once. As long as the animation-iteration-count property is included and the animation-delay property does not have a negative value, the animation will repeat the number of times given by the property's value, which can be any number or the key term infinite. If the numeric value is not an integer, the animation will be terminated midway through its final cycle if this is the case. The animation will continue to play, but it will be cut off in the middle of the final iteration. A value of 1.25 means that it will loop over the animation 1.25 times, taking out 25 percent of the animation on the second iteration, for example. If the number is 0.25 and the animation is 8 seconds long, the animation will play about 25% of the way through before stopping after 2 seconds. Numbers that are negative are not valid. A negative value, like any other invalid value, will result in a single repetition by default, just like any other invalid value.

Surprisingly, the animation-iteration-count property accepts the value zero as a valid value. When the value is set to zero, the animation still occurs, but only once. It works in a similar way as determining the duration of an animation: When it is 0s, it will cause both an animation start and an animation finish event to be fired. If users are connecting more than one animation to an element or pseudo-element, include a comma-separated list of values for the animation-name, animation-duration, and animation-iteration-count attributes: animation-name, animation-duration, and animation-iteration-count

```
.flag {
 animation-name: red, white, blue;
 animation-duration: 2s, 4s, 6s;
 animation-iteration-count: 3, 5;
}
```

When assigning values to the iteration-count property value (and all other animation property values), the values will be assigned in the order that the comma-separated animation-name property value is specified. Any other values will be disregarded. If any values are missing, the present values will be repeated until the missing values are found. The declaration will be nullified if any of the values are incorrect.

Because there are more name values than count values in the preceding example, the count values will iterate more than once: red and blue will iterate three times, while white will iterate five times. Because there are the same number of name values as there are duration values, the duration values will not be repeated in any way. The red animation lasts two seconds and iterates three times, resulting in a total duration of six seconds for the animation. A total of 20 seconds is spent watching the white animation, which lasts four seconds and iterates five times. Each iteration of the blue animation lasts six seconds, with the value repeated three times, for a total of 18 seconds of animation. If we wanted all three animations to end at the same moment, despite the fact that their durations differ, we might use the animation-iteration-count property to accomplish this:

```
.flag {
 animation-name: red, white, blue;
 animation-duration: 2s, 4s, 6s;
 animation-iteration-count: 6, 3, 2;
}
```

Each of the three animations in that example will last for a total of 12 seconds: red will animate over 2 seconds, iterating 6 times, for a total of 12 seconds; white will animate over 4 seconds, iterating 3 times, for a total of 12 seconds; and blue will animate over 6 seconds, iterating 2 times, for a total of 12 seconds. The number of iterations required to have one effect persist as long as another can be calculated using simple arithmetic. Keep in mind that the value for the animation-iteration-count parameter does not have to be an integer.

✓ **The animation-direction Property:**

Users can adjust whether the animation goes from the 0 percent keyframe to the 100 percent keyframe or from the 100 percent keyframe to the 0 percent keyframe by modifying the animation-direction parameter. In order to control whether all iterations progress in the same way, users must first select whether every other animation cycle should progress in the opposite direction.

The animation-direction property specifies the way the animation will go through the key frames as it progresses through them. There are four possible values for this variable:

animation-direction: normal: Each iteration of the animation goes from the 0 percent keyframe to the 100 percent keyframe when this option is set to normal (or omitted, which defaults to normal).

animation-direction: reverse: The reverse value causes each iteration to play in reverse keyframe order, always proceeding from the 100 percent keyframe to the 0 percent keyframe, as defined by the previous value. Reversing the animation direction also has the effect of reversing the animation-timing-function, as previously stated.

animation-direction: alternate: In this case, the first iteration (and each subsequent odd-numbered iteration) should progress from 0% to 100%, while the second iteration (and each subsequent even-numbered cycle) should reverse direction, going from 100% to 0%.

animation-direction: alternate-reverse: The alternate-reverse value is similar to the alternate value, with the exception that the animation iterations for odd-numbered iterations are in the reverse direction, and the animation iterations for even-numbered iterations are in the standard direction. alternate-reverse switches the direction of each repetition, starting with reverse, and continues in this manner. The first iteration (and each subsequent odd-numbered iteration) progresses from 100 percent to 0 percent; the second iteration (and each subsequent even-numbered cycle) reverses the direction, travelling from 100 percent to 0 percent: the first cycle.

```
.ball {
 animation-name: bouncing;
 animation-duration: 400ms;
 animation-iteration-count: infinite;
 animation-direction: alternate-reverse;
}
@key frames bouncing {
from {
 transforms: translateY(500px);
```

```
}
to {
transforms: translateY(0);
}
}
```

The ball is being bounced in this example, but we want it to start by dropping it rather than throwing it up in the air: we want it to alternate between going down and up rather than going up and down, thus animation-direction: The value alternate-reverse is the best appropriate for our requirements.

- ✓ **The animation-delay Property:**

Using the animation-delay property, users can specify how long the browser should wait once an animation has been associated to an element before starting the first iteration of the animation. The default value is 0s, which means that the animation will begin immediately after it has been placed to the canvas. The start of the animation will be delayed until the mandated time period, which is specified by the value of the animation-delay property, has elapsed when the value of the animation-delay property is positive. A negative value will cause the animation to begin immediately, however it will only begin partway through the animation if the value is greater than zero.

The animation-delay property specifies the amount of time, measured in seconds (s) or milliseconds (ms), that the animation will wait between the time that the animation is attached to the element and the time that the animation begins to be executed. Iteration of the animation begins immediately once it is applied to the element, with a zero-second delay between iterations.

In contrast to the animation-duration property, a negative value for the animation-delay property is acceptable. The use of negative values for animation-delay can result in some intriguing results. A negative delay will cause the animation to be executed instantly, but it will only begin animating the element after it has progressed halfway through the connected animation. For example, if the animation-delay property is set to: When the animation timers -4s and animation-duration: 10s are set on an element, the animation will begin instantly, but it will begin roughly 40 percent of the way through the first animation, rather than at the beginning.

```
div {
 animation-name: move;
 animation-duration: 10s;
 animation-delay: -4s;
 animation-timing-function: linear;
}
@key frames move {
 from {
 transform: translateX(0);
 }
 to {
 transform: translateX(1000px);
 }
}
```

A 10-second linear animation with a four-second delay is shown in this example of linear animation. As a result, the animation will begin immediately, 40 percent of the way through the animation, and the div will be moved 400 pixels to the right of its original location.

- ✓ **The animation-timing-function Property:**

The animation-timing function property, which is similar to the transition-timing-function property, indicates how the animation will progress over the course of one cycle of its duration, or one iteration.

The Bézier curve accepts four values, each of which specifies the starting location of the two handles. In CSS, the anchors are located at positions 0, 0 and 1, 1. The x and y coordinates of the first point or handle of the curve are defined by the first two values, and the x and y coordinates of the second point or handle of the curve are defined by the last two values. The x values must be in the range of 0 to 1, otherwise the Bézier curve is deemed invalid. When constructing users own Bézier curve, keep in mind that the steeper the curve, the faster the motion is going to be. The slower the motion is the flatter the curve must be. In contrast to the x values, which must be between 0 and 1, by utilising y values larger than 1 or less than 0 users can produce a bouncing effect, causing the animation to bounce up and down between values rather than going in a single direction consistently:

```
.snake {
 animation-name: shrink;
 animation-duration: 10s;
 animation-timing-function: cubic-bezier(0, 4, 1, -4);
 animation-fill-mode: both;
}
@key frames shrink {
 0% {
 width: 500px;
 }
 100% {
 width: 100px;
 }
}
```

This is due to the fact that one y coordinate is positive and the other is negative, giving the impression of a snake, travelling up and down and back up again on the same line. A Bézier curve with an arc shape is formed if either of the two inputs is more than one or both are less than one. The Bézier curve goes above or below one of the values set, but it does not bounce out of limits on both ends, as is the case with the s-curve above.

The timing function stated for the animation-timing-function is the timing function for the normal animation direction, which is the timing function for when the animation progresses from the 0 percent mark to the 100 percent mark. It is important to note that while an animation is being played backwards, that is, from the 100 percent mark to the zero percent mark, the animation timing function is reversed:

```
.ball {
 animation-name: bounce;
 animation-duration: 1s;
 animation-iteration-count: infinite;
 animation-timing-function: ease-in;
 animation-direction: alternate;
}
@key frames bounce {
 0% {
 transform: translateY(0);
 }
 100% {
 transform: translateY(500px);
 }
}
```

Consider the flip book. A flip book is a book with a series of pictures. Each page contains a single drawing or picture that changes slightly from one page to the next, like one frame from a movie reel or cartoon stamped onto each page. When the pages of a flip book are flipped through rapidly (hence the name), the pictures appear as an animated motion. Users can create similar animations with CSS using an image sprite, the background-position property, and the steps() timing function. Figure 6.14 depicts an image sprite having numerous images that change just little over time, similar to the illustrations on the individual pages of our flip book.

Figure 6.14: Sprite of dancing

✓ **The animation-play-state property:**

The animation-play-state parameter defines whether the animation is running or halted. When set to the default running, the animation goes as normal. If set to paused, the animation will be paused. When paused, the animation is still applied to the element, halted at the progress it had made before being interrupted. When set back to running or reverted to the default of running, it restarts from where it left off, as if the "clock" that regulates the animation had stopped and began again. If the property is set to animation-play-state: paused during the delay phase of the animation, the delay clock is likewise paused and resumes expiring as soon as animation-play-state is set back to running.

✓ **The animation-fill-mode Property:**

The animation-fill-mode property specifies which values are applied by the animation before and after the iterations of the animation are completed, and it is used to describe the behaviour of the animation. The animation-fill-mode attribute allows us to specify whether or not the values of an element's property values are applied by the animation outside of the scope of the animation execution. The duration of the animation execution is determined by multiplying the number of iterations by the duration and subtracting the absolute value of any negative delay from the result.

By defining the effect of the animation on the element on which it is set before and after the animationstart and animationend events are fired, we can control how the animation affects the element on which it is placed. When the animation end event is fired, we can specify whether the property values set in the 0 percent keyframe are applied to the element during the expiration of any animation delay, and whether the property values that exist when the animationstart event is fired are applied to the animated element after the animation's conclusion, or if the properties revert to the values that they had in their initial state before the animation was attached.

By default, if the animation-delay is set to a positive value, an animation will not change the property values of the element immediately after it is started. It is instead applied after the animation-delay expires and the animationstart event is fired that the animation property values are changed. In the default configuration, the animation property values are applied until the last iteration has completed: that is, until the animationend event is fired at the conclusion of the animation. Property values for the element are reset to their nonanimated values at that point.

This property allows us to apply the property values of any from or 0 percent key frames to an element from the time that the animation is applied to that element until the animation delay has expired. We can also keep property values at 100 percent or key frames after the last animation cycle is completed, from the time the animationend event is fired until the element is removed from the animation loop, or until the animation is removed from the element.

- ✓ **The animation Shorthand Property:**

The animation shorthand property allows us to define all of the animation attributes on an element in a single line, rather than eight lines previously. The value of the animation property is a list of values for the various longhand animation attributes that are separated by spaces. Include the numerous space-separated animation shorthands on an element or pseudo-element as a comma-separated list of animations if users are setting several animations on the same element or pseudo-element.

It accepts as its value all of the other preceding animation properties, including animation-duration, animation-timing-function, animation delay, animation-iteration-count, animation-direction, animation-fill mode, animation-play-state, and animation-name, and returns the following result:

#animated {

animation: 200ms ease-in 50ms 1 normal running forwards slidedown;

}

is the equivalent of:

#animated {

animation-name: slidedown;

```
animation-duration: 200ms;
animation-timing-function: ease-in;
animation-delay: 50ms;
animation-iteration-count: 1;
animation-fill-mode: forwards;
animation-direction: normal;
animation-play-state: running;
}
or:
#animated {
animation: 200ms ease-in 50ms forwards slidedown;
}
```

Unlike in the animation shorthand, we didn't have to define every single variable; instead, any values that weren't stated were set automatically to their initial, default, or default-like values. The first shorthand line was lengthy, and three of the attributes were set to their default values, so they were not required to be included.

6.6 CONCLUSION:

I hope this chapter has helped users to better understand how CSS can be used to add a little movement and smoothness to user's web pages and applications. CSS transitions provide users with a way to build simple animations that always begin as a result of a CSS property change being triggered by the user. Transitions can only animate between two states: the start state and the end state, and each state is governed by the values of existing CSS property values.

CHAPTER 7

CSS TECHNIQUES

"The world always seems brighter when you have just made something that wasn't there before."

-Neil Gaiman

Chapter Learnings:

CSS Techniques will be better understood by the reader. It starts with some basic web developer strategies like cleaning away browser styles with a CSS reset, utilising images instead of text (only when necessary!), and employing CSS sprites to reduce the number of server queries. It then continues on to general style methods and particular characteristics for forms and tables. Finally, in step-by-step activities, reader will learn how to use media queries to develop a responsive site.

7.1 INTRODUCTION:

Users should now be able to write style sheets with confidence. Users may use floats to build page layouts, style text and element boxes, and even add subtle movement effects to user's designs. Before users go any further, there are a few popular CSS approaches that want users to be aware of. As users may be aware, browsers have their own built-in style sheets (known as user agent style sheets) that are used to render HTML elements. If users don't specify styles for a h1, users can be confident that it will display as large, bold text with plenty of space above and below it on screen. However, the exact size and amount of space available may differ from browser to browser, resulting in uneven outcomes. Furthermore, even if users do offer users own style sheet, it is possible that parts in users document will inherit some styles from the user agent style sheets, resulting in unanticipated outcomes.

This is why many designers employ a technique known as CSS Reset, which is a collection of style rules that override all user agent styles and establishes a starting point that is as neutral as possible. In order to ensure that no styles from the browser interfere with user's document's font, text, margin and padding styles, users must specifically declare font, text, margin and padding styles for every element in users document. It was written by Eric Meyer (the creator of far too many CSS books), and it is the most often used reset. It is provided here, and have also attached a copy of it at the bottom of this page.

```
/* http://meyerweb.com/eric/tools/css/reset/
 v2.0 | 20110126 License: none (public domain)*/
html, body, div, span, applet, object, iframe,
h1, h2, h3, h4, h5, h6, p, blockquote, pre,
a, abbr, acronym, address, big, cite, code,
del, dfn, em, img, ins, kbd, q, s, samp,
small, strike, strong, sub, sup, tt, var,
b, u, i, center, dl, dt, dd, ol, ul, li,
fieldset, form, label, legend,
table, caption, tbody, tfoot, thead, tr, th, td,
article, aside, canvas, details, embed,
figure, figcaption, footer, header, hgroup,
menu, nav, output, ruby, section, summary,
time, mark, audio, video {
margin: 0;
padding: 0;
border: 0;
font-size: 100%;
font: inherit;
vertical-align: baseline;
}
```

```
/* HTML5 display-role reset for older browsers */
article, aside, details, figcaption, figure,
footer, header, hgroup, menu, nav, section {
display: block;
}
body {
line-height: 1;
}
ol, ul {
list-style: none;
}
blockquote, q {
quotes: none;
}
blockquote:before, blockquote:after,
 q:before, q:after {
content: '';
content: none;
}
table {
border-collapse: collapse;
border-spacing: 0;
}
```

Place these styles at the top of user's own style sheet if users want to use the reset feature. Users can use them exactly as users see them here, or users can make changes to them to suit user's project's needs. CSS resets aren't for everyone, and that's okay. It's possible that user will decide to want to rely on the browser for some basic styling rather than having to create styles for everything. However, if users want to be certain that all of the styles that appear are users own, a reset may be the best option.

7.2 IMAGE REPLACEMENT TECHNIQUES:

Before online fonts became a feasible choice, users had to rely on images whenever users wanted text to be shown in a typeface other than Times New Roman or Helvetica. As a result, users can now create highly elegant headlines and text treatments without having to rely on images, which is a huge improvement. Every now and then, though, even a web font will not enough, and an image will be required in place of a few words of text. In the case of user's company name, users might want to use a stylised logo instead of text links, or users might want to utilise familiar icons in place of text links.

A terrible choice is to remove the text entirely and replace it with an image element because this would result in the loss of valuable content for eternity. This can be resolved by employing a CSS-based image replacement technique that uses the image as a backdrop in the element and then shifts the text out of the way so that it does not appear on the page. Search engines, screen readers, and other assistive devices may read the text content since it is kept in the file for the benefit of search engines, screen readers, and other assistive devices. One excellent picture replacement technique comes from Scott Kellum (it was dubbed "The Kellum Technique" by Jeffrey Zeldman), and it was developed by Scott Kellum. Using the text-indent property, it is able to move the text content completely to the right and outside of the visible element box (Figure 7.1).

What users see:

What's actually happening:

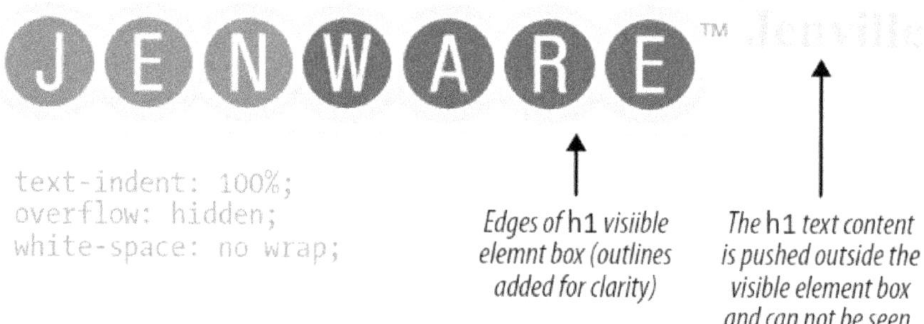

Figure 7.1: The Kellum image replacement technique hides the HTML text by pushing it out of the visible element box with a text indent.

The elegant Jenware logo will be used in place of the h1 "Jenware" HTML text in this example, as shown below. The mark-up is straightforward:

```
<h1 id="logo">Jenware</h1>
```

The style rule is as follows:

```
h1#logo {
 width: 450px;
 height: 80px
 background: url(jenware.png) no-repeat;
 text-indent: 100%;
 white-space: no-wrap;
 overflow: hidden;
}
```

There are a couple of items to take note of in this section. First and foremost, because the h1 element is shown as a block by default, users can simply adjust its width and height to match the dimensions of the image that serves as the background of the webpage. This property causes the word "Jenville" to be pushed to the right by the entire width (100 percent) of the element by the text-indent property. The white-space attribute has been set to no-wrap, which ensures that long strings of text will not wrap around and appear in the element box again after they have been rendered. Overflow: hidden tells the browser that anything outside the element box (such as our h1 text) should not be displayed. Actually, there have been perhaps a dozen or so different picture replacement techniques developed throughout the years. Phark is one of the most popular techniques because it makes advantage of an exceptionally large negative text-indent value (usually -9999px) to push the HTML text all the way to the left of the viewable region.

```
h1#logo {
 width: 450px;
 height: 100px
 background: url(jenware.png) no-repeat;
 text-indent: -9999px;
}
```

Because browsers are compelled to compute and draw the wide element box even if it will not be rendered, this strategy has the drawback of slowing down page load times and performance overall. However, if users come across an example of text that has a background image and an indent of –9999px, user understand what's going on. The disadvantage of any image replacement strategy is that it requires an additional request to the server for each image that is used. In the following part, we'll look at a method for reducing the number of needless queries.

7.3 CSS SPRITES:

CSS Sprites are a collection of pictures that are bundled into a single file that an HTML document can access. These photos are then called into use within the HTML code to be displayed on the website. The number of queries users page makes to the server can be reduced, which will enhance the overall performance of users site (HTTP requests). When it comes to decreasing the amount of picture requests, one method is to consolidate all of users little images into a single large image file, so that only one image is requested each page load. A CSS sprite is a big image that contains several images and was coined by the early computer graphics and video game industries to describe this type of image. The background-position property is used to position the picture in the element in such a way that just the appropriate area of the image is displayed. This should be demonstrated by an example.

The Velocity Conference website, which was developed by O'Reilly Network, had nine social media icons that are widely found on websites, as illustrated in Figure 7.2. One of the tactics taken by Tony Quartorolo and Zebulon Young in an effort to improve the site's efficiency was to combine those nine icon visuals into a single sprite, so reducing the number of HTTP requests made by the site. They arranged the icons in a single stack, with two pixels of space between each icon, as shown in the image.

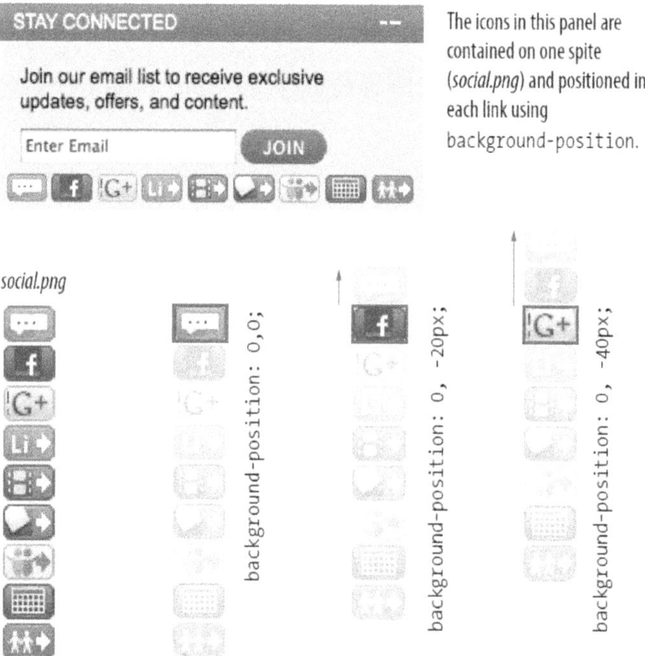

Figure 7.2: Replacing separate graphic files with one CSS sprite image cuts down on the number of HTTP requests to the server and improves site performance.

However, the styles and syntax seen here are a simplification of the code used on the Velocity website, and the end effect is the same.

The markup

```
<ul>
 <li><a href="" class="hide twitter">Twitter</a></li>
 <li><a href="" class="hide fb">Facebook</a></li>
 <li><a href="" class="hide gplus">Google+</a></li>
 <li><a href="" class="hide linkedin">LinkedIn</a></li>
 <li><a href="" class="hide blip">BlipTV</a></li>
 <li><a href="" class="hide lanyrd">Lanyrd</a></li>
 <li><a href="" class="hide slides">Slideshare</a></li>
 <li><a href="" class="hide sched">Schedule</a></li>
 <li><a href="" class="hide attendees">Attendee List</a></li>
</ul>
```

The styles

```
.hide {
 text-indent: 100%;
 white-space: nowrap;
 overflow: hidden;
}
li a {
display: block;
width: 29px;
height: 18px;
background-image: url(social.png);
```

```
}
li a.twitter { background-position: 0 0;}
li a.fb { background-position: 0 -20px;}
li a.gplus { background-position: 0 -40px;}
li a.linkedin { background-position: 0 -60px; }
li a.blip { background-position: 0 -80px; }
li a.lanyrd { background-position: 0 -100px; }
li a.slides { background-position: 0 -120px; }
li a.sched { background-position: 0 -140px; }
li a.attendees { background-position: 0 -160px; }
```

Each item in the mark-up has two different class values. The conceal class is used as a selector for the image replacement technique, which is used when it is loaded. The other class name is unique to each social networking link on the page. By using unique class values, users can put the CSS sprite in the most optimal location for each link. Users should be able to distinguish the image replacement styles at the top of the style sheet. Take note of the fact that the background image for all link (a) components is social.png in the following rule. Finally, users come to the styles that are responsible for the bulk of the work. For each link in the list, a new background position is specified, and the visible element box behaves like a small window that shows a bit of the background image. The first item has the value "0,0," which places the top-left corner of the picture in the top-left corner of the element box. The second item has the value "0,1," which positions the bottom-left corner of the image in the bottom-left corner of the element box. In order for the Facebook icon to be visible, users must move the image up by 20 pixels, which means that its vertical position is set to –20 pixels (its horizontal position of 0 is fine). As the image is transferred up the CSS sprite stack in 20-pixel increments for each link, image portions that are further and further down the CSS sprite stack are revealed.

All of the icons in this example have the same proportions and stack up well, although this is not a must. On a single CSS sprite, users can combine images with a variety of different proportions. The technique of determining the element's size and then aligning the CSS sprite properly with the background-position property is the same for both elements.

7.4 STYLING FORMS:

Web forms can appear a little haphazard straight out of the box when no styles are added (see Figure 7.3), so user will want to use CSS to give them a more professional appearance. Not only do they appear better, but studies have shown that when the labels and inputs are aligned properly, forms are significantly easier and faster to use. Various form elements can be styled in this part, and we'll also look at how to align form elements without the use of tables. Designing forms can be somewhat difficult due to the wide diversity of methods in which browsers handle form components. However, the time and effort invested in making users forms look as professional as the rest of user's website will be well worth it.

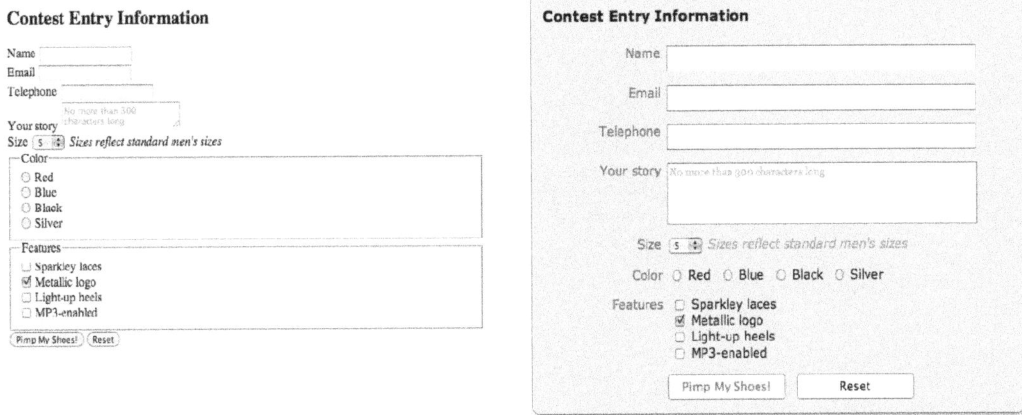

Figure 7.3. Forms tend to be ugly and difficult to use with HTML alone (left). A little CSS can make a big difference (right). This section walks users through the styling of this form step by step.

Forms don't have any unique stylistic attributes; instead, users should use the usual colour, background, font, border, margin, and padding properties that has been learned about in the previous chapters to create the look users want. The following is a quick review of the types of things users can perform with each form control type, organised by control type.

Text inputs (text, password, email, search, tel, url): Change the appearance of the box itself by adjusting the width, height, backgroundcolor, background-image, border, border-radius, margin, padding, and box-shadow properties of the element. The text inside the entry box can also be customised by changing the colour and the various font attributes of the text.

The text area element: This type of field can be styled in the same way that text-entry fields can be. Users will need to modify the default font for text area components to something that matches the font used for the rest of user's text-entry fields. A line-height can also be specified because there are several lines in the document. It's worth noting that some browsers display a handle in the lower-right corner of the text area box, indicating that it is resizable; however, users can disable this feature by including the style resize: none;

Button inputs (submit, reset, button): Users can use any of the box properties on the submit and reset buttons, including the width and height of the box as well as the border, background, margin, padding, and box shadow. It should be noted, however, that by default, buttons are configured to use the border-box sizing paradigm, which means that width and height values are applied border to border. Most browsers also include a small amount of padding by default, which can be adjusted by entering a custom padding value in the address bar. Additionally, users can customise the text that displays on the buttons.

Radio and checkbox buttons: When it comes to radio and checkbox buttons, the best practise is to leave them alone. At the most, Internet Explorer will display a small circle of colour around the box, which looks a little strange. If users are particularly determined, users could use JavaScript to completely redesign the buttons.

Drop-down and select menus: It is possible to specify the width and height of a select element, but keep in mind that it by default uses the border-box box-sizing model to determine its size. It is possible to apply colour, background-color, and font properties to options in some browsers; however, it is generally recommended to leave them alone so that they can be rendered by the browser and operating system.

Field sets and legends: The border, background, margins, and padding of a fieldset can be adjusted just like any other element box in the layout editor. It is possible to keep users form appearing neat while still maintaining semantics and accessibility by turning off the border fully on the form. It is unfortunate that browsers make it difficult to change how legend components are displayed by default. By default, legend elements are placed on an indent, centred vertically with the top edge of the fieldset. Using a span or an element within the legend and applying styles to the confined element can produce more predictable outcomes, according to some developers.

7.5 STYLING TABLES:

Using the various font, text, and background settings, users may alter the appearance and alignment of the material contained within the cells, just as users would with any other text element on user's page. In addition, users may apply padding, margins, and borders to the table and cells itself to make them more appealing. Although not expressly for tables, there are a couple of CSS attributes that have been designed to work with them. This section focuses on table display properties that have a direct impact on the appearance of the table, notably the treatment of table borders.

7.5.1 SEPARATED AND COLLAPSED BORDERS:

CSS provides two techniques for displaying borders between table cells: separated and collapsed. Separated borders are the default setting. A border is drawn on all four corners of each cell when borders are separated, and users can specify the amount of distance between the borders when they are split. Collapsing border models are used when the borders of adjacent borders "collapse" such that only one of the borders is visible and the gap between them is eliminated (Figure 7.4).

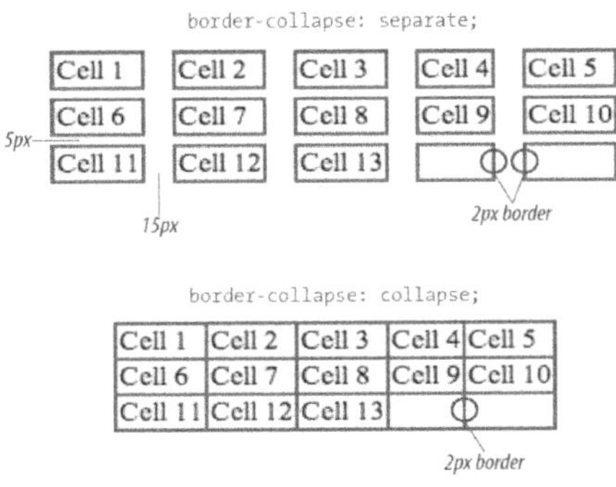

Figure 7.4: Separated borders (top) and collapsed borders (bottom).

The border-collapse property enables users to select which of these border-rendering approaches they want to utilise for their borders.

Separated border model: Tabular data is rendered with separated borders by default, as illustrated in the top table in Figure 7.4. The border-spacing attribute allows users to determine the amount of gap that should appear between cells in a row or column. There are two length measurements used to determine border spacing. The horizontal value is the first one to be calculated and is applied between columns. The second measurement is used to determine the distance between rows. The value users enter will be utilised both horizontally and vertically if users only give one. The default option is zero, which causes the borders to overlap the inside grid of the table by a factor of two. In Figure 7.4, the top table shows the style rules that were utilised to build the custom border spacing that is presented in the bottom table.

```
table {
 border-collapse: separate;
 border-spacing: 15px 3px;
 border: none; /* no border around the table itself */
}
td {
 border: 2px solid purple; /* borders around the cells */
}
```

Collapsed border model: When the collapsed border model is used, only one border appears between each table cell when the table is displayed. Specifically, this is the style sheet that was used to generate the bottom table in Figure 7.4.

```
table {
 border-collapse: collapse;
 border: none; /* no border around the table itself */
}
td {
```

```
border: 2px solid purple; /* borders around the cells */
}
```

It is important to note that, despite the fact that each table cell has a 2-pixel border, the borders between cells measure a total of two pixels, rather than four pixels. In a 4-pixel border between cells, two pixels will fall in one cell and two pixels will fall in another. Borders between cells are centred on the grid between cells. When there are odd numbers of pixels, the browser determines where the extra pixel should be placed. When two or more adjoining cells have distinct border styles, a sophisticated pecking order is used to select which border will appear on the screen. If the border-style for either of the cells is set to hidden, then no border will be displayed for that cell. Following that, the width of the border is considered: broader borders take precedence over narrower borders. Finally, when everything else is equal, it boils down to a matter of personal preference. CSS's users ranked the border styles from most to least important in the following order: double, solid, dashed, dotted, ridge, outset, groove, and (at the bottom) inset (the least important).

7.5.2 EMPTY CELLS:

The empty-cells attribute allows users to specify whether or not empty cells should display their backgrounds and borders in tables with separated borders. Text, pictures, and non-breaking whitespace are all prohibited from being contained within a cell that is considered "empty." It is possible that it will contain carriage returns and space characters. Figure 7.5 depicts the previous separated table border example with its empty cells (what would be Cells 14 and 15) set to conceal in the previous separated table border example.

```
table {
 border-collapse: separate;
 border-spacing: 15px 3px;
 empty-cells: hide;
 border: none;
}
td {
```

```
border: 1px solid purple;
}
```

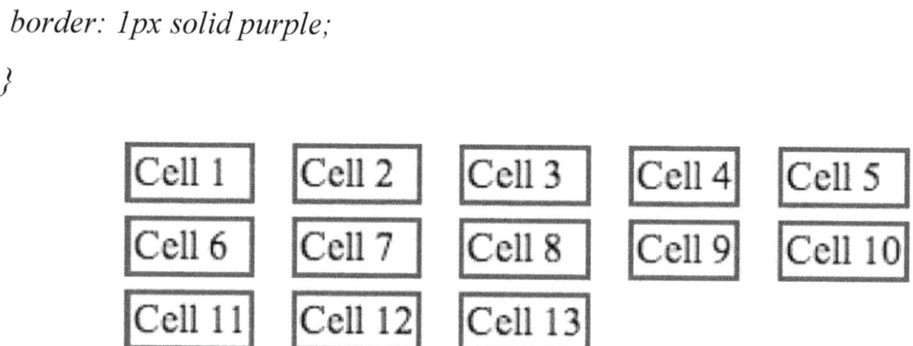

Figure 7.5: Hiding empty cells with the empty-cells property

7.6 BASIC RESPONSIVE WEB DESIGN:

Responsive web design is a technique that makes use of CSS to change the layout of a page depending on the size of the screen being used. It is only one of the strategies users are employing to deal with the staggering diversity of screen sizes available. Without a doubt, responsive design is a massively complex subject that could (and has) been the subject of entire books. What I'm going to do here is introduce users to the fundamental components of a responsive website so that users can get a sense for the process of creating one. The method of responsive design provided by Ethan Marcotte in his seminal book Responsive Web Design serves as the foundation for the methodology discussed here.

7.6.1 A SIMPLE EXAMPLE:

In this part, we'll work together to make the Jenware page more responsive to different devices. The image in Figure 7.6 depicts how the same Jenware HTML page will appear on a narrow screen, a tablet screen in both portrait and landscape orientations, and a huge desktop monitor by the time users are finished with it. In order to fit on a smartphone screen, the page has a one-column style with extremely narrow side margins. When using a tablet in portrait mode, there is more room for slightly more liberal margins and wrapped text than when using landscape mode. At 1,024 pixels wide, there is enough area for a second column, and in extremely wide browser windows, the width of the content is regulated by the max-width attribute to ensure that line lengths do not become uncontrollably long, as seen in the example. These are minor tweaks when compared to the sophisticated responsive designs created by professionals, but they should be sufficient to demonstrate how it works.

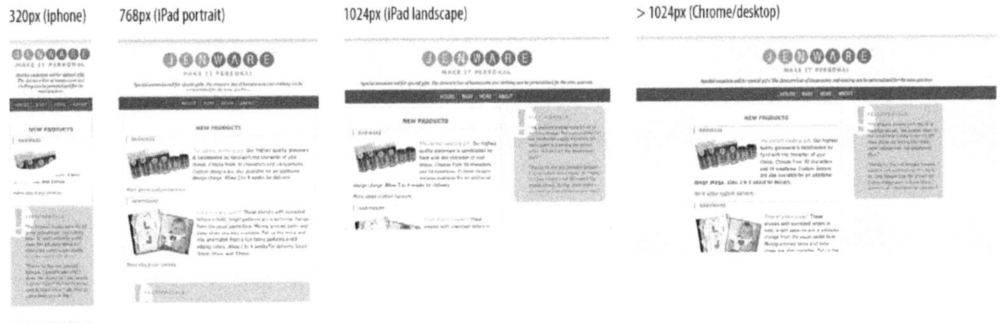

Figure 7.6: The newly responsive Jenware site. Users can look at it on users own mobile devices at www.learningwebdesign.com/rwd/.

How it works: Responsive design as first proposed by Mr. Marcotte has three core components:

✓ **A fluid layout:** A fluid layout is a style of webpage design in which the layout of the page resizes in response to changes in the size of the browser window. In order to accomplish this, percentages are used to define regions of the page rather than set pixel widths.

✓ **Flexible images:** When the layout is scaled down, the photos and other embedded media must also scale down in order to be visible; otherwise, they will be hidden from view. Make sure the Jenware graphics are scaled down to fit in this area.

✓ **CSS media queries:** In web design, media queries are a means of applying styles to a document based on the medium through which it is displayed. Queries begin with questions such as "Is the document being printed?" and "Is the document being printed?" Then make use of these styles that are suited for printing." Alternatively, "Is the document displayed on a screen, and is the screen at least 1,024 pixels wide and in landscape mode?" Then make use of the following styles.

7.7 CONCLUSION:

To summarise, web design is the heart and soul of any website. It has a significant impact on the overall performance and success of a website. This is one of the reasons why web designers devote a lot of time and effort to commercial web design. A well-designed website attracts more visitors and improves a website's search engine rating. In this chapter, users will learn how CSS may be used to enhance the creation of online applications. The use of CSS, or cascading style sheets, has made the building of web pages significantly simpler. CSS makes it simple to create hyperlinks to other documents on a website. Using CSS, users can have complete control over the appearance of the various elements on the various web pages of users site. CSS merely determines the structure and presentation of material on a website, not the content itself. A website's design has absolutely nothing to do with this issue. The CSS, on the other hand, has an impact on how the design will seem after the final process is completed. A whole website's typeface, positioning, colour, and style information can be controlled by a single CSS sheet, which can be accessed through any web browser.

CHAPTER 8

WEB GRAPHICS

"What separates design from art is that design *is meant to be... functional.*"

— Cameron Moll

Chapter Learnings:

This chapter provides an introduction to the principles of web visual development, beginning with a discussion of the many methods that can be used to locate and create images. After that, it walks users through the various file formats that are available for usage with online graphics and assists users in selecting one to utilise. In addition to that, it discusses SVG, which stands for Scalable Vector Graphics. This chapter also refers to the strategies and tools that are available for reducing the file sizes of web graphics as much as possible through a process known as optimising, while still preserving an image quality that is acceptable.

8.1 INTRODUCTION:

The integration of web graphics into any website is just as important as the website's actual content. A customer might get better and more original thoughts of what they are seeking for by looking at a graphic that has been designed exceptionally well. The use of online graphics enables website designers to improve their work by incorporating more colours and visual attractions, as well as by lending an artistic and professional touch to their original ideas. Visitors are less likely to stick around on websites that are lacking in online graphics. The successful use of web graphics is contingent upon their strategic and strategic placement on websites. Not only does the strategic positioning of images draw in end-users, but it also contributes to the website's overall attractiveness.

When used correctly, the tools in Photoshop, Flash, Dreamweaver, and Fireworks are extremely helpful in the process of designing and generating one-of-a-kind graphics. These graphics, which were designed by a professional, represent the inventiveness of the website's designer and help to improve the website's overall quality. In most cases, images are utilised to explain facts and concepts that cannot be articulated via the use of words alone. An example of this would be a shopping or e-commerce website that employs a lot of visuals to display the photographs of the things they sell.

People are able to quickly and readily comprehend anything written in a graphical language because it provides specifics about specific products. The simplified and more easily understood material is made possible by the product visuals that are associated to it. Assume that users of userswebsite have access to product descriptions; in this case, clients should also have access to the associated graphic depiction of the product. It is preferable to employ logos, cartoons, graphs, and charts whenever possible, provided that doing so makes logical sense.

The following are some graphic design fundamentals and guidelines:

- ✓ **Clarity in web page:** In an organised web design, the components should be laid out in accordance with the importance they hold, and the components that are related to the content should appear to be relevant to it.
- ✓ **Imagery:** Because images play such a crucial part in the design of websites, it is important to select ones that are relevant to the content of the site in order to make the most positive impression possible on site visitors.
- ✓ **Colour:** Every hue speaks in its own distinct dialect. Different colour combinations and their permutations pique people's interests in a variety of topics. Because of this, the choice of colours is another facet of web design that is quite significant. Web pages would appear lifeless and unappealing if they lacked colour. Web pages can have an appealing appearance that is lively and welcoming to users if they employ colour schemes that are balanced.
- ✓ **Colour Contrast:** It is of the utmost importance to pick colours that contrast sufficiently between the text and the background. Therefore, it is essential to make use of colour contrast that is pertinent and must be tailored to the type of website and visuals that are employed. Websites can be made to look more appealing and aesthetically acceptable by using colour contrast in the suitable ways.
- ✓ **Readability:** The size of the fonts that are utilised on a website serves as an important differentiator and plays an important role. Something significant or a

new section is indicated by the size of the typeface. It is recommended that a sans-serif face be used for the entire body copy. Important points can be brought to the reader's attention by emphasising them with underlines, bold, and italics, but users should only do so sparingly.

- ✓ **Effective text**: When creating websites, HTML text is utilised more frequently. In comparison to the other visual word, it is more effective. Text possesses a multitude of benefits when utilised in an online environment. Text is often more effective than pictures in achieving the desired objectives in a variety of contexts.
- ✓ **Page Layout:** When users decode Websites, users pay close attention to the layout of the components on the screen since this imparts a great deal of significance. The concept of relationships on a wide variety of distinct levels is implied by the relative position. As a result, it is essential to exercise a great deal of caution while designing page layouts. When it comes to communicating information about products and services, the order in which text, visuals, and images are presented is critically significant.
- ✓ **Alignment:** On web pages, alignment ought to be made clearly obvious in some way. It appears to be straightforward and readily apparent. Text that is aligned to the left is simpler to read than text that is right-aligned. Therefore, it is recommended that, when developing a website, one adhere to web alignment standards.
- ✓ **3D Effect on the graphic design:** The use of 3D generates the illusion of space between the various pieces of text and components. The use of 3-D illusion effects is a potent method that can produce excellent outcomes. They could potentially be contributing to the total size of the page's file.
- ✓ **Navigation Buttons:** The visitors to the website can navigate the site more easily thanks to the navigation buttons. The navigation button ought to be positioned either at the very top of the page, directly beneath the corporate logo, or farther down on the left side. Because they will not be able to get the information that they were seeking for on the website, visitors become frustrated when it is difficult to find links on the website.

8.2 IMAGE SOURCES:

Users need to have an image in order to save a picture, therefore let's have a look at several different methods users can obtain photos in the first place. There is a wide variety of choice accessible to the user, such as scanning, photographing, or illustrating the images by themselves; making use of the available stock photos and clip art; or just employing someone else to make images on user's behalf. Making users own photographs from scratch is almost always going to be the most time- and money-efficient approach to generate images for userswebsite. The fact that designers are granted unrestricted permission to utilise the photos is an additional attractive feature. Imagery can be generated by designers using devices such as scanners, digital cameras, or drawing programmes.

- ✓ **Scanning:** The collection of source material can be done very effectively by scanning. Users are able to scan practically anything, including flat art as well as three-dimensional things. Be wary, on the other hand, of the temptation to scan and use photographs that users have found. Keep in mind that the majority of the photographs that users uncover are undoubtedly protected by copyright and cannot be used without the owner's consent, even if the images are modified quite a bit.
- ✓ **Digital Cameras:** Using a digital camera, users may take pictures of the environment around users and import them into an image editing tool without any additional steps. It is not necessary to make a significant financial investment in high-end equipment due to the low-resolution nature of the Internet. Depending on the kind of imagery users need to capture, users might be able to acquire the required level of quality using a regular consumer digital camera.
- ✓ **Electronic Illustrations:** Users can create user's own images using a drawing programme or a picture editing programme if users have the abilities necessary to illustrate them. Every designer has her own go-to resources and methods that she prefers. After creating our logos, graphics, and type effects in Adobe Illustrator, users import the image into Photoshop to make a version that is suitable for the web. Nevertheless, for the majority of image kinds, Photoshop offers all Users require, and as a result, it is where Users spend the most of my time designing.

8.2.1 FORMATS:

Once users have some photographs in user's possession, users will need to convert them to a format that is compatible with being displayed on a website. The world wide web is home to dozens of different file formats for graphic files. For instance, if users use Windows, users might be familiar with BMP graphics. On the other hand, if users are a print designer, users might make frequent use of images in TIFF and EPS format. On the World Wide Web, user's sole options are GIF (pronounced "jif"), JPEG (pronounced "jay-peg"), and PNG (pronounced "ping"). Users will be familiar with the differences between a GIF and a JPEG by the time users reach the conclusion of this session. The following is a brief summary:

- ✓ When it is necessary to have transparent images or motion, as well as when images need to have firm edges and flat colours, GIF images are the best option.
- ✓ JPEGs are ideal for use with pictures and other images that have seamless colour transitions.
- ✓ PNG files are frequently recommended as a suitable alternative to the GIF format because of its versatility and ability to store any kind of picture. They are also able to hold images that contain sections that are transparent or partially transparent.

These formats have become the de facto standard due to the fact that they are platform-independent (that is, they can run on operating systems such as Windows, Macs, and Unix) and they compress data very efficiently, making it simple to transport it across a network. In the following paragraphs, users will discuss terminology and go into greater detail regarding the characteristics and capabilities of each format. If users have a good understanding of the technological nuances, users will be able to create online graphics of the greatest quality with the shortest file sizes.

8.2.2 THE UBIQUITOUS GIF:

The Graphical Interchange Format (GIF) file is commonly considered to be the best option for Websites. Despite the fact that it was not created with the web in mind explicitly, it was the first format to become widely used on the web due to its adaptability, small file sizes, and cross-platform compatibility. GIF files can also be transparent and have the capacity to incorporate animations that are quite basic.

Because the GIF compression method is so effective at compressing images with flat colours, it is the ideal file format for usage with logos, line art, graphics including text, icons, and other similar types of graphics (Figure 8.1). Users have the ability to save pictures or textured images as GIFs as well; however, the saving process for these types of images is not as efficient, which results in bigger file sizes. These should be saved as JPEGs, which is the format users shall discuss in the following section. On the other hand, GIF works quite well for images that have a mix of a relatively small amount of photographic imagery and a relatively large amount of flat colour. It is necessary to be knowledgeable with the inner workings of GIFs as well as the capabilities they possess in order to create really outstanding GIFs.

Figure 8.1: The GIF format is great for graphical images comprised mainly of flat colours and hard

- ✓ **8-bit, indexed colour:** GIF files are indexed colour images that include 8-bit colour information. This is the technical definition of a GIF (they can also be saved at lower bit depths). GIFs can have up to 256 colours if they are 8 bits, which is the maximum amount of colours that 8 bits of information can specify ($2^8 = 256$). Lower bit depths lead to fewer colour options and also result in a smaller file size.

When a picture has indexed colour, it indicates that the collection of colours that make up the image, known as the palette, is saved in a colour table, which is also referred to as a colour map. Each pixel in the image is assigned a numeric reference (also known as a "index") that corresponds to a specific location in the colour table. A straightforward illustration of this point ought to clear up any confusion. The presentation of a 2-bit (4-color) indexed colour image is illustrated in Figure 8.2, which shows how the image references its colour table. There are 256 spots available in the colour table for images that are 8 bits.

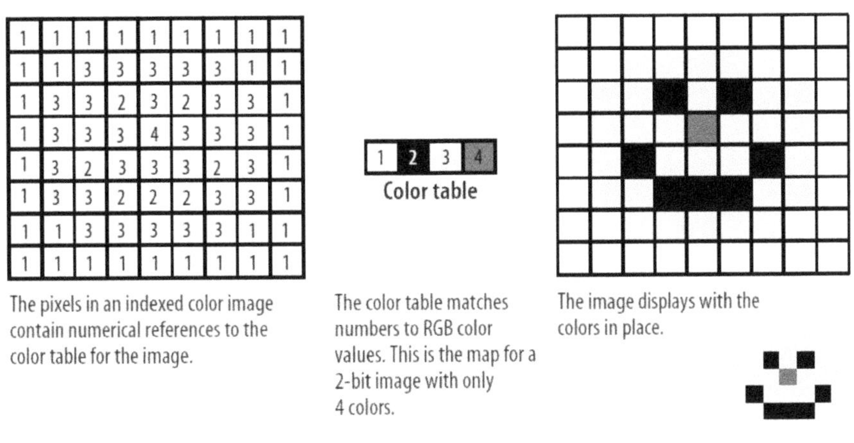

Figure 8.2: A 2-bit image and its colour table

When users open a previously saved GIF in Photoshop, users may inspect (and even alter) its colour table by selecting Image Mode Color Table from the drop-down menu (Figure 8.3). Within Fireworks, the Optimize panel is where user will find the colour table presented. The vast majority of source pictures (scans, illustrations, photographs, and so on) begin in the RGB format; therefore, in order for them to be saved as GIFs, they need to be converted to indexed colour. When a picture is converted from RGB mode to indexed mode, the colours in the image are scaled back until they fit on a palette that contains 256 colours or fewer. In Photoshop, Fireworks, and Image Ready, the conversion occurs when users save or export the GIF. However, users are able to view a preview of the final image along with its colour table before the conversion takes place. Users may be required to manually convert the image to indexed colour by some other image editing tools before users can move on to the second step of exporting the image as a GIF. In either scenario, users will be prompted to choose a colour palette for the image that will be shown using indexed colours. The most common image editing programmes all include a variety of colour palettes users can choose from, and this sidebar provides an overview of those selections. For the best results with the vast majority of picture formats, it is suggested that users use the Selective or Perceptual filter in Photoshop, the Adaptive filter in Fireworks, and the Optimized Median Cut filter in Paint Shop Pro.

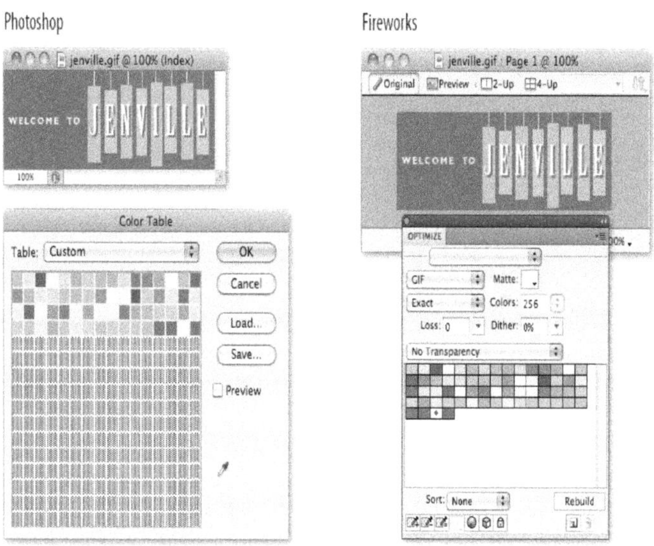

Figure 8.3: A view of the Colour Table in Photoshop and Fireworks.

GIF compression:

GIF compression is considered "lossless," which means that no picture information is lost during the process of compressing the indexed image (although some image information may be lost during the conversion of an RGB image to an image with a limited colour palette). Second, it makes use of a method of data compression known as "LZW," which stands for "Lempel-Ziv-Welch," and it capitalises on the occurrence of repetition in the data. When it finds a series of pixels with the same hue, it is able to condense all of that information into a single data description. Ones that have big regions of flat colour compress better than images that have textures because of this reason. To illustrate this point with an overly simplistic example, the compression strategy comes up with a shorthand notation that refers to "14 blue pixels" whenever it finds a row that contains 14 blue pixels that are all the same. When it comes across another group of 14 blue pixels in the future, it will merely employ the code shortcut (Figure 8.4). In contrast, when it comes across a row that has a gradual transition from blue to aqua and green, it needs to store a description for every pixel along the way, which necessitates the storage of additional data. This makes the process more time-consuming. When developing GIF images with the goal of achieving the highest possible level of compression, this example serves as a helpful mental model to keep in mind. What actually occurs in technical terms is, of course, more difficult.

8.2.3 THE PHOTOGENIC JPEG:

JPEG, an acronym that stands for Joint Photographic Experts Group, is the second most common graphics format used on the World Wide Web. JPEG was developed by the standards organisation of the same name. JPEGs, on the other hand, use a compression method that favours colours with gradients and blended tones, as opposed to GIFs, which use a scheme that performs particularly poorly with flat colours and sharp edges. Because of its ability to store full colour and its compression strategy, JPEG is the format of choice for photographic photographs.

24-bit TrueColor images: JPEGs don't employ colour palettes like GIFs. Instead, these are 24-bit images, which have the ability to depict any one of the millions of colours that are included within the RGB colour space. They come with every hue a user could possibly require, which is one of the reasons why they are perfect for taking images. Users do not need to worry about being restricted to 256 colour options while working with JPEGs, as is the case when working with GIFs. JPEGs are noticeably less complicated than other image formats.

Lossy compression: The JPEG compression system is a lossy compression method, which means that during the process of compression, some of the image information is lost. Thankfully, this loss is not detectable for the majority of images when compressed to the majority of settings. When a picture is compressed using high levels of JPEG compression, users will start to notice colour blotches and squares as a result of the way the compression scheme samples the image. These are typically referred to as artefacts.

Progressive JPEGs: Progressive JPEGs are displayed in a series of passes, much like interlaced GIFs, beginning with a low-resolution version that gradually improves in clarity as more passes are displayed, as seen in Figure 8.4. Users are able to determine the total number of steps required to complete an image using certain graphic design systems.

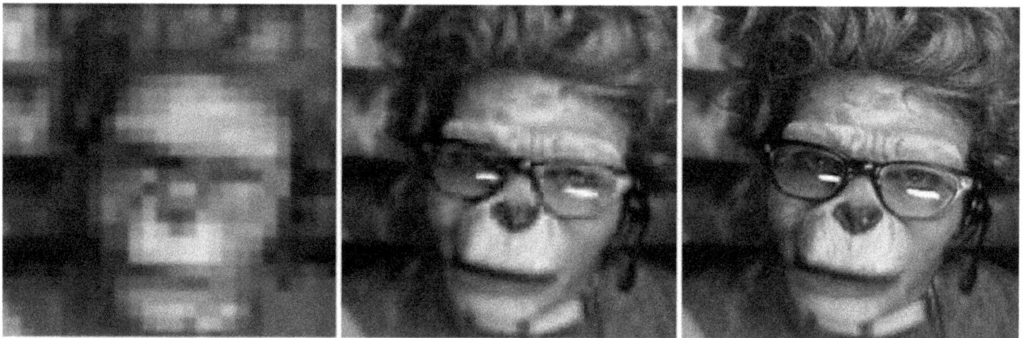

Figure 8.4: Progressive JPEGs render in a series of passes

The use of progressive JPEGs has the benefit of allowing viewers to see a preview of the image before the file has finished downloading completely. In most cases, making a JPEG progressive will result in a minor reduction in the file size of the image. The drawback is that they require more processing power and can cause the final display to move more slowly.

Decompression: Because JPEGs need to have their compression removed before they can be viewed, it takes a web browser more time to decode and assemble a JPEG than it does a GIF of the same size. However, because the difference is typically not noticeable, this should not be seen as a reason to avoid using the JPEG format.

8.2.4 THE AMAZING PNG:

PNG, a versatile graphic format, is the final graphic format to join the roster of web graphics (Portable Network Graphic). PNGs are now supported by every browser that is currently being utilised, despite having a very sluggish beginning. In addition, image editing software is now able to produce PNG files that are as compact and feature-rich as they should be despite their reduced file size. PNGs are at last attaining the level of public appeal that they really deserve.

PNGs provide an astonishing array of features, including the following:

- ✓ The capacity to store images with a bit depth of 8 bits, 24 bits for RGB, 16 bits for grayscale, and even 48 bits for colour.
- ✓ A compression method that does not suffer any loss.

- ✓ Either a straightforward on/off transparency, like a GIF, or several gradations of opacity
- ✓ Progressive display (similar to GIF interlacing)
- ✓ Adjustment information regarding gamma
- ✓ Text that is embedded in order to attach information about the author, copyright, and other related topics.

Multiple image formats: PNG was developed to replace GIF for use in online applications, while TIFF was designed to be used for the storing and printing of images. PNG files are capable of storing a wide variety of picture formats, including 24- and 48-bit RGB colour, 16-bit grayscale, and 8-bit indexed colour.

8-bit indexed colour images: PNG files, much like GIF files, are capable of storing indexed images with a maximum of 256 colours per. They can also be preserved with a depth of 1, 2, or 4 bits respectively. In common parlance, indexed colour PNGs are referred to as PNG-8 files.

RGB/True colour (24- and 48-bit): Each channel in a PNG file (red, green, and blue) can be described by information with either 8 or 16 bits, which can result in images with either 24 or 48 bits of the RGB colour space. PNG-24 is the designation given to 24-bit RGB PNGs while working in graphics programmes. It is important to highlight that photographs with 48 bits of resolution cannot be utilised on the web, and even images with 24 bits of resolution should be used with caution. JPEG provides reduced file sizes while maintaining a picture quality that is suitable for RGB photographs.

Grayscale: PNGs can also support 16-bit grayscale images, which can have as many as 65,536 different shades of grey (216). This allows black-and-white photographs and illustrations to be stored with an incredible level of subtlety of detail; however, these images are not suitable for use on the web.

Transparency: PNGs can also support 16-bit grayscale images, which can have as many as 65,536 different shades of grey (216). This allows black-and-white photographs and illustrations to be stored with an incredible level of subtlety of detail; however, these images are not suitable for use on the web. The following illustration compares the identical PNG file against two distinct background images. The drop shadow has many levels of transparency, ranging from almost opaque to completely transparent, in contrast to the orange circle, which is completely opaque. The drop shadow may be made to blend in perfectly with any background thanks to the many transparency levels that are included in the PNG file.

Figure 8.5: Alpha-channel transparency allows multiple levels of transparency, as shown in the drop shadow around the orange circle PNG.

Progressive display (interlacing): PNGs also have the capability of being encoded for an interlaced display mode. If users choose to use this feature, the image will be displayed using a total of seven different layers. In contrast to interlaced GIFs, which only fill in the rows horizontally, PNGs do so in both the horizontal and vertical dimensions. In most cases, interlacing is not required, thus if users want user's files to be as tiny as possible, users should disable interlacing display. This will reduce the file size.

Gamma correction: The brightness setting of a display is referred to as its gamma (see note). Because the gamma values of different platforms are different, the graphics users generate may not seem to the end user the way users intended them to. PNGs have the ability to be tagged with information about the gamma setting of the environment in which they were produced. The software that is showing the PNG can then analyse this information and perform suitable gamma compensations for the image. When this is done on both the creator's end as well as the end user's end, the PNG maintains the brightness and colour intensity that was intended for it. As of the time of this writing, unfortunately, the support for this functionality is lacking.

Embedded text: PNGs additionally feature the capacity to save strings of text in their files. This is helpful for permanently attaching text to a picture, such as information on copyright or a description of what is contained in the image. Sole Corel Paint Shop Pro and the GIMP are capable of adding text annotations to PNG graphics. Corel Paint Shop Pro is the only tool. The meta-information contained in the PNG file should, ideally, be accessible by right-clicking on the graphic within a browser; however, this functionality is not yet available in most modern browsers.

8.3 IMAGE SIZE AND RESOLUTION:

Images saved in GIF, JPEG, and PNG format are all bitmapped images, which are often referred to as raster images. This is one thing that all three formats have in common. When users zoom in on a bitmapped image, users will notice that it is constructed similarly to a mosaic, with numerous individual pixels making up the whole (tiny, single-colored squares). These are not the same as vector graphics, which are comprised of clean lines and areas that are filled in and are created using mathematical methods. Figure 8.6 is an illustration of the distinction between bitmapped graphics and vector graphics.

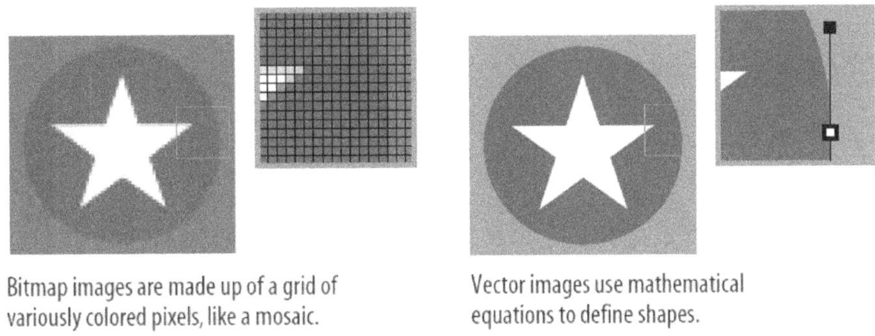

Bitmap images are made up of a grid of variously colored pixels, like a mosaic.

Vector images use mathematical equations to define shapes.

Figure 8.6: Bitmapped and vector graphics.

Users might be familiar with the term resolution if users have ever utilised bitmapped pictures for print or on the web. Resolution refers to the amount of pixels that are packed into one inch. Image resolutions of between 300 and 600 pixels per inch (ppi) are typically used in the printing industry. Images, on the other hand, have to be made at significantly lower resolutions in order to be used on the web. In spite of the fact that 72 ppi has become the industry norm, the concept of "inches" and, by extension, "pixels per inch," are rendered meaningless while working within an online environment. The actual pixel measurements of an online image are the only measurement that may be considered meaningful in the end. When an image is displayed on a web page, the display resolution of the monitor is mapped one-to-one with the pixel dimensions of the displayed image. Due to the fact that the monitor resolution might differ based on the user and the platform, the image may appear larger or smaller depending on the settings.

Because of this, conceiving of content on the web in terms of "inches" is a pointless exercise. Everything depends on context. And because there are no inches to measure with, the whole concept of "pixels per inch" is rendered meaningless as well. The only thing about the graphic that users can say for certain is that it has a width of 72 pixels, and this means that it will have a width that is twice as broad as a graphic that has a width of 36 pixels. Following this illustration, it ought to be obvious why photographs that have just been extracted from a digital camera are not suitable for use on websites. Users typically capture photos with a resolution of 180 ppi and a dimension of 1600 by 1200 pixels. All of those extra pixels are superfluous given that the normal width of a browser window is just 800 pixels, which means that if users used them, half of the image would dangle off the edge of the window. In order for users to see it, they would need to scroll both vertically and horizontally. Even while some current browsers reduce the size of the image such that it fits within the browser window, this does not solve the issue of forcing consumers to download an unnecessary large file when they could be downloading a lot smaller file instead.

Because of this, thinking about content on the web in terms of "inches" is a pointless exercise. Everything is viewed in a relative context. And because there are no inches to measure with, the concept of "pixels per inch" may also be tossed out the window. The only element about the graphic that users can state with absolute certainty is that it has a width of 72 pixels, meaning that it will have a width that is twice as broad as a graphic that has a width of only 36 pixels. The preceding illustration ought to have made it abundantly clear why photographs that have just been extracted from a digital camera are not suitable for use on websites. Images are often captured by users with a dimensions of 1600 by 1200 pixels and a resolution of 180 pixels per inch. All of those extra pixels are superfluous given that the normal width of a browser window is only 800 pixels, which means they would cause half the image to dangle over the edge of the window if it were used.

In order for users to view it, they will need to scroll both vertically and horizontally. Even while some current browsers reduce the size of the image such that it fits within the browser window, this does not solve the problem of forcing consumers to download an unnecessary large file when they could be downloading a lot smaller file instead.

8.4 INTRODUCTION TO SVG:

Scalable Vector Graphics is the abbreviation for SVG, which is an XML syntax for stylable graphics that can be used as an XML namespace. Scalability refers to the ability to rise or decrease in a consistent manner. In the context of graphic design, "scalable" refers to the quality of not being constrained to a particular, predetermined pixel size. On the World Wide Web, the term "scalable" refers to a specific technology's capacity to expand to accommodate a big number of files, a large number of users, and a broad range of applications. As a graphics technology for the Internet, SVG is scalable in both the literal and figurative senses of the word. Because SVG graphics are scalable to different display resolutions, they can be displayed at the same size on screens that have varying resolutions but still use the full resolution of the printer, for example. On a single web page, the same SVG graphic can be used in a variety of various sizes, and it can also be reused on other pages in a variety of different sizes. It is possible to magnify SVG graphics in order to view finer details or to assist people who have low eyesight. SVG graphics are scalable due to the fact that the same SVG material can be a stand-alone visual or can be referenced or included inside other SVG drawings. This allows a complicated illustration to be built up in pieces, possibly by multiple different persons. The capabilities of symbols, markers, and fonts encourage the re-use of graphical components, optimise the benefits of HTTP caching, and eliminate the requirement for a central register of recognised symbols.

Objects such as lines and curves are examples of vector graphics' geometric components. This allows for greater flexibility as compared to raster-only formats (such as PNG and JPEG), which are required to hold information for each and every pixel that makes up the visual. SVG is not an exception to the rule that most vector formats may also incorporate raster images and can combine those raster pictures with vector information such as clipping paths to make a comprehensive depiction. Since all contemporary displays are raster-oriented, the primary distinction between raster-only and vector graphics lies in the location at which they are rasterized. Rasterization occurs on the client side for vector graphics, whereas rasterization occurs on the server already for raster-only graphics. SVG grants control over the rasterization process, which can be used, for instance, to enable anti-aliased artwork that does not exhibit the unsightly aliasing that is common of vector implementations of low quality. Moving to a vector format does not result in the loss of commonly used effects like soft drop shadows because SVG also includes client-side raster filter effects.

The vast majority of the currently available XML grammars either describe textual information or represent raw data such as financial information. They often offer just the most fundamental graphic capabilities, which are frequently inferior to those offered by the HTML 'img' element. SVG was developed to address a need in the industry by delivering a comprehensive and well-structured description of vector and mixed vector/raster graphics. This not only allows it to be used independently, but also as an XML namespace in conjunction with other grammars.

The extensible mark-up language (XML), which was developed to facilitate the transmission of structured data, has recently seen a surge in adoption rates and is now extensively used. Because it is written in XML, SVG relies on this solid foundation and receives many benefits as a result. These benefits include a solid framework for internationalisation, robust structuring capacity, an object model, and many more. Grammars that are based on XML can be implemented without requiring a significant amount of time or effort to be spent on reverse engineering because they are built on specifications that have already been implemented correctly.

A viewer that is dedicated solely to SVG would be quite beneficial to have. However, SVG can also function as a single component within an XML application that makes use of several namespaces. Because of this, the power of each of the namespaces that is used is multiplied, which makes it possible to generate inventive new content. For instance, SVG graphics might be used in a document that makes use of any text-oriented XML namespace, including XHTML. This would be possible because SVG is an open standard. For the purpose of displaying mathematical content, for instance, MathML might be utilised in a scientific document. When used together, SVG and SMIL may provide presentations that are visually appealing, time-based, and rich in animation. Any multi-namespace grammar that requires the use of graphics should consider using SVG because it is a good component for broad use.

The benefits of using style sheets, which include greater presentational control, greater flexibility, faster download speeds, and enhanced ease of maintenance, are now commonly acknowledged and recognised. This is particularly true for their application with text. This control is brought into the domain of graphics through the SVG standard. For animation, interactive features, and presentational effects, a mix of scripting, DOM, and CSS is frequently referred to as "Dynamic HTML," and it is utilised extensively. Both the document tree and the style sheet are susceptible to script-based manipulation, which is supported by SVG.

8.4.1 THE BASIC SVG DOCUMENT:

An SVG document is, at its core, an XML document. That means that SVG documents have certain basic attributes:

• All tags must have a start and end tag, or must be noted as an empty tag. Empty tags are closed with a backslash, as in <rect />.

• Tags must be nested properly. If a tag is opened within another tag, it must be closed within that same tag. For example, <g><text>Hello there! </text></g> is correct, but <g><text>Hello there! </g></text> is not.

• The document must have a single root. Just as a single <html></html> element contains all content for an HTML page, a single <svg></svg> element contains all content for an SVG document.

• The document should start with the XML declaration, <?xml version="1.0"?>.

• The document should contain a DOCTYPE declaration, which points to a list of allowed elements. The DOCTYPE declaration for an SVG 1.0 document is:

```
<?xml version="1.0"?>
<!DOCTYPE svg PUBLIC "-//W3C//DTD SVG 1.0//EN"
"http://www.w3.org/TR/2001/REC-SVG-20010904/DTD/svg10.dtd">
<svg width="200" height="200" xmlns="http://www.w3.org/2000/svg">
<desc>All SVG documents should have a description</desc>
```

```
<defs>
<!-- Items can be defined for later use -->
</defs>
<g>
<circle cx="100" cy="100" r="75" fill="green"/>
</g>
</svg>
```

8.5 CONCLUSION:

This chapter offers an introduction to the fundamentals of web visual creation, beginning with a discussion of the several techniques that can be implemented in order to identify images and produce new ones. After that, it guides users through the numerous file formats that can be used to online graphics and assists them in selecting one of those formats. In addition, participants will receive instruction on the principles of picture resolution, scaling, and transparency during the duration of this course. In conclusion, the design of websites is a matter that should not be taken lightly due to the significance it has. We can improve our chances of generating a positive impression on prospective customers by having a website that has been built with careful consideration. Additionally, it can help us cultivate leads from consumers and acquire additional conversions, which is a huge benefit. However, the most important benefit is that it provides website visitors with a positive experience and makes it easier for them to navigate and access the various sections of the website. Therefore, the Internet is capable of accommodating any content that users may place on it. Because of this, users need to make sure that their content is up to par with the standards of the web.

CHAPTER 9

CONCLUSION AND ITS FUTURE

"We love what we do and we do what our clients love & work with great clients all over the world to create thoughtful and purposeful websites."

— ProWeb365

Chapter Learning:

This chapter concludes the web designing concepts and animation. Also share information regarding the security precautions taken in site designing process. The last portion explains future of web designing sector.

9.1 CONCLUDE:

Maintaining a website design that is compatible with a variety of device sizes and resolutions has been difficult and will continue to be difficult in the future. If it is created correctly, a responsive website will increase the user experience, adjust itself to the size of the user's device, be mobile-friendly, and be ready for devices that have not yet been invented. This has been made feasible because to three fundamental building elements of web design, namely media queries, flexible and scalable media (pictures and videos), and most significantly fluid and adaptable grids. All of this has been made possible. Heavy websites were a challenge for mobile devices since mobile web browsers had fewer capabilities than desktop web browsers. This made it difficult for mobile devices to access some websites. After that, a fourth important building element was added to web design, and that was dynamic content. Dynamic content is what enables web design approaches such as slow loading and selective content loading. To have dynamic content, user's semantic web content needs to be correctly organised and structured, which in and of itself is a laborious process that includes document structuring and the development of a content hierarchy that corresponds to the structure.

There are already-made frameworks that are responsive that developers may use to simplify their work by taking care of content organisation and hierarchical planning without having to worry about the underlying tiresome work that is involved in web design principles. The selection of any such framework is contingent on the requirements and demands of the user. Because of this, it is up to the developer to decide which framework would work best for their website. This is the most crucial aspect, as switching to a different framework in the middle of or after the development process will require starting a brand new web project. In the event that it was necessary, experienced developers and designers might also construct their very own responsive framework. Additionally, in order to avoid issues in the future, a responsive website requires on-the-go device agnostic testing during the development process as well as before to the actual launch. Even prefabricated frameworks, if not managed correctly, have the potential to throw the developers into a state of disarray.

Web design, as it is now understood, refers to the process of creating a website that is capable of adapting itself to different screen sizes and resolutions. User sought to be required to take our responsive websites one step further in the direction of a responsive philosophy, according to which a website would not only adapt to different screen sizes, but also adapt its content to suit different contexts of user behaviour or user needs. This would be required of us if users want our websites to be truly responsive. In a nutshell, those days are not far away when responsive web design with responsive philosophy would be declared a standard for websites. Users have seen Google rating websites in their search results based on mobile-friendly test, and in the future it will rate websites as human-friendly, websites which would layout and shape their content based on user preferences, user behaviour, location, age, gender, and cultural values. This is because Google has seen that responsive web design with responsive philosophy would be declared a standard for websites. In the next paragraphs, a discussion of web security, an essential component of website design, is provided in more detail.

9.1.1 A REVIEW OF THE USER BASED WEB DESIGNING:

Web technology refers to the tools and tactics used to communicate online between devices. Web browsing requires a browser. Web browsers show text, data, graphics, animation, and video. In a short time, the Web has become an indispensable business and leisure tool. Many people now utilise the Internet instead of the phone to find information. Internet allows fast, accurate, detailed information sharing. Most radio, TV, and print ads now include online addresses, giving clients a more targeted way to learn and make decisions. Today's Web is more than an information source. People use Web-based applications to manage their business and personal life. The ability to link directly with other people and organisations via a widely utilised and easy-to-use computer network technology can enhance company efficiency and ease numerous previously complicated processes. Web designers ensure a site or app carries the intended message and is usable by the target audience. Web design is as vital as content and functionality.

Designers aren't just for web. Technical and non-technical professionals (and their support staff) must understand Web design to remain competitive. Modern workers will help develop the information infrastructure. Web design tools and technology abound. Designers must grasp Web design's technical components to choose technologies that give their organisations a competitive edge. They must also understand design and be able to produce usable Websites.

Most Web designers are self-reflective. They aim to market themselves using mass advertising parallels. The Internet allows one-on-one relationships. Website visitors respond better to customised information and products.

Everyone should know that the Internet lets users choose what information to receive and when to view it. Internet is a one-to-one rather than broadcast media. The Internet doesn't always follow mass media concepts and applications. Passive media dominate. Its objective is to stimulate the viewer's or reader's curiosity so they will make a purchase (such as buying an advertised product). There's a gap between reading and buying. Customers don't interact directly with TVs or newspapers. Mass media content requires a different strategy than Internet content. Internet is transactional. Transactions and interactivity underpin the whole Internet experience, from logging on to Web browsing. Internet is nonlinear. The user makes transactional decisions when travelling to the site, searching (typically in the site's integrated databases), completing e-commerce, and returning to the site. Users can switch sites and businesses at any time.

Web Performance Optimization (WPO), often called website optimization, speeds up the download and display of web pages in a user's browser. Souders (2008) established performance principles to boost web page speed. Faster-loading websites enhance visitor loyalty and enjoyment. This is true for those with slow

Internet connections and mobile devices. Web performance reduces data transmission, which reduces website power usage and environmental effect.

First decade of internet progress focused on optimising website code and pushing hardware boundaries. Early approaches, like simple servlets or CGI, expanded server RAM and enhanced packet detection and retransmission. These theories comprise a substantial part of the optimised foundation of internet apps, but they differ from modern optimization theory since less effort was taken to improve browser display speed throughout their development. Souders created WPO (2008). WPO is projected to have a large impact on the web, with sounders forecasting fast-by-default websites, consolidation, Web performance standards, environmental impacts, and speed as a competitive difference. Souders says the front-end structure accounts for 80% of the time it takes to download and explore a website. This delay can be decreased by understanding browser and HTTP behaviour (HTTP).

The sheer amount of online pages, how sites are designed, and how browsers consume information were three of the biggest performance issues. Second, most websites can't meet users' page-load expectations. Website performance affects both users and developers. Website speed matters to customers. A poll of 1500 consumers found that 75% of internet shoppers would prefer visit a competitor's site than wait. 88% of internet shoppers won't return to a site after a terrible encounter. Half of those surveyed had a less positive image of the company after a single unpleasant experience. Page load time and availability affect consumer satisfaction directly. Visitors won't stick around if a page takes too long to load. It's unprofessional and could cost the developer a lot of money.

Anyone can make a website that loads quickly and functions well, and that, if done correctly, may even be visually pleasing to the untrained eye. Nonetheless, determining whether or not the usability objectives have been realised in the design and development of a valuable and measurably usable Website requires assessing the target audience, identifying the common tasks that they will complete, and empirically evaluating the Website's usability. The order in which tasks are completed is less important than if the developing Website has been thoroughly reviewed at each stage of the process and is progressing toward these quantitative usability goals as a result of the testing. In order to retain a high level of expertise, an accomplished professional web designer works to anticipate the creation of a usable Website that meets clearly defined needs and to be able to repeat this activity on future projects. Design approaches that have been proved to be effective in user interface design for other topic domains should be utilised during the Website design process to ensure the usability and productivity of future Websites.

The formal specification and building of consistent solutions for technologies and capabilities that have already been in use through various hacks and plug-ins proposed by web developers is being formalised through the overarching concept of HTML5 and other tools presented in this chapter 4. Adobe Flash technology, which was supported by all of the major browser vendors at the time of publishing, was used to create modern rich and interactive web designs. The Flash plug-in offers excellent multimedia functionality, notably for animations and animated interfaces. It was also completely free. HTML5 makes it easy to add this type of functionality by providing native browser support.

The most notable new trend on the Internet right now is the inclusion of semantics into web content. Because internet content is designed to be read and understood by humans, a computer cannot provide considerable aid by analysing, searching, or processing the data. The incorporation of semantics will eventually lead to the establishment of the Semantic Web, the third generation of the Web. Recent advancements in web development practises, rich web content, and the need for semantics in web documents are already being seen in practise. The introduction of semantics in the form of microdata and ARIA characteristics, support for RIA through the introduction of new form widgets, support for multimedia, and dynamic graphic rendering, among other things, are some of the most significant new features of HTML5.

CSS transforms, CSS transitions, and CSS animations are all separate CSS specifications that can be used in combination. CSS transitions and animations are more about making things move over time than they are about having things move instantly. Users can specify the transition between two or more states of an element using transitions and animations. In web design, transitions and animations are used.

Transforms change the look of an element by translating, rotating, scaling, and skewing it; however, they are not time-based. The CSS transform property can be used to change the coordinate space location of an element in the CSS visual for matting model, but transitions or animation are necessary to make the change appear to happen over time. The CSS Transforms section goes through the transform property in depth.

While animation can be accomplished with JavaScript, learning CSS3 transitions and animations will save users time and work if they ever need to animate something on the Web. In general, it will save users' CPU and battery life as compared to JavaScript. When applied correctly, CSS animations and transitions may give life and depth to a user's online app. The goal of this chapter is to show users how to use transitions and animations in their papers. Understanding when to employ animation, on the other hand, can assist consumers improve their experience (UX). By introducing the sense of time, an animated user interface can help users communicate on a deeper level.

The incorporation of web visuals into a website is equally as crucial as the information itself. Looking at a graphic that has been designed exceptionally well may provide a customer with better and more creative ideas of what they are looking for. The usage of online graphics allows website designers to better their work by adding more colours and visual appeal, as well as giving their original ideas an artistic and professional touch. Visitors will be less likely to stay on a website that lacks online graphics. The clever and strategic arrangement of web graphics on websites is critical to their success. The strategic placement of photos not only attracts visitors, but it also adds to the overall appeal of the website.

The tools in Photoshop, Flash, Dreamweaver, and Fireworks may be highly useful in the process of designing and creating one-of-a-kind graphics when utilised appropriately. These professionally made graphics demonstrate the website's designer's creativity and serve to boost the website's overall quality. Most of the time, visuals are used to clarify facts and concepts that cannot be expressed in words alone. A retail or e-commerce website that uses a lot of visuals to display the photos of the items they offer is an example of this.

Because it provides specifics about certain products, people can quickly and easily comprehend anything written in a pictorial language. The product graphics that are associated with it enable the material to be streamlined and more easily understood. Assume that users of users website have access to product descriptions; in this instance, customers should also have access to the product's accompanying graphic representation. When possible, use logos, cartoons, graphs, and charts, as long as they make logical sense.

9.1.2 CSS TECHNOLOGY IN DESIGNING WEBSITES:

A set of rules or a file method with a style that is specifically designed to govern the appearance, description, and other features of Web pages written in HTML and XML markup languages, as well as the way in which those documents are shown in a web browser. CSS allows you to modify the design of hundreds of Web pages by editing only one file. It also allows you to control how text is written, font size and colour, and margins and justification using both edges and fonts. CSS allows Web page programmers to link CSS and HTML pages together. CSS style is based on W3C recommendations and is supported by the newest browser versions. Since the 1970s, when SGML was first introduced, style sheets have existed in various forms.

Cascading Style Sheets (CSS) were created as a way to standardise the delivery of style information for web publications. HTML evolved throughout time to include a broader range of aesthetic capabilities to fulfil the needs of web developers. This advancement allowed the designer more control over the site's aesthetic, but it also made HTML more difficult to develop and maintain. Because of differences in web browser implementations, it was difficult to maintain an uniform site design, and users had less control over how web content was shown. Nine different style sheet languages were presented to the W3C's www-style mailing list to increase online presentation capabilities. Two of the nine suggestions, Cascading HTML Style Sheets (CHSS) and Stream-based Style Sheet Proposal, were chosen as the foundation for what became CSS (SSP). In October 1994, Hkon Wium Lie (now the CTO of Opera Software) proposed Cascading HTML Style Sheets (CHSS), a language that resembles CSS today. Bert Bos was developing Argo, a browser that included its own style sheet language called Stream-based Style Sheet Proposal (SSP). Lie and Bos collaborated on the CSS standard (the 'H' was dropped from the name because the style sheets could be used with languages other than HTML). CSS, unlike other style languages such as DSSSL and FOSI, allows many style sheets to influence the style of a document. One style sheet might inherit or "cascade" from another, allowing the site designer and user to influence stylistic preferences equally. In 1994, Hkon presented his proposal at the "Mosaic and the Web" conference in Chicago, Illinois, and again in 1995 with Bert Bos. Around this time, the World Wide Web Consortium (W3C) was forming; the W3C was interested in CSS development and hosted a workshop chaired by Steven Pemberton to that goal. As a result, the W3C added CSS work to the HTML editorial review board's deliverables (ERB).

CSS is a basic syntax that specifies the names of many style properties using a number of English keywords. A style sheet is a collection of rules. One or more selectors plus a declaration block make up each rule or rule-set. In braces, a declaration-block is a list of semicolon separated declarations. A property, a colon (:), a value, and a semi-colon make up each declaration (;). Selectors, a type of match expression, are used in CSS to declare which items a style applies to. Selectors can match all elements of a certain kind or only those that match a specific attribute; elements can be matched based on how they are nested within the document object model or how they are situated relative to each other in the markup code.

A significant level of flexibility may be incorporated into content submission forms by integrating CSS with the capability of a Content Management System. This lets a contributor who may not be familiar with or capable of editing CSS or HTML code to choose the layout of an article or other page they are contributing on-the-fly in the same form. For example, an article or page's contributor, editor, or author may be allowed to choose the number of columns and whether or not the page or article would include an image. This information is then provided to the Content Management System, where the computer logic evaluates the data and determines how to apply classes and IDs to HTML elements based on a set of combinations, styling and positioning them according to the pre-defined CSS for that layout type. When working on large-scale, complex sites with a big number of contributors, such as news and informational sites, this advantage has a significant impact on the project's viability and maintenance. A global stylesheet can be used to impact and style items site-wide when CSS is used correctly in terms of inheritance and "cascading." If the styling of the elements has to be updated or adjusted, it is simple to do so by altering a few rules in the global stylesheet. This type of upkeep was more complex, expensive, and time-consuming before CSS.

CSS2, the most recent Cascading Style Sheets guideline, also includes mechanisms for better non-graphical and non-visual device interpretation. The following is a brief list of features: (i) Mechanisms that allow a user-created style sheet to override all higher-level style sheets in a cascade, allowing the end user to have complete control over presentation. The user can develop a custom style sheet to display pages based on their specific requirements. (ii) Support for downloaded fonts - removing the temptation to hide text in visuals to improve the page's aesthetic. Content and presentation are further separated by positioning and alignment methods. These style sheet restrictions are intended to prevent the usage of HTML tags for unique presentation effects. The HTML tags can be used to logically structure the page, making it easier for nonvisual agents to understand. (iii) A suite of settings for rendering audio from web-based content. (iv) Improved navigation devices, such as the ability to place numbered markers for orientation purposes throughout a page.

9.2 ROLE OF SECURITY IN WEB DESIGNING:

WEB applications have made their way into people's lives and places of work ever since the information age began, and application programmes that are based on WEB are now being used extensively in a wide variety of fields, such as the management of the internet, the control of facilities, and other areas. Any information or data transferred via the Internet today requires the use of the WEB service. Since the World Wide Web is so widely utilised today, programmes and data that are based on Web applications are the targets of the majority of hacker attacks on computer networks. The Internet's data vulnerabilities have been identified as one of the most important factors in ensuring secure dissemination, according to the relevant publications. As of recently, browsers and web applications have been the targets of hacking attempts, with 75 percent of all Internet threats being associated with web applications. These concerns about safety have resulted in significant financial losses in the affected regions. Next, a more in-depth analysis and discussion of the various security technologies that are based on web applications will take place in this part.

The so-called authentication technique refers, for the most part, to the procedure that splits it into two topics, with one of those subjects acting as a clear confirmation of the other. When the identification of a user is the topic of discussion, that user is required to utilise authentication technology to verify their identity. If the verification is successful, the user is allowed to continue accessing the resource; otherwise, access is denied. After authentication, users can refer to this process as authorisation if the subject in question possesses the right to follow-up access as well as the access privileges involved. Authorization is comprised primarily of two components: first is the information that controls access to the resources, and second is the information that pertains to the subjects. After encryption, users are able to send data, but other users are unable to read the information that has been transferred. This is true even when using a network protocol analyser. This technique is primarily hidden in the user information without authorisation application.

The client and the server are the two primary components that make up a web application. The client comes first, followed by the server. In order to accomplish data transfer and processing, it mostly relies on the support provided by the TCP/IP protocol layer. The web browser is the client application that is utilised by the most people. The Web server can access the various resources available on the Web. The static text file, the document of hypertext mark-up language, the media file, the client code, and the dynamic script are the five primary components that make up web resources. Figure 9.1 illustrates the manner of operation for a Web application.

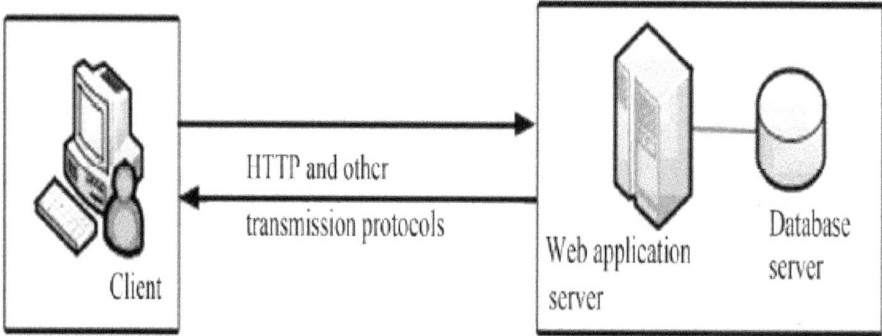

Figure 9.1 Mode of Web application

The term "browser" is typically used to refer to the application that runs on the client host and is responsible for catering to the requirements of the Web server while also displaying and processing the data and information that is provided by the Web server. Before, the browser only needed to provide the display function for HTML static pages. However, with the rapid development of scripts and plug-in technology, scripts and plug-in technology with ActiveX and FLASH model have been used comprehensively. This provides the conditions for the enhance of the browser's performance, but it is followed by the gradually increasing security problems in the process of Web application. Because the browser is the most important component of the Internet, malicious network hackers frequently exploit vulnerabilities in browser software to plant viruses, launch attacks on clients, and put Web clients in danger.

One type of XSS assault is known as a persistent attack, and the other is known as a reflection attack. Both of these attacks are common. The term "persistent attack" most commonly refers to the fact that the attacker stores the virus in the database that crosses over with the programme for the Web application. Then, when users use it, the Web application will communicate the potential infection to the user. When the user runs the programme, the information about the user that is pertinent to the attack will be given to the attacker. The most important aspect of a reflection attack is that the perpetrators do not save the virus on the server side but rather reflect it directly to the user instead. They mostly make use of harmful scripts that have been given to them by third parties, copy viruses into them, and then use those viruses to steal information from users when those users click to those viruses. This attack will not persist after it has been stopped.

The term "clickjacking" most commonly relates to a sort of visual trickery. Hackers typically add transparent Web elements to a web page. When users link to the web page, they are unaware that they have clicked on the transparent Web elements; as a result, information can be accessed or stolen. In order to obtain a desired supply performance, network hackers typically utilise deception to get users to click the performance button on various web elements without first informing them of the relevant information. For instance, link jacking attacks can not only steal information, but after carrying out a number of laborious steps, hackers with access to a network can eventually take control of a camera.

As soon as there are security issues on the server side, it will lead to security issues with web apps, web servers, and the database. Once the complexity of Web applications steadily rises, the security awareness of Web programmers and the management staff corresponding to those Web apps gradually decreases. This provides the circumstances for an attacker to launch an attack on the system. Under typical conditions, the primary security risks posed by the web server side can be broken down into two categories. (1) The potential security risks posed by the data and files stored on the server side, such as the disclosure of sensitive information such as bank account and credit card numbers, etc. Assuming that the intruders have obtained this knowledge, they will be able to commit fraud by way of role playing, and then they will be able to reap the economic gains that are associated with this fraud. (2) Web applications running on the server side can be compromised if malicious code is allowed to be preserved, making them vulnerable to attack by a web page's version of a Trojan horse. SQL injection attacks, assaults that include remote code execution, and other types of attacks are among the most common online dangers users face.

The potential for a security vulnerability is present whenever there is an inappropriate action, whether it be on the user side or the server side of the data transfer process. The active assault and the passive attack are the two most common types of attacks that humans face. The active attack is the more aggressive of the two. The term "active attack" most commonly refers to a data attack carried out within a network. This attack primarily modifies user information on the user side or on the server, which then allows for the effect of the attack to be realised. The term "passive attack" most commonly refers to the act of reading data from the network. This type of assault typically reads the most vital information from the network, such as user names, user passwords, and users' personal information, among other things.

The browser version and the real-time patch update of the operating system should be well done in the link of security in order to enhance the security of both the host operating system and the browser. Additionally, the vulnerabilities of both the browser and the operating system should be repaired as soon as possible. This is because of the security threats posed by both the browser and the host operating system. Because the Web client script poses a security risk, the Web client's capacity for defending against attacks should be improved; a detection system should be included in the Web client script; and detection should be performed on a frequent basis. The first type of detection technology for harmful web pages is known as static detection, while the second type is known as dynamic detection. In general, there are two kinds of detection technologies for malicious web pages.

Analysis of the website's code enables the static detection technique to identify potentially harmful code. Dynamic detection has relatively poor effectiveness in comparison to static detection, but it has significant pertinence, which enables it to effectively identify dangerous code embedded within a page. The aim of protection can be attained even if the malicious code is altered or encrypted because dynamic detection can read the relevant information in the bad code, analyse the characteristics of the behaviour, and then accomplish this. As a result, dynamic detection has a high degree of precision.

When the original security system of a Web application is compared to the AJAX protection mechanism, there are certain aspects of both that are similar in nature. These aspects include the ability to query data by interacting with the data, the response ability of data transfer, the capability of data transmission and information call, and so on. In order to avoid the situation in which only the user side is validated, it is necessary to validate all of the information provided by clients and servers. This includes checking the HTTP header, validating cookies, validating parameters, validating data, and checking the length and specification of user data. The protection mechanism is primarily comprised of the following four components: first, the application system mechanism on the user end; second, the mechanism of the external programme of a third party; third, the data call mechanism; and fourth, the protection mechanism of data processing. In most cases, before the filtering of a firewall or the HTTP layer, it is unable to defend against an assault on Web services. As a result, it is necessary to play the role of resistance in the filter and supervision of the SOAP layer. The information of WSDL date could not be leaked because it is one of the key sources; however, its enforcement mechanism primarily includes two aspects: the first is that during the process of programme design, it needs to provide the corresponding function, and the second is that it is only used in SSL. The protection mechanism incorporates five distinct components: first, the R&D staff of the system are responsible for WSDL access control; second, security assertion mark-up language is applied; third, a WS-Security certificate is utilised; fourth, SOAP filtration is carried out; and fifth, data is transferred.

When constructing a TCP in HTTP, link to it. When the user side offers a demand, the server will deliver a corresponding reply. HTTPS is primarily used to refer to running HTTP based on SSL. The structure that results from this fusion is called

HTTPS. In order to apply SSL, the user side needs to construct a TCP, link to it, construct an SSL channel on it, and send the same need to the SSL channel. The server side will then make a response that corresponds to the SSL channel. Due to the fact that not all servers are able to implement SSL, the information that can be accepted by SSL is considered to be spam when compared to the regular HTTP server. As a result, in order to guarantee the accuracy of the data, it is necessary to choose the right application channels when carrying out the application process. For SSL to be applied, the website's address must begin with the letters "HTTPS," so that users may access it.

SRTP protocol primarily investigates and develops the safety performance of the two contents, the first of which is the audio stream, and the second of which is the video stream. Additionally, SRTP supplies the encryption options and cognitive methods that correspond to AES. Therefore, the SRTP protocol's primary purposes are to provide security and to operate in real time. Although SRTP is compatible with both TCP and UDP, its most common implementation is in UDP due to the fact that UDP is the protocol most commonly used for the transmission of speech and video. Protection of data authenticity and integrity: MAC-SHA1 is, in most cases, the authentication technique that RTP employs. After the results of the calculation have been communicated to the data packet, the side that is receiving the data will choose a reasonable label value of M based on the results of the computation, and then compare this value with the label value that was received.

The RTMPS protocol, also known as the security protocol, is the protocol that is obtained after SSL encryption has been performed. The protocol can support data transport. The provision of a security protocol for network communication that guarantees the integrity of data is the primary objective of the secure sockets layer. To encrypt the network link, SSL relies heavily on the transmission layer as its primary method of operation. 443 is the default port number.

In general, the application programmes that are based on the Web have steadily developed, and they have become an important standard of the contemporary computing platform. This development coincides with the rapid expansion of Internet technology. Web applications have infiltrated our work, living, and learning, become an indispensable part of our daily life, and played an important role in the provision of network information service ever since the advent of web mail, online commerce, and online media. Applications that are tied to the Web have gotten more complicated as a result of the rapid growth of Web technology, which also contributes to the gradual emergence of security vulnerabilities. In order to ensure the safety of Internet applications, it is necessary to conduct a comprehensive security analysis of the Web application, as well as develop an effective and dependable method for preventing attacks, in order to ensure the safety of programmes and data. Only then can the safety of Internet applications be guaranteed.

9.3 RESPONSIVE WEB DESIGN IN FUTURE:

Because it is essential to examine both the past and the present in order to accurately anticipate the future, the preceding discussion was chosen quite extensive. Users may now declare that in 2015, it is not even close to being viable to reject the necessity of a responsive website. When web designers and developers refer to "web design," they are referring, of course, to responsive web design. But being device agnostic, which means being able to adjust to screens of varying sizes, is merely the first step in developing a web that is responsive to the next generation. Users anticipate having a web experience that takes into account specific characteristics, such as their location, the time of day, the content that they have previously visited (their web browsing history), and the activities that are occurring in real time in their immediate environment. Because of this, responsive thinking on the web is where the future of responsive web design rests. Users who purchase a series of print publications of a printed magazine may become aware that each edition features a unique layout and design, indicating that the publication possesses the capacity to respond to any combination of events that are taking place around it. This capability is lost from the modern responsive web in some respects. The layout of the majority of websites, which ranges from four to twelve columns, remains the same for the entirety of the most significant events as well as on a daily basis. Because of this, a website should not only respond to the sizes of the devices accessing it; rather, both the website and the content should be able to adapt and reformat themselves depending on the context. For example, the homepage of the website for Web Directions South 2012 was designed based on the participants' physical locations. Once a participant has arrived at the location, the homepage of their website is modified to display the schedule for the event.

The number of senior citizens and other older individuals using the internet is the demographic that is expanding at the highest rate. Web designers have a responsibility to customise websites in consideration of the requirements of this big and expanding demographic. Because of their advanced age, these web users have several usability challenges that come along with them. These concerns include the way information is arranged and presented on design-rich websites; text colour, style, and size; accessing information while on the go; and other similar issues. It is not as simple for an older adult to become proficient on the internet in a shorter amount of time in comparison to users falling in the age range of 45 to 55, and it is a natural phenomenon that younger individuals are capable of learning and adapting to new things easily. Therefore, users now have another context that calls for web developers to design complex and clever algorithms that are savvy enough to recognise previously saved user profiles and to format and style the content in a way that makes it easy for senior adults to read, browse, navigate, and comprehend. The majority of the most popular social networking sites and email providers, such as Twitter, Facebook, and Gmail, have algorithms that actively check to see if a new user has registered. After successfully login in, a new user will be given some pointers and instruction on how to start making use of their services as soon as possible. That is a context-aware serving of services, in which they have a new user context, but what if that specific new user is an elderly person who might become confused by their somewhat difficult introductory tutorial? Therefore, in addition to simply identifying the type of user, web developers will also need to focus on the ageing aspect. Users are able to state that if a user is new to this website, then this content should be served first. Additionally, if the user is new AND falls into this age category, then this content should be presented first in that layout AND using these style standards, etc.

Another possible scenario is a website that caters to multiple cultures. Every culture has its own distinctive set of norms, values, and ethics, in addition to a characteristic way of living. The proliferation of online commerce and communication technology, as well as social networking and news websites, have all, to a greater or lesser extent, contributed to the mixing of cultures and the subsequent formation of a global culture. All of these instructional websites have been made more easily navigable and friendly to users thanks to responsive web design. This has presented significant challenges for emerging nations like Pakistan in their efforts to safeguard their cultural traditions.

Developing countries such as ours are making an effort to fight back against this cultural shift; but, the world as a whole is heading in the direction of greater globalisation, and technology has already begun to build its own global culture. The industrialised nations of the world are, for the most part, the ones behind the wheel when it comes to the development, manufacturing, and dissemination of information and communication technologies. This has a significant impact on global culture. Before the development of flexible web design, websites such as news, articles, blogs, networking platforms, and online shopping were inaccessible to individuals who did not have access to computers. Following the implementation of responsive design on these websites, there was a noticeable spike in the number of people using those websites. The global community of today is not relying on mobile devices to maintain communication; rather, they are engaging in a great deal more activity. People have raised a great deal of awareness through social media websites; in fact, they had even organised a revolution through the use of these platforms; as a result, the governments of some countries, such as Pakistan, have decided to prohibit access to these websites within their borders. Because of this, it should come as no surprise that responsive web design, which makes websites more accessible and increases their availability, has had a significant effect on the way people live their lives.

Culture therefore becomes another context in responsive web design, where, for instance, an online shopping website based in a western country that is accessed would not show the content that is not permitted by our religious cultural ethics and values. This is because our religious cultural ethics and values are based on a set of values that have been handed down through the generations. If, however members of minority groups who live in Pakistan are interested in accessing the whole version of the content on the website, there has to be some means for this behaviour to be overridden.

This is just one example of how users could use cultural context in responsive web design; however, if it is implemented correctly, it will assist web users from religious families in accessing the web content on websites that they otherwise feel uneasy browsing in public. This is due to the fact that only the text and figures on such online shopping websites will violate their cultural values. One of the parameters that has been explored here is the practise of concealing content that violates a religious prohibition whenever it is seen in such a zone; however, there may be many more.

Therefore, in order to create a website that is flexible across multiple cultures, responsive web designers and developers need to take into mind factors such as these. On a more upbeat note, site designers might even offer content that focuses on and expresses the culture and cultural values of their users, no matter where in the world those users are located and what section of the web they are accessing. This will have a beneficial impact on the goodwill that users already have for companies in their view.

REFERENCES:

1. Beaird, J., Walker, A., & George, J. (2020). *The principles of beautiful web design*. Sitepoint.
2. Cyr, D., Head, M., Lim, E., & Stibe, A. (2018). Using the elaboration likelihood model to examine online persuasion through website design. *Information & Management*, *55*(7), 807-821.
3. A little history of the world wide web. (n.d.). Retrieved April 16, 2022, from Www.w3.org website: http://www.w3.org/History.html
4. Marcotte, E. (2017). *Responsive web design: A book apart in 4*. Editions Eyrolles.
5. Iyengar, A., Challenger, J., Dias, D., & Dantzig, P. (2000). High performance Website design techniques. *IEEE Internet Computing*, *4*(2), 17-26.
6. Mockapetris, P. V. (1987). Rfc1035: Domain names-implementation and specification.
7. Kwan, T. T., McGrath, R. E., & Reed, D. A. (1995). NCSA's worldwide web server: Design and performance. *Computer*, *28*(11), 68-74.
8. Athuraliya, S., 2002. A note on parameter values of REM with Reno-like algorithms. *Networking Laboratory, Caltech.*
9. Calongne, C. M. (2001, March). Designing for Website usability. In *Proceedings of the twelfth annual CCSC South Central conference on The journal of computing in small colleges* (pp. 39-45).
10. Mayhew, D. J. (1999, May). The usability engineering lifecycle. In *CHI'99 Extended Abstracts on Human Factors in Computing Systems* (pp. 147-148).
11. Souders, S. (2008). High-performance Websites. *Communications of the ACM*, *51*(12), 36-41.
12. Huang, M. H. (2005). Web performance scale. *Information & Management*, *42*(6), 841-852.
13. Killelea, P. (2002). *Web Performance Tuning: speeding up the web*. " O'Reilly Media, Inc.".

14. Barford, P., & Crovella, M. (1999). Measuring web performance in the wide area. *ACM SIGMETRICS Performance Evaluation Review, 27*(2), 37-48.

15. Meyer, M. H., & Zack, M. H. (1996). The design and development of information products. *MIT Sloan Management Review, 37*(3), 43.

16. Nielsen, J., & Sano, D. (1995). SunWeb: User interface design for Sun Microsystem's internal web. *Computer Networks and ISDN Systems, 28*(1-2), 179-188.

17. Atzeni, P., Mecca, G., & Merialdo, P. (1998, March). Design and maintenance of data-intensive Websites. In *International Conference on Extending Database Technology* (pp. 436-450). Springer, Berlin, Heidelberg.

18. Chen, P. P. S. (1976). The entity-relationship model—toward a unified view of data. *ACM transactions on database systems (TODS), 1*(1), 9-36.

19. HTML5 differences from HTML4, W3C Working Draft, 24. 6. 2010, http://www.w3.org/TR/html5-diff/, accessed 7. 2010

20. World Wide Web consortium. CSS specifications. http://wwww.w3.org/Style/CSS/ current-work.

21. Mozilla Developer Network, "Web developer survey research," https:// hacks.mozilla.org/2010/11/its-all-about-web-developers/, Mozilla, Tech. Rep., 2010.

22. Web Technology Surveys. Usage of CSS for websites. http://w3techs. com/technologies/details/ce-css/all/all.

23. H. W. Lie and B. Bos, Cascading Style Sheets: Designing for the Web, 3rd ed. Boston, MA, USA: Addison-Wesley Professional, 2005.

24. D. Mazinanian, N. Tsantalis, and A. Mesbah, "Discovering Refactoring Opportunities in Cascading Style Sheets," in Proceedings of the 22nd ACM SIGSOFT International Symposium on Foundations of Software Engineering (FSE), 2014, pp. 496–506.

25. Bucketbranch, R. (2017). *Transitions & Animations in CSS.* https://www.academia.edu /35302495 /Transitions and_Animations_in_CSS.

26. Ferekides, C. S., Marinskiy, D., Viswanathan, V., Tetali, B., Palekis, V., Selvaraj, P., & Morel, D. L. (2000). High efficiency CSS CdTe solar cells. *Thin Solid Films, 361*, 520-526.

27. Duckett, J. (2011). *HTML & CSS: design and build websites* (Vol. 15). Indianapolis, IN: Wiley.

28. Meyer, E. A (2006). CSS: *The Definitive Guide: The Definitive Guide*. O'Reilly Media, Inc”.

29. Meyer, E. A. (2006). *CSS: The Definitive Guide: The Definitive Guide*. " O'Reilly Media, Inc.".

30. Stolley, K. (2020, November). CSS instruction enhanced by objective typography. In *Proceedings of the 2020 ACM SIGPLAN Symposium on SPLASH-E* (pp. 23-28).

31. Meyer, E. A., & Zeldman, J. (2002). *Eric Meyer on CSS: Mastering the language of web design* (p. 322). New Riders.

32. Zeldman, J. (2003). *Designing with web standards*. New Riders.

33. Marcotte, E. (2017). *Responsive web design: A book apart n 4*. Editions Eyrolles.

34. Robbins, J. N. (2012). *Learning web design: A beginner's guide to HTML, CSS, JavaScript, and web graphics*. " O'Reilly Media, Inc.".

35. Larsen, R. (2018). *Mastering SVG: Ace web animations, visualizations, and vector graphics with HTML, CSS, and JavaScript*. Packt Publishing Ltd.

36. Zhao, N., Cao, Y., & Lau, R. W. (2018, October). Modelling fonts in context: Font prediction on web designs. In *Computer Graphics Forum* (Vol. 37, No. 7, pp. 385-395).

37. Xiaojie X, Yang X, Shuo J., Research and Design of Web Application Firewall Based on Feature Matching. Netinfo security, (11)53-59,2015

38. Ziqian W, Bo W., Research on technology taking use of vulnerability of information security in Web application system. Electronic Product Reliability and Environmental Testing, (6):30-33, 2015

39. Dongjiao Z, Ping W., Analysis on the security technology of Java Web application program. Computer fan, (3):48-49,2016.

END OF PAGE

www.ingramcontent.com/pod-product-compliance
Ingram Content Group UK Ltd.
Pitfield, Milton Keynes, MK11 3LW, UK
UKHW061952290726
14090UKWH00021B/1185

9 789359 899589